Lars Blinkenberg

The Middle East Conflict
From Bad to Worse to WAR

Lars Blinkenberg

The Middle East Conflict

From Bad to Worse to WAR

Syddansk Universitetsforlag 2006

© The author and University Press of Southern Denmark 2006
Printed by Narayana Press
ISBN 87-7674-049-8
EAN 9788776740498

Published with support from:
Lillian og Dan Finks Fond
G.E.C. Gads Fond
VELUX-fonden
Politiken-Fonden

On the front page the Israeli flag in the middle is surrounded by the flags of the neighbouring Arab nations: Egypt, Jordan, Lebanon, Syria and the PLO, as seen from above and from left to right.

University Press of Southern Denmark
Campusvej 55
DK-5230 Odense M
Phone: +45 6615 7999
Fax: +45 6615 8126
Press@forlag.sdu.dk
www.universitypress.dk

Distribution in the United States and Canada:
International Specialized Book Services
5804 NE Hassalo Street
Portland, OR 97213-3644 USA
www.isbs.com

Distribution in the United Kingdom:
Gazelle
White Cross Mills
Hightown
Lancaster
LA1 4 XS
U.K.
www.gazellebooks.co.uk

Contents

Foreword 9

Introduction 13

Conflicts and little hope   19

I.   The origins of the conflict 21
     A. Zionism 21
     B. The Arab Fight for Recognition and Independence 40
     C. Pan-Arabism 47
     D. The Creation of Israel, Born in War 50

II. Fragile peace efforts, and widening conflict, 1949-55 63

III. The 1956 war 77
     1. Collusion with Britain and France 77
     2. October 1956 War 81
     3. Aftermath 84

IV. The militant policies of the Arab League 89
     1. Arab Summit of 1964 91
     2. Terrorism 92

V.   The decisive War of 1967 95
     1. The Background 95
     2. The Impressive Victory 100
     3. Aftermath 105

VI. The PLO and Inter-Arab fights 111
     PLO and Jordan 111

VII.	War of attrition Between Egypt and Israel, 1969-71	115
VIII.	The october 1973 war	121
	1. Secret Preparations by the Arab Powers	121
	2. Surprise Attack	128
	3. Aftermath	131
IX.	Lebanon's war, 1975-90, Spillover of the conflict	137
	A. Background and Interference from Abroad in the Civil Wars	137
	B. Essence of the Civil War	149
X.	The Egyptian peace opening, 1977-78	155
	A. Sadat's Great Plan	155
	B. The Isolation of Egypt	165
XI.	Slow Arab recognition of Israel	169
	1. Arab League Summits	169
	2. Abortive American Peace Proposals	170
	3. The First *Intifada*	172
	4. PLO's Recognition of Israel	173
XII.	The Madrid Peace Conference	175
XIII.	Oslo talks and agreements	179
XIV.	The peace treaty between Israel and Jordan of 1994	185
XV.	Deterioration of the conflict under Netanyahu, 1996-99	189
	1. Right-Wing Victory at May 1996 Elections	189
	2. Worsened Conditions with Regard to the Arabs	191
	3. The Palestinian Problem	192
	4. The Syrian/Lebanese Relationship	195
	5. The Jordanian and Egyptian Relationship	198
	6. Internal Disagreements	199
XVI.	Barak's abortive peace efforts	201
	1. Resumption of the Peace Process	203
	2. Negotiations with the PA	203
	3. Negotiations with Syria	204
	4. Doldrums in 2000 – 2001	207

XVII.	THE BRUTALISATION OF CONFLICT UNDER SHARON	213
	1. Man of War	213
	2. After 11 September 2001	219
	3. Dangerous Years, 2002-2004	222
	4. The 2003 War in Iraq	236
XVIII.	NEW OPENING FROM THE ARAB LEAGUE SUMMIT	239
XIX.	JOINT MEDIATION EFFORTS BY THE EU, RUSSIA, THE UN AND THE USA	243
XX.	LATEST DEVELOPMENTS	247
	2004 – 05	247
	The Death of Arafat	253
XXI.	INDEPENDENT PEACE EFFORTS	259
	1. The Geneva Accord of 2003	259
	2. The Copenhagen Declaration of 1997	260
	3. International Folk High School	262
	4. Neve Shalom	262
POSTSCRIPT		265
SELECTED BIBLIOGRAPHY		267
INDEX		270

Foreword

This study is intended to render the history of the long-standing conflict between Israel and her immediate Arab neighbours. It spans the period from 14 May 1948, the day of the Declaration of Independence of the new Jewish nation, Israel, to the re-election of Ariel Sharon as Prime Minister in Jerusalem in early 2003, as well as the War in Iraq which soon followed, with its consequences, if any, for the Middle East conflict.

It was written during the last four years, while Ariel Sharon, as Prime Minister of Israel, has turned his back on the Peace Process — albeit with the excuse (which some would find legitimate) of the unhappy increase in terrorist acts in Israel — and made a mockery of the relationship with the Palestinian administration, supposedly the forerunner of a Palestinian state, which most countries will recognise as such, as soon as it is established. The fairly recent election result in Israel, which prolongs Sharon's rule and thus the unsolved conflict, does not offer much hope of a solution in the near future. More violence and the continuation of the vicious circle are to be expected.

At the time of writing both the easy, American-led victory in the War against the dictatorship of Saddam Hussein in Iraq and its difficult aftermath have lent new momentum to the already existing uncertainty, but may also imply a faint hope of solution.

My point of departure is my personal knowledge of the region, of both Israel and its neighbouring countries, where I have lived or which I have visited on several occasions. I can only try to present the history of this long conflict as objectively as possible from an unbiased point of view, that is, without feelings of sympathy or enmity for either side. I have concentrated mostly on the high points of the conflict, not burdening the reader with too many details.

Over the years, I have become fond of the Middle East, especially its more peaceful areas untouched by the conflict. They do exist, even if most people who observe the region from a distance do not believe it. As a young man I felt great sympathy for the Zionist vision because of the horror of the *Holocaust*, but at that time, I — like many Jews and others in our part of the world — was ignorant of the untold sufferings created by the Jewish intrusion into Palestine.

It has been my ambition to demonstrate understanding for all parties in the conflict, and even to express sympathy for them, if at all possible. My hope, therefore, is to be seen as unbiased and to avoid being accused of anti-Semitic feelings. Only uninformed or ill-willed persons can nurture such negative feelings over the years, and as we should know, the ethnic backgrounds of Jews and Arabs are not that far apart. Their two religions and languages and many of their old traditions have a lot in common (some of them also shared by Christians). At any rate, I have to a great extent based my account on books written by modern Jewish historians whom I regard as the most well-informed and on reports by well-known journalists with a Jewish background.

In the years 1996 to 1999, I served as Denmark's ambassador to Syria, Jordan and Lebanon, residing in Damascus. My stay in the area lasted for only a little more than the period of government of Benjamin Netanyahu, whose Prime Ministership was looked upon with frustration by most Arabs and by many Israelis, as well. I went back to all the involved countries in 2000, 2001, and 2002.

By the time this book is published, I shall long have ceased to be a serving diplomat, having retired from the Danish Foreign Service in September 2000. It must be stressed, nonetheless, that whatever opinions I have expressed in this study are mine and no one else's, certainly not those of the Danish Ministry of Foreign Affairs or any other public institution.

I have previously studied another of the world's most difficult conflicts, the one between India and Pakistan, and the result was the publication of my book, *India-Pakistan, The History of Unsolved Conflicts*, in 1998 by Odense Universitetsforlag, Denmark. At the time of writing the present book, that dispute remains as unsolved as ever, even if there now seems to be some new hope. Are similarities to be found in the two conflicts? Some, but not many, even if some people might pretend that both conflicts derive from the fact that two religions are opposed: In the present case, Judaism and Islam, in the other conflict, Hinduism and Islam. This is only partly correct, but in both conflicts there are many cultural, social and even political factors that are, if not identical, then surely very similar. All in all, I feel sure that there are more differences than similarities between these two stubborn conflicts.

I have received financial contributions from the following foundations, without which it would have been difficult to make public this work:

Lillian and Dan Finks Fond; C.E.C. Gads Fond and VELUX fonden. I am indeed grateful for this valuable help.

Persons who want to know more about the recent history of the countries concerned in this Conflict can read my second volumen, which will be published seperately under the same title *The Middle East Conflict, From Bad to Worse to War*, with the addition **SECOND BOOK, Brief History of the Involved Countries**.

I want to thank several persons for their help and assistance: Many of my former colleagues in the region, who gave me advice and help/hospitality, especially Ambassador Christian Oldenburg (previously in Cairo, now in Baghdad), also

INTRODUCTION

Israel celebrated her 50th anniversary in 1998. The enmity that met her coming into being remains a factor to be reckoned with in many Arab and Islamic countries. The crisis which originally surrounded the creation of this new state has therefore turned into a permanent conflict which influences most political problems in the Middle East, whether or not the countries involved have accepted Israel. The so-called peace process has already brought about peace agreements with a few countries, but a real, comprehensive and just peace in the whole area is still as elusive as ever. Moreover, Israel is not yet recognised as a full-fledged nation within the region. At the time of writing, not only has the Second *intifada*, with its many terrorist attacks, brought untold sufferings upon many Israelis, but the frequent retaliation acts by the Israeli Defence Force, the IDF, have also resulted in even more casualties on the Palestinian side. These developments fully illustrate the difficulties for Palestinian and Israeli co-existence, which are probably worse today than ever before.

In this book, I concentrate on the relationship between Israel and her immediate neighbours: Egypt, Jordan, Syria, Lebanon and the PLO/PA. My definition of the Middle East is therefore limited to this difficult area, with its most dramatic conflict between Arabs and Israelis. It purposely ignores Israel's relationship with such other Arab countries as Saudi Arabia, Iraq and many more, except when it occurs naturally in the course of the account of events. It is my point of departure that there are few studies by outsiders who have tried to look at the conflict from this limited regional angle while trying to study the long-standing confrontation on the basis of the most well-informed views and against the background of personal knowledge of both sides.

This work relates the history of the conflict, including the history of *Zionism* and of the Arab fight for recognition and independence from former domination. While it renders the conflict's ups and downs from 1948 to 2004, it also presents short accounts of the wars between the involved parties, providing more details of the conflict as we approach recent developments, sadly showing a decrease in the progress, or a complete stop, of the Peace-Process.

Nowadays, we have to admit that Israel has grown up as a nation in her own right; this is a development which no one can or should deny. This fact is even recognised by the Arab world and confirmed as recently as the Arab League Summit in Beirut at the end of March 2002. It was to have given the green light for collaboration between Israel and her neighbours on the basis of mutual respect, but the Arab offer was immediately rejected by the Sharon government. The election victory of his right-wing government in early 2003 by no means gives it any right to continue the illegal occupation of the West Bank or Gaza, already the longest lasting in the world. We must here recall that ten years ago, in 1993, Israel accepted that Palestine should have autonomy. It is beyond any doubt that the population of the occupied territories wants to have a nation fully recognised among others. A small but viable Palestine, living side by side with Israel, is also what the EU, Russia, the UN and the USA have all recognised as a must and have stated they will try to promote in their recent *Quartet* efforts. Let us hope that this goal will eventually be achieved, despite the serious delays over the last years. The very recent (October 2003) unoffical Geneva Agreement between liberal, peace-oriented Israelis and Palestinians may offer a new opening, even if it was immediately rejected by the Sharon government.

Currently, the perspectives for peace therefore seem more confusing and frustrating than they have in a very long time, but there may be light at the end of the tunnel. Whereas the government in Jerusalem is still dominated by the powerful Israeli general who was looked upon negatively by most Arabs from the very beginning and who has contributed to an unhappy deterioration of the conflict during his five-year Prime Ministership, Sharon will not be in power for ever; born in 1928, he is no young man.

It is a fact that his main opponent during most of the time, Yassir Arafat, was not helpful, either, in easing the difficult situation. Shortly before his death in November 2004 the PLO leader accepted that his power be shared with a Prime Minister. Arafat's recent death constitutes a new picture of the conflict that give us some hope.

Since the Israeli dominance and the illegal settlements in the occupied territories constitute the basic problems of the conflict, no PLO leader can change any essential factor in the conflict as long as the Israeli government does not acknowledge this main problem as a point of departure. The disastrous developments in Israel and Palestine while Sharon has been in power received new impetus with the war in Iraq in the first part of 2003. To some, however, this war constitutes a new opening for peace, as has also been stressed by President Bush. But in the first many months after the fall of the Saddam Hussein regime, no new development took place at the official level between the Israeli government and the PLO. And the Washington administration still seems hesitant and not decisively pro-peace, unless on Sharon's conditions. It is therefore still relevant maintain my book's subtitle: *From Bad to Worse to War*.

If the new nation, Israel, was not accepted by the Arab World from the outset, when its establishment became common knowledge, differences soon developed in the various Arab capitals. The immediate reaction of Israel's neighbours to her declaration of independence was to reject it and begin an undeclared war in the same negative way as they had rejected the UN resolution of November 1947, which divided the British mandate of Palestine into two entities and thereby made possible the creation of the State of Israel. Most Arabs would tolerate neither the partitioning of Palestine nor the creation of a Jewish nation. Nevertheless, they might have accepted a secular, multi-ethnic nation which also comprised the Jews who had already arrived in the country.

Whereas at the beginning of the conflict the Arab neighbours *seemed* united and all fought together against the intruding nation, there is a new situation today: Egypt made peace with Israel many years ago, in 1978, but remained isolated in the Arab world for a period of time afterwards. The PLO and Jordan have also made agreements with their former enemy, in 1993 and 1994 respectively (though the 1993 agreement was only preliminary). In addition to these two countries (Egypt and Jordan) which now maintain diplomatic relations with Jerusalem, a few other Arab states have entered into some form of relationship with their former enemy.

Even Syria and Lebanon have accepted that Israel is a *fait accompli*, since Damascus and Beirut have declared their willingness to negotiate a peace agreement with Jerusalem and talks have been going on during some periods.

All Arab states point out, however, that the various UN resolutions must be respected before a final and comprehensive peace agreement can be reached, especially the one demanding the withdrawal of Israeli forces from the occupied territories. The majority still do not accept the Egyptian/Jordanian/PLO endorsement of something less than this global arrangement if Arab aspirations are to be satisfied. Nevertheless, the Arab League recently demonstrated at its meeting in Beirut in March 2002 that all the member states are willing to reach out to Israel and open up relations, in the same way as the two Arab nations had already done. Their only condition was that the Israeli forces be withdrawn from the occupied territories and that some other serious problems be taken up before a final solution can be reached.

Although the division in the Arab world was significant in the 1970s and 1980s, it is now more formal than real. But the nationalistic Israeli government in place in Jerusalem today, harassed by terrorism, stresses only the importance of security, without which it finds that no normal peace arrangement can be achieved. Therefore, the Sharon government immediately rejected the offer from the Arab League in March 2002. The Arab answer regarding the demand for security is that it cannot be achieved as long as Israel illegally maintains domination over more land than is accepted by the rest of the world, i.e. Arab land outside the pre-1967 borders. The Golan must thus be returned to Syria and most of the occupied land of Palestine made fully free of Israeli domination and soldiers.

The Arab governments find that the arbitrary Israeli measures to dominate and often humiliate the fragile government of the PA cannot continue if any serious talk of a comprehensive peace agreement is to be resumed. The Arab governments have many UN resolutions and, increasingly, world opinion, even in the Western nations, behind them. The EU has thus recognised the PLO's right to a Palestinian state, and even the USA has come round to an acceptance of this perspective, if very slowly.

There was some genuine hope in Prime Minister Barak's time that the peace process between Israel and the PA could be resumed and converted into a real understanding or peace, but after the take-over of Sharon there has been an all-round worsening of the conflict, as already mentioned. The new *intifada* that began in September 2000, and the Israeli counter-measures, have made the situation more tense than ever.

If one compares the Arab side with that of Israel, it is easy to establish that only on the new nation's side may we talk of real democracy, even if to a Scandinavian observer, Israel's political and military ways are very often far from being acceptable as genuinely democratic. We may even claim that over the years, Israel has come to resemble other Middle Eastern countries much more than it did at the beginning when it was still under the influence of the first idealistic founding fathers. It is a fact that Egypt, Syria and most other Arab countries have never really known democratic ways, though with the possible exception of Lebanon, which nowadays enjoys fairly good government based on free elections, a credible press and an open society. This is often forgotten by those who maintain that no Arab country has ever known Western democratic government. We must also recognise that undisputed and authoritarian leaders like (the late President) Hafez Assad, the Egyptian presidents or the kings cannot completely ignore the feelings of their people.

Whereas Egypt and Syria remain authoritarian regimes without many liberties, Israel's two other neighbouring countries, Jordan and even more so Lebanon, enjoy fairly free debates and have both seen conditions improving in this regard over the last few years.

In many ways, we have come to a watershed in the region. Young leaders have taken over in Jordan and Syria after the disappearance of the long time leaders, King Hussein and President Hafez Assad, in 1999 and 2000 respectively.

The right-wing government took over in Israel under Ariel Sharon in early 2001, at the same time that President George W. Bush was installed in Washington. The fairly recent re-election of the nationalistic, insensitive and even brutal Prime Minister, General Sharon, allowing him to continue at the helm of affairs, does not give much hope for new priority being granted to the resumption of negotiations with the Arab side. Initially Sharon enjoyed the full support of the new Bush Administration in Washington, which has been more reluctant to interfere than the former President, Bill Clinton, who gave high priority to resolving the Middle East conflict. If only the US government, together with its partners in the "Quartet" would insist on a solution to this conflict, which has lasted over 50 years, it might actually be solved. But the American government must put *real* pressure on the Israeli government, and not just use soft talk and kind words with their allies in Jerusalem, as has so often been the case.

For the Arabs, the Sharon government in Jerusalem has led to new frustrations and a revival of old hatreds that many had hoped were eliminated forever. This, combined with the obvious lack of direction from Washington and the Administration's pro-Israeli policies, has often created even more pessimism. The Americans have their own serious worries after the cruel terrorist attacks of 11 September 2001 on the World Trade Towers in New York and the Pentagon in Washington, culminating in the conflict with, and military intervention in, Afghanistan, and very recently the war with Iraq.

We may interpret the terrorist attacks as the desperate sign of utter frustration in the Arab world and in the third world in general, with regard to the USA. But the terrorists represent neither responsible Arab governments nor Islam as such. There is no real clash of civilisations, I find, and all civilised people round the world condemn meaningless acts of terrorism. On the other hand, we have to admit that what has been called "state terrorism" must be equally condemned, because it involves the killing of innocent persons in order to eliminate one or a few dangerous opponents, and utilises excessive force by a government.

There is no doubt that the dramatic events of the 11 September 2001 catastrophe and its wake are linked in some way to the Middle East conflict; therefore, pessimists again prevail with regard to this long-term conflict between Israel and her immediate neighbours, especially the Palestinians.

During the recent war in Iraq, the Bush Administration promised to solve the Palestinian problem when the war with Iraq was over, but at the time of writing this book, there seems to be little hope of a just and comprehensive peace in the Middle East, unless Washington radically changes its policies with regard to the area. When the then British Foreign Secretary, Robin Cook, resigned at the outbreak of military intervention in Iraq, he correctly pointed out that the West had never shown the same impatience with Israel as with Iraq and compelled it to respect the many relevant UN resolutions. This was even more surprising, he implied, since the Jewish Nation had ignored a multitude of them, just as much as, or even more than, Iraq. My personal comment to this, however, would be to emphasise the great differences between the madman's regime in Iraq and the democratically elected, albeit heavily criticised Sharon government, which often does not respect international law or the geo-political relations in the area. But eventually the latter will have to accept that the use of sheer power cannot solve the conflict in the Middle East.

We may also quote a former American President and Nobel Peace Prize winner, Jimmy Carter, who played a prominent part in the first peace treaty between any Arab country (Egypt) and Israel, and who has recently declared (in *Time*, 8 December 2003) that "[t]he (Bush) Administration has hurt the Arab-Israeli peace process, abandoning what was in the past a bipartisan [i.e. in the USA] commitment to a relatively balanced position in trying to find peace. It's been an ostentatious alliance between the White House and the Sharon government".

I end this *Introduction* by quoting from an article written by Jonathan Freedland in the *Guardian* on 18 October 2000, in which he states: "The Middle East Conflict is a tragedy, putting against each other two needy peoples whose causes are both just. When both sides see each other that way, then may-be they will decide to share the land, not only because they have to, but because it is right".

Conflicts and little hope

I. The origins of the conflict

A. Zionism

1. *The Original Movement*

It is a well-known fact that the Jews, throughout their long diaspora, which began with their expulsion from Jerusalem by the Romans during the first and second centuries, upheld the dream of a return to that holy city. *Next year in Jerusalem* was the ritual prayer of the Jews without a recognised nation, which they used in order to keep their spirits up. *To come back to Zion* was the eternal hope of the Jews, who often suffered persecution or at least felt different from the people around them, the gentiles.

The fate of the Jews was often sad, but not always. In many countries, including Arab ones, they could often lead a decent life, and in the period of the Omayad splendour in Andalusia, the Jews played an important role in a society of mixed Arab, Christian and Judaic cultures living together in the South of Spain. With the expulsion of the Jews by the Catholic kings and their bigotted followers from that important region in the late 1400s and the beginning of the following century, many Jews went to Eastern Europe or to the Ottoman Empire. There, clever kings (and other leaders), found out that they could use the craftsmanship and skills of the Jews in order to modernise the state, at a time when progress was occurring in many European nations, unfortunately often combined with an increasing religious intolerance. Anti-Semitic (Anti-Jewish) measures were thus already common in many Western countries such as France, Germany and Italy in the Middle Ages, especially around the period of the Crusades.

In the course of the eighteenth and nineteenth centuries, however, religious intolerance also grew in Eastern Europe, combined with the increasing nationalism that excluded the Jews, not only in the minds of local inhabitants, but in their own. Jews were without land in two ways. Not only was their nation a faraway dream, but in their countries of residence, they were not allowed to own land. For these understandable reasons, internationalism appealed, generally speaking, to

Jews,[1] especially those who were educated, whether the ideologies/movements to which they adhered were Socialism or Communism or others.

Terrible *pogroms* (massacres) were often initiated against the Jews by those higher in society, because it was easy to divert the anger felt by the downtrodden peasantry and other lower classes in Russia and Ukraine (Poland was no longer a recognised state in that period) which was caused by their low status, by accusing the odd and different Jewish community of being responsible for their misery. The majority would often accept this denigration of the Jews and perhaps even participate in organising new pogroms. This happened, for instance, after the first, abortive Russian Revolution of 1905, when the Imperial Court accused the Jews of being behind the revolt. It was therefore almost with official backing that some of the worst massacres took place in the aftermath of that rebellion.[2]

Sometimes the initiative to the pogroms was taken by the lower classes themselves. As we see expressed in the famous play *Waiting for Godot*, it is sometimes easy for downtrodden people to find someone of even lower status than themselves to despise and attack.

The Zionist movement as such arose in the late nineteenth century, but it had its roots far back in history.[3] In a remarkable way, Jews had managed to survive spiritually by creating the feeling of a sort of nationhood that represented more than the belonging to a common religion based on the hope of the return of the Messiah. Many became influenced by the ideas behind the French Revolution of 1789, and as already mentioned, Jews were generally in favour of international movements, for instance those that they hoped could protect them against narrow nationalistic arrogance and suppression.

Even if there had been some forerunners who had written about a return to the Holy Land in a religious sense, the first person to really formulate the political desire to come back to the lost homeland, *Zion*, was the Austrian-Hungarian Jewish journalist and writer, Theodor Herzl, who published his famous book, *Der Judenstaat* in 1896. This was some ten years after the first, small wave of Jewish settlers had arrived in Palestine and around the same period that saw the beginning of the great emigration of millions of poor Russian Jews to the USA because of dreadful pogroms.

---

1 See *Cual es el futuro de Israel* , a book containing interviews with Shlomo Ben-Ami, former Minister of Foreign Affairs of Israel (in the Barak government), published in 2002, p 247: El universalismo era la manera de salvarse para los judíos. (Universalism was the way for Jews to save themselves.)
2 Benny Morris, *Righteous Victims*, New York 2001, p. 25. He writes that *the Regime tried to thwart the revolutionaries by diverting popular anger from the monarchy to the Jews*.
3 David Fromkin, *A Peace to end all Peace*, Owl books, New York, 1989, p. 271.

Founder of the political Zionism, Theodor Herzl.

Herzl was far from being a religious man himself and lived a secular life as a correspondent for an Austrian newspaper in Paris. There, he was shocked by the massive anti-Semitic campaign in French conservative circles during the Dreyfus drama, and this motivated him to promote the Zionist cause. The idea soon gathered momentum after the publication of his above-mentioned book on the Jewish State. A Zionist Organisation was established soon after, in 1897, in Basle, during the first Zionist Congress, which was led by Herzl. Later on it took the name of *World Zionist Organisation*.

Whereas the founder, in his original proposals for a Jewish nation, did not necessarily intend to create it in Palestine — other countries, such as Argentine and African colonies (Uganda) were also envisaged — the first Congress decided to strive for the creation of a home for the Jewish people in Palestine, secured by public law. Herzl was chosen as the first President and remained so until his early death in 1904 at the age of 44. He was very energetic in discussing the Zionist cause with well-established politicians and even heads of state in Europe; he saw the German Emperor twice and even visited the Ottoman Sultan. The latter, however, would not accept the Zionist plan, undoubtedly because he had enough problems with the Arabs in his multi-ethnic empire. In retrospect, it is curious to learn that the German Emperor, for his part, showed some sympathy for the Zionist cause. Herzl himself never saw any tangible results coming of these talks, but managed to visit the envisaged Jewish homeland in the then Turkish-Ottoman dominated Palestine.

It is evident that only very few of the Eastern or Central European Jews who took the initiative at that time to create a Jewish nation had any in-depth knowledge of Palestine, which was generally regarded as belonging to a fairly backward region without any special identity and governed from far-away Istanbul. The motto soon adopted by the Zionists was that it was simply in accordance with an idea of justice that they, as a people (nation) without land should strive back to the place from which they came and which (at that time) constituted a land without a people.[4] In this day and age, with easy travel, it is difficult to understand that the very idea of going back to an area that the Jews had left two thousand years ago could arise without any deeper knowledge of the region. But it was a well-known fact that the dominating power of the Ottoman Empire was declining during this period, when the Balkan nations were fighting for their independence in a struggle that would give rise to a successful war of liberation just before the First World War.

At the same time, the two dominant European powers, France and the United Kingdom, were eager to fortify their domination over less developed countries. Even well before the First World War, London and Paris were thinking in these terms, which later allowed them to take over from the Ottomans in the Middle East, and the most well-informed Jews were of course aware of this.

A delegation of rabbies from Vienna did go to Palestine in the early part of the twentieth century in order to see for themselves what the country of their dreams was like. They sent a telegram home stating, "the bride is beautiful, but she is married to another man"[5].

If this delegation realised that the land of Palestine was not vacant, it did not deter the Zionists in general from their long-term plan. They aimed at obtaining approval from the main colonial power, of their desire to establish a homeland – the word *state* was not yet employed – in Palestine. The first Zionist Congress deliberately avoided the word *state*, in order not to antagonise the Ottoman regime, with whom a solution was still being sought by Herzl – in vain, as we already know.

---

4 Strangely, we learn from Morris that it was a slogan created by an Englishman, Lord Shaftesbury, in the middle of the nineteenth century, but later adopted by the Zionists, see op.cit., p. 42.

5 See Avi Shlaim, *The Iron Wall*, Penguin Books, London, 2000, p. 3.

Herzl was aware that Palestine was not an uninhabited land and that it would be necessary to convince the Arabs there that the Jewish wish to settle in Palestine was not to be seen as directed against the interests of the people already there. He wrote a personal letter to one of the local leaders, Yusuf Zia-el Khalidi, in Jerusalem, emphasising that the Zionists did not pose a threat of displacement for the Arab inhabitants of Palestine. But he also declared to his co-Zionists that it might be necessary to displace Arabs to make room for the newly-arriving Jews. In his liberal mind, however, he only envisaged expropriating land *in a gentle way,* i.e. with full compensation, but also supplemented by the Zionists' financing of the expatriation and employment in other countries of the poor local Arabs.

It is interesting to learn that after the first Zionist Congress, Herzl had written in his diary that he was sure that the Jewish state would soon materialise, perhaps after five, but surely not later than after 50 years. Indeed, it took 51 years in reality (1897 – 1948).

Inspired by the declared gentle methods of the founding Zionist, Herzl's spiritual heir, Chaim Weizmann, soon took over as one of the leaders of great importance for the Zionist movement. He was born in Russia in 1874, but established himself in England in 1904 (the year Herzl died) and eventually became a recognised chemist there, working for the government during the war years in order to improve the quality of shells. He later became President of the Zionist Organisation (1920) but was, as early as the first stages of Zionism, already an important member of the organisation, particularly because of his good relations with the British leaders. Herzl himself had recognised that his efforts to achieve results from his contacts with the Ottoman, German and other leaders had been without result; therefore, he finally turned his attention to the British government. Sadly, he did not live long enough, as we remember, to see any results from his personal endeavours, and the Zionists became utterly divided after Herzl's early death. Accordingly, it took thirteen years more to arrive at a solution through the *Balfour Declaration*.

Weizmann, who first lived in Manchester, had made influential acquaintances such as the editor of the *Manchester Guardian,* C.P. Scott, who soon understood and favoured Zionism, and wrote about it in his prestigious paper. He was considered one of Lloyd George's closest political confidants. As a lawyer, the latter had already had close contact with the first Zionist leader, Herzl, and therefore understood the motives behind the Jews' wish to gain their homeland and leave the *diaspora*. England, for quite some time, had the problem of a growing political movement, and even fight, for Irish independence, so the atmosphere was conducive to understanding the importance of such national movements, which were equally active in the British dominions of Australia, Canada, New Zealand and South Africa, and also supported by the American President Woodrow Wilson. This American leader had very liberal ideas and was one of the promoters behind the establishment of the *League of Nations* after the First World War, but remained sceptical of British

Chaim Weizmann, President of the Zionist Organisation from 1920. First President of Israel.

colonial aspirations or endeavours. He was therefore not initially in favour of the Zionist scheme as promoted by the United Kingdom, even if he understood the Jewish wish for a homeland. Eventually he praised the Balfour Declaration in a letter to the representatives of American Jews in September 1918.

Most of the already three million Jews in the USA during that period did not favour Zionism, because they had arrived safely from Eastern Europe to a new haven far from both Europe and Palestine and had no wish to turn their backs on their new homeland. American Zionists, however, soon became a force to reckon with. But in geo-political terms the USA was still no major power then — far from it.

Weizmann — together with another influential British Zionist, Lord Rothschild — was the driving force behind those who eventually managed to persuade Lloyd George of the virtues of Zionism. This important liberal politician, who became British Prime Minister in late 1916 and had already shown some understanding of the need of a homeland for the Jews, was eventually responsible for the Balfour Declaration that was issued in 1917. It was won through hard work on many sides

— Jewish and non-Jewish — and the declaration became a turning point in Jewish/Zionist history.

The Balfour Declaration is quoted here in its entirety because of its utmost importance for later developments. It was issued in a letter dated 2 November 1917 from the then Foreign Secretary, Arthur James Balfour, to one of the leading Zionist representatives in England, Lord Rothschild:

Dear Lord Rothschild,

I have much pleasure in conveying to you on behalf of H.M.'s Government the following declaration of our sympathy with Jewish Zionist aspirations which has been submitted to, and approved by, the Cabinet.

> *"H.M.'s government views with favour the establishment in Palestine of a national home for the Jewish people, and will use their best endeavours to facilitate the achievement of this object, it being clearly understood that nothing shall be done which may prejudice the civil and religious rights of existing non-Jewish communities in Palestine, or the rights and political status enjoyed by Jews in any other country".*

I should be grateful if you would bring this declaration to the knowledge of the Zionist Federation.

Yours sincerely
A.J. Balfour

One of the episodes that had frightened European Jews, some of whom had fled the pogroms of Russia, was the above-mentioned scandalous Dreyfus affair in France in the mid-1890s and early 1900s that demonstrated the latent anti-Semitism in the West. However, the leading French Jews were not in favour of a homeland solution as promoted by Zionists, because many were highly integrated into French society and generally nervous about drawing more attention than there was already to the Jews in the aftermath of the sad Dreyfus affair. Knowing this, the French government was equally sceptical about the proposals, not least because of their delicate relationship with the UK in the always latent competition between the main colonial powers, despite the fine days following the *Entente Cordiale* (from 1904).

It is evident that the Balfour Declaration was not only intended to satisfy the Zionists' dreams, but was also part of a British wish to dominate the Middle East area after the expected fall of the Ottoman Empire. The later British High Commissioner in Palestine, Sir Herbert Samuel, himself a Jew, had prepared a memorandum to the British Cabinet as early as 1915, in which he recommended the establishment of a Jewish homeland in Palestine as *a cornerstone of British policy in the region*, but it was not adopted at this stage. Nevertheless, his suggested policy remained an important element in British policy, not only as a prerequisite for the fulfilment of the Balfour Declaration, but also as a political necessity in the wake of the First World War.

The Westernised Jews who — mainly through the diplomatic skills of Weizmann — had managed to persuade the British leaders of their just cause also gave the impression that in their coming Zionist homeland they would represent Western ways of thinking in a difficult and unsettled area and even be regarded almost as an extended arm of the Empire. More or less at the same time, the British government established a Jewish Fighting Unit within their armed forces to take part in the defence of the allied cause against that of Germany, Austria, Turkey and others. This unit participated in the battles for the liberation of Palestine in late 1917.

When the Balfour Declaration was issued, it had the backing of most members of the British Cabinet, but some of the Arabists in the Foreign Office or elsewhere in the Colonial establishment were not amused by this idea. They probably foresaw some of the troubles that a Jewish homeland was bound to create. This was undoubtedly not the only obstacle to the decision to grant a homeland to the Jews.

The British government had of course obligations to its main ally, France, and vice-versa, and talks had been going on between highly placed representatives of the two nations, Sir Mark Sykes (UK) and F.G. Picot (France), about the future of the Middle East; the talks had materialised in the agreement of May 1916 bearing the two names, Sykes-Picot. We have already mentioned that the French government was sceptical about the Zionist scheme and neither of the two allied governments played with open cards. It was only at a late stage that Weizmann learned about this secret bilateral agreement. But through the bilateral contacts between the governments, especially via the two already mentioned *éminences grises*, the French government eventually came round to a more positive attitude about a Jewish solution in Palestine, probably also under the impression of the powerful British influence in the Jewish set-up, and generally speaking in the area of the Middle East, where France wielded fairly limited influence compared to the United Kingdom.

The war effort also weakened France to a larger extent than Britain because French territory constituted the main theatre of war, with its extensive battlefields. Therefore France could hardly afford to think in such expansionist ways outside Europe, as the United Kingdom was able to.

Weizmann, who had prepared the first draft of the declaration, was somewhat disappointed because it had been watered down, as such declarations tend to be in diplomatic life. But Zionist-minded Jews now had a declaration of the greatest importance because it legalised their dreams of a return to Zion, and a general euphoria soon spread in Jewish circles around the world. It came at a time of great uncertainty during the persistent and horrible First World War, when the battles on the Western front still did not give much hope of a final break-through for the Allied cause, even as late as early 1918. At the same time, Russia was in turmoil because of the fall of the Tsarist regime in late 1917 and the uncertainties caused by the Russian revolution. The Arabs were still mostly dominated by the Ottoman power that had not yet given up and still hoped for a victory of the two Central European powers, Germany and Austria. The main Arab country, Egypt, was dominated by the British and could not openly speak out against the Balfour Declaration, but it is likely that intellectual circles took the decision as a warning signal.

Considering that the British had already promised the Emir/Sharif of Mecca, Hussein, that they would support independence of the Arab Nation after the War, it is clear that the government in London was going to be haunted by these irreconcilable promises to both Arabs and Jews.

2. Zionism between the Balfour Declaration and Israeli Independence

Now that the Zionists had won approval from the powerful British government and were thus given "a golden key to unlock the doors of Palestine",[6] the movement had to put forward more precise plans for their coming homeland. Naturally there were divisions with regard to the future, and we must initially stress the fact that many Jews in the Western countries had no wish to settle in Palestine, even if it was now going to be possible. One of the most important decisions of the Zionist Organisation was to provide money for the purchase of land in Palestine. During the fifth Zionist Congress in 1901, well before the Balfour Declaration, a Jewish National Fund had already been set up to finance the purchase of land in Palestine.

The British began their administration of Palestine, which they had conquered in 1917, as soon as the Great War was over, and assured the inclusion of the Balfour Declaration in the mandate given by the League of Nations, granting the UK the responsibility as the protecting power of Palestine after the Ottomans, effective 1923. But the new masters of Palestine soon realised how many problems were involved in ruling a country whose century-long Arab population had not been consulted before the Balfour Declaration and was now of course opposed to the coming intrusion of foreign immigrants. Despite his promises, the first Zionist leader, Herzl, had convinced very few, if any, of the Arab leaders in Palestine. And with the rising sun of Zionism in Palestine, the roots of the later open conflict were bound to find fertile soil in the otherwise not easily cultivable land.

Many of the Jews who came had put aside some means and were therefore able to buy land from low-income farmers or from more well-to-do local chieftains who wanted to get rid of land that was not regarded as fertile enough to be cultivated.

---

6   Avi Shlaim, op.cit., p. 7.

In many cases the immigrants could obtain financial support from the abovementioned Jewish National Fund. For the Zionists from the East, the sole fact of being able to buy and own land was the fulfilment of a dream. Many of the early pioneers were influenced by socialist thinking and wanted the new immigrants to be educated in a farmer-soldier orientation. David Ben-Gurion, who was later to become Prime Minister, was one of these original leaders who held such ideas, which soon became the basic approach for the new waves of immigrants and for the first Israeli governments. Ben-Gurion had come to Palestine as a young man as early as 1906, long before the Balfour Declaration.

It was to be expected that it would be difficult to establish harmonious relations between the intruding Jews and the original Palestinian Arabs, whether of Christian or Muslim faith. Some Jews felt that the very fact of their coming would give the Arabs many advantages because of the higher standard of living it would entail, and accordingly, that the Palestinians would eventually welcome the Zionists. Others realised that this dream of harmony was false, and Ben-Gurion was among those who soon discovered this, when, at an early stage, he was attacked and lightly wounded by an Arab. "They surely hate us" was his reaction.[7] Like all colonisers, most Jews felt a mixture of fear and animosity (sometimes based on a superiority complex) with regard to the Arabs, and many ugly episodes arose from time to time. Morris quotes a Zionist comment on some of the dramatic episodes in which Arabs had been suffering, accordingly: "We Jews who ourselves suffered from persecution and ill-treatment for thousands of years [... —] from us a minimally humane approach could have been expected, not to beat unarmed and innocent people with a whip, out of mere caprice".[8]

The original Zionist settlers had the idea, based on their philosophy that the culture of land was an essential element in their lives, that they should not be dependent on the Arab workforce. In many cases, however, this principle was easily forgotten. Morris tells us that, generally speaking, the Arab labourers were "docile and hardy"[9], whereas Jewish workers tended to be "more expensive and weaker". It was therefore soon evident that it was advantageous for employers to engage local Arab workers. Either way, problems were bound to arise, and we must understand that the increasing immigration of Zionists made problems worse everywhere around the Jewish settlements. Morris writes that "the villagers continued to nurture a deep, lasting resentment toward the newcomers",[10] even in

---

7 Morris, op.cit., p. 60.

8 Ibid., p. 53. His comment is equivalent to a remark King Hussein once uttered, also expressing his surprise that Jews — despite their long suffering — rarely showed compassion for other peoples' problems.

9 Ibid., p. 52.

10 Ibid., p. 55.

those rather exceptional cases where the intruders were met with some amount of acceptance — read resignation — from the Arabs. If the Palestinians were generally docile, this must be seen in the light of their status as downtrodden peasants or landless labourers in the Ottoman period, a very feudal one.

Around the time of the First World War, the Jewish population amounted to 56,000 people,[11] many of whom had recently arrived from Russia after the failure of the first Russian revolution in 1905. The Arab population, on the other hand, amounted to 600,000 at the time. In 1925, the Jewish population had grown to 108,000, in 1939 to 446,000, and at Independence in 1948, Jews counted for about 30% of the total population of Palestine. This steady increase of Jewish immigration (called *Exodus*), also in clandestine ways, naturally gave rise to Arab riots on and off: not only the first ones in 1921 and 1926, but especially the much more serious revolt in the years preceding the Second World War, 1936 – 39. This last-mentioned revolt, which involved many killings on both sides, compelled the British government to reconsider all the difficult problems related to its responsibilities in Palestine.

In July 1937, a commission under Lord Peel came out with a report indicating the necessity of dividing Palestine into a small Jewish entity and a larger Arab one. The Zionists were not pleased, of course, but Ben-Gurion managed to persuade a majority to support the resolution adopted that year by a Zionist Congress to the effect that the organisation accepted the proposals as a basis for negotiations with the British. This was his pragmatic approach, which he employed throughout his life.[12] As we shall see later, it also gave the impetus to the final preparations for a take-over of power in Israel, however limited the Jewish area would be. The British decision became the basis not only for negotiations, but also for the coming conflict between all parties, Arabs, British and Jews. We may conclude that at this stage, there was no solution in sight to this problem, since the disagreements between Arabs and Jews had taken on a degree of seriousness beyond the point of no return.

Whereas the aim of the Balfour Declaration was eventually achieved by the British government — though with some 30 years' delay in its complete form — the Sykes-Picot agreement was initially more difficult for the British government to adopt. The Prime Minister, Lloyd George, was very hesitant with regard to the necessity of respecting the terms of the agreement which granted France the control over what is today Lebanon and Syria, especially after the liberation of Damascus by British/Arab forces. But the very influential civil servant, Sykes,

---

11   Avi Shlaim, Ibid., p. 7 points out that it was at the time of the Balfour Declaration in 1917.

12   Shlaim tells us that it is not relevant to study in depth the many articles by Ben-Gurion on the subject of Arab-Jewish relations, because he would say one thing in private and another in public. Op.cit., p. 17.

aided by pressure from the French, managed to get the terms of the agreement carried through. Sykes was something of an idealist and in many ways a forerunner with regard to de-colonisation. He realised that the time of imperialism was lapsing, but for the two main powers it took almost thirty years more to respect the wishes of the young, long dominated nations to obtain their freedom.[13] We shall elaborate on the Arab aspirations in a later chapter, and the support some of their princes received from the government in London.

Weizmann, who reluctantly supported Ben-Gurion in his acceptance of the Peel Commission's proposals, eventually became the first President of Israel. Among Zionists he is generally considered a moderate, but more in form than in substance, as Shlaim tells us.[14] His aim was to obtain as much as possible for the Jews in Palestine, but in accordance with the initial Zionist decisions, he was careful for a long time not to antagonise the Arabs in Palestine by talking about a state. He had discussions with Prince Feisal, the later King of Syria (for a short while) and then of Iraq, and in 1919 signed an agreement with him which endorsed the Balfour Declaration and "foresaw the most cordial goodwill and understanding" between the two parties, Arabs and Jews.[15] But because of fierce opposition from the Arabs, the Prince soon had to send out a declaration to the effect that the Balfour promises to the Jews were not acceptable to the Arabs. History would repeat itself 30 years later when Feisal's brother, Abdullah, the first King of Jordan, was unable to carry through his wish to honour an understanding he had reached with Golda Meir.

Weizmann had played the British card, but soon had to realise that the foreign policy pattern of the UK did not allow London to ignore the interests of the Arabs completely, especially after the serious riots in Palestine against the British immigration policies in the late thirties which angered both Arabs and Jews — the former because they thought too many Jews had already come and the latter because they accepted no restrictions whatsoever on Jewish immigration. This dramatic dilemma became explosive with the Holocaust in the 1940s which led to a substantial increase in the need for the surviving, persecuted Jews, particularly those who had been in extermination camps, to find a safe haven.

Not only did the Holocaust dramatically increase the need for a national home for the Jews, but the Western powers and others finally realised that the wishes of the Jews could no longer be ignored. Only few thought then of the aspirations of the not yet independent Arab nations and the confrontation which was bound to

---

13 For those interested in learning about the details of the many intrigues, not only between the British and the French, but also internally within the UK, I can recommend David Fromkin's above mentioned book, *A Peace to End All Peace.* .

14 Op.cit., p. 9.

15 Ibid, p. 8.

Founder of the new Zionist party, the World Union of Zionist Revisionists, Zeev Jabotinsky.

occur between Jews and Arabs in the aftermath of the Second World War because of the increased Jewish intrusion into Palestine.

Weizmann therefore also ran into many difficulties before the end was in sight. He was not the only leading figure among the Zionists, and we shall here look into other key persons in the fight for a sovereign state that was eventually achieved in 1948.

Zeev Jabotinsky was born in Russia in 1880 and soon became the most ardent nationalist among the Zionists, one of those in opposition to Weizmann and eventually the spiritual father of the right-wing circles in the movement and later in Israel. He was elected to the Zionist Executive in 1921 and opposed the British White Paper of 1922 drawn up by Winston Churchill, which limited the scope of Jewish aspirations in Palestine. Jabotinsky founded a new Zionist party, the World Union of Zionist Revisionists, which later became the New Zionist Organisation. Generally speaking, he represented the growing militancy of some Zionists, eventually becoming leader of their *Irgun* militia. Jabotinsky died in 1940, before Independence, but his spiritual and political influence was felt for a long time. He advocated that the Jews should openly declare that they belonged to Western culture and regarded themselves as an extended arm of the West in the Arab world. This was a typical *Ashkenazim* view, whereas the *Sephardim* Jews (of non-Eastern European origin),[16] who became more influential at a later stage, understandably did not agree.

Jabotinsky published two important articles in 1922 under the title *The Iron Wall*, which Shlaim used as the title for his interesting book, published in 2000. Jabotinsky did not foresee any likelihood of an easy compromise between the Zionists and the Arabs, whereas those in agreement with the main faction of Zionists, led by Weizmann, still hoped for a solution based on such a compromise.

Jabotinsky advocated that the Zionists would have to build an *Iron Wall* around their coming state, at least spiritually, in order to protect their interests. Only in this way, he emphasised, would the Arabs accept the coming Jewish nation as *a fait accompli*. Shlaim stresses that Jabotinsky based his philosophy on the idea that the Jews had a moral right to return to Palestine, which the Arabs of course never accepted: "The Iron Wall was not an end in itself but a means to end Arab resistance to the onward march of Zionism".[17] One can trace a direct line from this self-assured leading politician to the Prime Minister of Israel today, Ariel Sharon, who also believes in military as opposed to political solutions. It is necessary to keep in mind, however, that if Jabotinsky's iron wall between Jews and Arabs was indeed realised in some ways after Independence and even more after the 1967 Arab debacle, it was not enough to secure peace and harmony between the two communities. It was Jabotinsky's wish that in the coming Jewish state, which he never lived long enough to see, the Palestinian Arabs should be granted some national rights, but he did not define his ideas clearly. Ironically, the Sharon government is building an iron wall (in cement and barbed wire) today to protect Israel from terrorist attacks.

An interesting fact about Zionism is that it was one of the later political leaders who settled in Palestine long before the Balfour Declaration, *Ben-Gurion*, who

---

16 *Ashkenazim* literally means *German* in Hebrew, whereas *Sephard* is the Hebrew word for *Spain*. There was a large majority of the former in Israel around Independence, but the proportion of *Sephardim* Jews has grown to nearly 50 percent today. They mostly represent the Jews from North African or other exotic countries that identified with the original mixed Arab/Jewish culture of Spain. Many of them still speak Arabic, just as the Jews expelled from Spain continued to speak Spanish/*Ladin* for centuries. In very recent years, the arrival of more than a million Russian Jews has again increased the proportion of *Ashkenazim* Jews in Israel.

17 Op.cit., p. 15, where a good analysis of this early movement is given.

Palestinian rebels during the revolt against the Jews and the British Government 1936-1939.

became the founding father of the new State of Israel, and not Weizmann or Jabotinsky, the two most important Zionists outside Palestine. Nevertheless, the pragmatism of Ben-Gurion led him to the same conclusion as that of Jabotinsky[18]: "It was essential for the Jews to have well-trained and strongly armed forces in order to convince the Arabs of the necessity of accepting the intruding Zionists", just as the American colonisers of the West or the old colonial powers in Asia or Africa based their survival on the superiority of their arms against the *natives*. In his pragmatic way, Ben-Gurion was willing to change the partners who acted as the Zionists' protecting allies, from the Ottomans before the First World War to the British in the period from 1917 to the 1950s, to the British/French in the 1950s and 60s and then finally to the Americans. He was also pragmatic in his accepting the partition of Palestine, which the political heirs of Jabotinsky never did.

The Zionists had one more setback before their final dream could be realised. It came in May 1939, just before the Second World War, when the British government failed to keep its promises deriving from the Balfour Declaration, accepting the Peel Commission's recommendations. The new White Paper suggested that the Jews should have only minority status in Palestine, and thus no state of their own.

---

18   Ibid., p. 19.

This negative decision, which was soon overshadowed by the War and the *Holocaust*, led to a meeting among American Jews in May 1942 at the Biltmore Hotel in New York, where Ben-Gurion and Weizmann were both present. The *Biltmore Program* that was passed there envisaged a Jewish state in the entire Palestinian territory and may be seen as a banner of revolt against the British policies of breaking old promises. This program was adopted shortly before the world learned about the horror of the Holocaust, which eventually gave strength to the Zionist idea, though not enough to make the Biltmore Program acceptable for the majority in the UN, which was soon going to take an important decision with regard to the Jewish-Arab conflict.

This final settlement was made on 29 November 1947, when the UN resolution 181 called for the division of Palestine into a Jewish and an Arab state. Nearly all the major powers voted in favour of this resolution, and as a rare case, the USA and the USSR both voted for it, while the UK abstained, strangely enough. Shlaim rightly calls this resolution, however imperfect it might seem to the Zionists, "a major triumph for Zionist diplomacy".[19] The Jewish Agency officially recognised the resolution, while the Arabs called it "absurd, impracticable and unjust" and therefore rejected it.[20]

It is a strange fact that many Zionists, especially the Ben-Gurion generation who were already established before Independence in what became Israel, initially never wanted to talk much about the Holocaust. There was sometimes even a tendency to criticise the East European Jews for being too docile and thus leading themselves to their own deaths in the extermination camps. Later politicians, on the other hand, especially Begin and his generation, tended to exploit their sad fate and (mis)use the Holocaust to their advantage. According to Thomas Friedman there is now a general policy in Israel, which he finds exaggerated, to exploit the sad past when the Nazis ruled Europe in their murderous way. He expresses it as follows: "Today — unfortunately — the teaching of the Holocaust is an essential element of Israeli high-school education and in the Israeli army course".[21] He quotes an Israeli expert on Holocaust literature who has written: "The Holocaust is no longer a trauma that affected certain families in Israel. It has become a collective pathology affecting the entire nation".[22]

---

19 Ibid., p. 25.
20 Ibid., p. 27.
21 Thomas Friedman, *From Beirut to Jerusalem*, Anchor Books, New York, 1989 (latest edition 1995), p. 280. Friedman is a well-known American journalist and writer, himself a Jew.
22 Ibid., p. 281.

3. Zionism after the Establishment of the State of Israel

When the creation of the new state in 1948 had become a fact of life, it was no longer easy to define what Zionism meant. We may even ask whether it had any meaning then. The Jews had achieved their national state, as the Zionist movement wanted it, and the world had generally accepted this accomplishment. The Jewish state was born with the approval of the UN, even if there have later been many reservations with regard to some of modern Israel's policies. It took some thirty years to come that far from the Balfour Declaration, and some fifty years from the publication of *Der Judenstaat* and the first Zionist Congress to fulfil the Jewish dream of a homecoming.

To answer my own question above, we cannot completely ignore the notion of Zionism, even today. If one has to define Zionism nowadays, it would be as follows: The State of Israel allows all Jews in the world, wherever they live, to come back to the Holy Land and settle there in accordance with the original Zionist philosophy. A committee of Rabbies has to decide whether the applicant is indeed a Jew, which will normally depend on the religious status of his or her mother. If the person in question is confirmed to be a Jew, he or she, but no other foreigner, has *the right* to settle in Israel. Generally speaking, this is what survives of Zionism today, and it is therefore relevant to those Jews who live in miserable surroundings abroad and want to settle in Israel, as was the case with a large number of Russian Jews after the fall of the Iron Curtain between East and West, not so long ago.

Almost a million Jews went to Israel from Russia, but whether they all were indeed Jews is a question which I am not qualified to answer. I know, however, that many Arabs and even Israelis doubt that this was the case. Arab leaders often ask why, if Israel could absorb so many Jews of doubtful origin in the 1990s, it cannot accept those Palestinian refugees who are able to prove that they lived in Palestine before Israel was born. The answer is, of course, that such an influx of Arabs would create a completely different balance between the two communities and in reality destroy the Jewish State as it was planned by the Zionists.

Radical-minded Arabs have misused the word *Zionism* for many years, for instance through resolutions in the UN that declared "Zionism equal to racism". This was of course not helpful with regard to reconciling Arabs and Israelis, but most of the Arab states did not have such a wish, either, in those days. Later on, this radical tendency slowly diminished and some Arab states even began to work for reconciliation. The more understanding policy is still not fully accepted, and the trend has been reversed under the recent right-wing governments in Israel. We shall return later to those promising steps that were taken with the agreements between Egypt and the Jewish state in 1978 – 79; with the Oslo process in 1993, which resulted in a limited but still important agreement between Jews and the Palestinians; and finally, with the peace treaty between Jordan and Israel in 1994.

A few of the radical Arab or Islamic regimes continue to use the phrase *Zionist entity* instead of *Israel*, simply to indicate that no recognition of that state will be granted. But this negative policy is no longer representative of the general Arab position.

In domestic Israeli politics, Zionism may still play a role, but for external observers it is not a very helpful term to employ beyond what has been written above. Many Jewish writers today seem to employ the words *Zionist* and *Jewish* as synonyms. The word *Israeli* has a different meaning, of course, including also the Arab citizens of Israel (now some 20% of the population) who are neither Zionists nor Jews. They are indeed Israelis, even if their rights are not on the same level as that of the Jews. They may be said to be second-class citizens, and this is one of the unacceptable aspects of modern Israel, as I and many other observers see it.

I shall now allow myself to turn to the American Jew, *Thomas Friedman*, from whose interesting book, *From Beirut to Jerusalem,* we have already quoted; he has also tried to define what is representative of modern Jews in Israel, under the amusing title: *Whose Country is this, anyway?* [23] It comes as no surprise when he tells us that Israel is far from being a homogeneous nation and that even among the Jews, it is difficult to find a clear notion regarding what they feel about being Israelis. Friedman's four categories are as follows: (here quoted in a slightly abbreviated form)

The first school of thought is represented by the secular and non-observant Israelis, men like Simon Peres and Yitzhak Shamir. They form about 50% of the Jewish population and for these *secular Zionists* (even here this term is used), being back in the land of Israel and erecting a modern society and army became a substitute for religious observance and faith.

The second major school consists of *religious Zionists* who form about 30% of the Jews in Israel. They see the state and the synagogue as being compatible.

The third school is made up by other *religious Zionists* who are of a more messianic bent. They comprise about 5% of the Jews in Israel and they see the state as a necessary instrument for bringing the Messiah.

The last category is represented by the *ultra-Orthodox non-Zionist Jews*, who comprise about 15% of the Jews in modern Israel. They are called *Haredim* and do **not** see the birth of the Jewish state as an event of major religious significance. They dress in the old-fashioned East-European way, do not send their children to the army (which the state generally accepts) and when they are engaged in politics will be on the extreme right and try to promote a more religious society. If they stay in Israel it is because they feel safer there than anywhere else — despite all their open criticism of the state.

If there is any shared characteristic of these strange patterns of Zionism or Jewish life inside modern Israel it is that "it is literally exhausting at times to be an

---

23 Op.cit., pp. 285 - 287.

Israeli Jew", according to Friedman. It is easy to agree with him, and many other observers have witnessed the same difficult inter-relationship among Jews, Zionists and Israelis. It has certainly become worse during the last generation or so. Shlomo Ben-Ami, the second Foreign Minister under Barak, who is also a historian, tells us that some of the innocence of the first pioneers went astray with the Arab debacle of 1967, when Israel so convincingly won over most of its enemies. He is definitely more pessimistic than earlier about the immediate future of Israel.[24] I may add that generally speaking, Jews like jokes about themselves and will often tell you that when two Jews or Israelis get together there will surely be at least three different opinions.

One conclusion I want to draw personally is the fact that the last category (4), which only represents 15% of the population, has managed to force Israeli society to accept religious norms to a surprising degree, and more so than what is normal in most Arab societies (except Saudi Arabia). In many places, especially in Jerusalem, of course, where the religious influence is by far the most eye-catching, the Sabbath has to be respected, and it may even be imposed in a violent way; public transport often cannot function and during *Passover*, the celebration of an important Jewish holiday equivalent in some ways to our Easter, no bread or beer made with yeast can be served in Israel, even in tourist establishments.[25] On the other hand, Friedman tells us how surprised he was when he assisted at a *bar mitzvah* religious ceremony of his Israeli cousin and the latter, at the following meal, asked for *white steak*, which is synonymous to pork meat, banned by Jewish Orthodox tradition. Apparently he could get it and Friedman rightly talks of "the irony of the moment".[26]

Some of the notorious Israeli terrorists who have shocked the world, like Baruch Goldstein, who killed many praying Arabs in Hebron; the murderer of Prime Minister Rabin or the fanatics who wanted to blow up the holy Mosques in Jerusalem in the 1980s but were fortunately arrested in time, are either members of the last-mentioned group, the *Haredim*, or spiritually close to them, in an utterly negative way. Rabin tells us in his memoirs how ashamed and shocked he felt when ultra right-wing politicians from the *Gush Emunin* party greeted Kissinger (himself a Jew) in the Knesset with insulting words and gestures.[27]

Some observers point out that the ultra-religious sections of the Jewish society, which are not completely — or at all — loyal to the modern state, must be seen

---

24 Op.cit., pp. 13 - 15.
25 This is in memory of the Jews´ enforced exile in Egypt thousands of years ago, when they had no time to wait for the yeast to make their bread rise. Flat bread without yeast may be served, though.
26 Op.cit., p. 313.
27 Y. Rabin, *The Rabin Memoirs*, University of California Press, 1979/98, p. 271.

as a latent danger to Israel, because these orthodox families have more children than the secular Jews. In the long run this will lead to an increasing influence by these extremist circles, to the detriment of the democratic society and to the Israeli relationship with the Arabs.

B. The Arab Fight for Recognition and Independence

1. *The Glorious First Arab Period*

While the history of Zionism over the last 100 years is fairly clear-cut, albeit complicated, the Arab fight for recognition is a much more complex affair. We have to recall here that Arab traditions developed over the last 1400 years, since the conquest of large parts of the world around the Mediterranean Sea by the successors of the Prophet Muhammed. The Omayad dynasty established in Andalusia in the eighth century soon showed great cultural and political power when its influence was at a peak, and it had no equal for the subsequent 200 years. Cordoba and Toledo were then the most important cities in the world, and later also Sevilla and Granada were brilliant civilised towns during the Viking period and early Middle Age. Literature, science and the arts were highly respected, and there was a remarkable harmony[28] among the three religions then in Spain: Islam, represented of course by the Arabs who settled there over centuries; Judiasm, by the important section of the population formed by the Spanish Jews in the diaspora; and finally Christianity, which was prevalent in the less developed regions of Northern Spain then, but also slowly, but increasingly, influenced the mixed cultural society of the South. It can of course be discussed whether the influence of the non-Muslim portions was more or less decisive, but there is no doubt about the great cultural importance of the Jews in this Arab-dominated setting, especially in Cordoba and Toledo.

Here it is relevant to recall that, generally speaking, Arabs have often shown a respect for the two other monotheistic religions, the Jewish and the Christian, which was hardly ever reciprocated, and no equivalent of the horrible *Inquisition* of Spain and other Catholic countries can be found in an Arab setting. This does not mean, however, that Arab regimes have always been tolerant of Jews and Christians. As in all societies there has been greater and lesser degrees of religious tolerance among

---

28 I do not write "full harmony", because we should avoid idealising these remote periods from which we have mixed information. But it is, at any rate, a fact that there was collaboration between the three sections of society and the Muslim leaders largely accepted the minority groups. Tolerance was therefore a fact of life, but not all practiced it.

leaders. But what should be stressed here is that in the earlier periods before the French Revolution, and even much later, Arab societies as a whole showed a good deal of tolerance — much more than Christian societies — towards members of the two other religious groups, especially the Jews.

2. The Beginning of the Arab Decline

This highly developed multi-cultural Arab society in Spain declined in the Middle Ages and eventually the final Christian conquest of the south of Spain, marked by the capture of Granada in 1492 and the eviction of Arabs and Jews in the following period, finally destroyed the remarkable degree of harmony that had existed in Andalusia for centuries. In the Eastern parts of the Arab world, the tide also turned against the Arabs, especially after the Turkish conquest in 1453 of the important old Byzantine capital, Constantinople, now almost without land outside the city walls (and named *Istanbul* shortly afterwards). This final conquest and elimination of the East Roman and Christian influence meant that in the sixteenth century the Ottoman regime could conquer old Arab land in what is today Syria, Lebanon, Jordan, Palestine, Iraq, Egypt and other countries. These countries had already seen a decline in their political influence in previous periods because of various Persian and Mongol intrusions, but they now came under a rising Ottoman Empire that up until the First World War was to dominate a huge area: not only the old Arab Empire — which was established in the aftermath of the first great expansion after Muhammed's death and which was not united for long periods — but also parts of Southeastern Europe, up to near Vienna, in the seventeenth and eighteenth centuries, up to the nineteenth.

The Turkish regime had taken Islam as its own religion and the *Koran* was read in Arabic so that the Muslim influence and to some extent Arab traditions survived in the conquered areas. The Arabs had not only spread their language after the conquest (even as far away as in Spain) but also settled in the occupied lands to a much greater extent than the Romans ever did in their Empire. This has given great importance and prestige to the Arab language, which is proud to trace its roots to the holy book, the *Koran*. But in the long run, and especially when the Ottoman regime was a dominant power in the period between around 1500 and 1850, it was more the Turkish than the Arab influence that dominated. Like many Empires, however, it could not remain very centralised. Thus Istanbul had to allow regional influences to some extent, especially in the nineteenth century, when the major European powers gained more political influence and eventually supported the liberation of the European part of the Ottoman regime, ending with the successful Balkan War just before the First World War. In the past twentieth century, these powers used their rising influence to promote Arab independence, but only hesitatingly.

3. First Attempts at Arab Revival

One of the areas in the Arab world where a certain autonomy was allowed by the Ottomans was in the high Lebanese mountains where the Christian Maronites[29] had established a stronghold and were allowed to keep their identity, not least because of the difficult access to these remote mountains. Parts of Syria, Lebanon and Palestine were administered from the important old city of Damascus, whereas the Egyptian Monarchy had been established as autonomous in the nineteenth century, albeit linked in some ways to Istanbul until the British became the dominant power.

With the increasing weaknesses of the Ottoman regime in the early part of the twentieth century, the Arabs wanted autonomy — a desire which was fortified by the Zionist movement's endeavours for recognition by the major powers, particularly the UK. In Damascus, Arab groups had been established in the course of the nineteenth century in order to obtain some form of autonomy, and the Society of Arts and Sciences was founded in 1857. The dominant figures were the Lebanese Christian writers and educators Nasif Yaziji and Butrus al Bustani. The latter preached that "Syria is our fatherland", including in this term his native Lebanon and other areas. His speeches of protest were perhaps inspired by a terrible massacre in 1860 in Lebanon of Maronites by Muslims and Druzes, which naturally gave rise to criticism of the Turkish authorities who had not been able to protect the Maronites.

In the period 1877 to 1878, when the Russians defeated the Ottomans and even threatened Constantinople for a while during an intervention to assist national upheavals in the Balkan area, many Arab conscripts died for a (Turkish) cause they did not accept; in order to exploit Ottoman weakness, a certain national movement arose again in Damascus and other cities in the area denouncing the Imperial tyranny, but it was not strong enough to survive when the Ottoman regime re-established law and order, and barely survived this dangerous Russian attack.

Arab nationalism revived in the early 1900s and the Aleppo-born (Syrian) Kawakibi is recognised as being the main herald of a modern, secular Pan-Arabism.[30] He died as early as 1902, but in his writings he talks of Ottoman despotism and the need for an Islamic revival based on Pan-Islamic unity. He admits weaknesses in Islam such as fatalism, religious rifts, intolerance, the ban on speech and the lack of education of women. Many of these accusations could be boiled down to

---

29 Called so because they follow the lessons of a Syrian Christian Monk, Saint Maron, who lived in the late fourth and early fifth centuries. They have their own patriarch in Lebanon, but respect the Pope in Rome.

30 Benny Morris, op.cit., p. 27. Note that "Arabism" and "Islam" were then used synonymously.

rising antagonism against continued Arab acceptance of an unjust Ottoman, feudal society that also gave rise to the Young Turks' revolt a few years later, in 1908.

Another nationalist-minded Arab was Rashid Rida, born in Lebanon, who spoke of Arabia as the heartland of an Arabism uncorrupted by a difficult Ottoman way of life. He lived most of his life in Cairo — far from the Ottoman centre — and published a pro-Arabist newspaper, *al-Mattar*, that promoted an Islamic revival. He founded the secret *Society of Arab Association* and openly declared the Turks the enemies of the Arabs. He served as President of the First Syrian-Arab Congress, held in Damascus in 1920, the year when the Ottoman power was fighting its last battles.

In a French setting, a Maronite, Najib Azouri, founded *la Ligue de la Patrie Arabe* in 1904, interestingly enough using *Arab* and not *Islamic* as the uniting term. He also published *Le Réveil de la Nation Arabe* in 1905, advocating secular Arabism, surely influenced by French thinking on secularism, which was at that time a new development in France and other European countries. When he had later settled in Cairo, just before the First World War, he asked French diplomats to provide him with arms in order to fight the Ottoman regime, but apparently Paris would not risk its entente with Britain at that stage. Or perhaps France had no confidence in the gifts of these nationalistic circles. France also had its own problems with the Arab societies in North Africa.

The reform policy of the Young Turks, who gained the upper hand in the revolution of 1908, had involved a Turkification that of course went against the Arabs' interest. Some scorn was even shown by the young regime in Istanbul towards what they called the "dogs of the Turkish nation", meaning the Arabs. No insult could be stronger to an Arab than the use of the word *dog*.

The Ottoman Party for Decentralisation was founded in Cairo in 1912, when the initiators still believed in the possibility of a reform of the Empire which would allow them more autonomy. In June 1913 the First Arab Congress convened in Paris, calling for political rights for the Arabs and a decentralised administration. An initial result was that senior Ottoman representatives travelled to Paris in order to find a compromise with the Arabs that included not only Muslim, but also Christian, representatives and even a Jew. This was one of the last efforts of reforming the dying Ottoman regime, which soon felt the strain of the First World War, in which Istanbul was an ally of the Central European powers. This regime eventually realised that it was on the losing side, which was underscored by its defeat in the final wars in the Balkan just before the outbreak of the Great War, which also aimed at the liberation of the last vestige of Ottoman power in Europe.

4. *British-French Supported Revolt*

All the aforementioned Arab attempts to obtain autonomy were undertaken mostly by academic circles and did not really involve the masses. There was therefore not yet any equivalent to the Zionist movement, which at the same time (early 1900s) had grown into a force which politicians in the West could not ignore. But just as the UK wanted Zionists to be their extended arm in the still Turkish-dominated Palestine, London also envisaged an Arab revolt during the First World War that could assist the Allied fight against the Turkish supporters of their dangerous enemy, the Central European powers.

In accordance with its imperial way of thinking, the British government decided to focus its attention on the Mecca-based Hashemite prince, Sharif Hussein, whom they regarded as intelligent and willing to liberate Arab land in collaboration with the British and French. He had two sons, Abdullah and Feisal, and the latter was eventually chosen to head the military efforts against the Turks, in which the young British officer called *Lawrence of Arabia* played an important role (although many scholars think that this role was later somewhat exaggerated by this exotic officer himself). Secret negotiations had been going on for some time with Sharif Hussein, and with the help of Allied assistance (money and arms) the Hashemite prince soon began a serious revolt against the Turks, in 1916. This was all the more easy because the Ottoman power had started a regime of terror in the Arab world, publicly executing (by hanging) Arab nationalists in several places (Damascus and Beirut, especially) and instituting a policy of deportations, also of Jews, almost at the same time.

The British promised the Hashemite prince that he or his son Feisal could occupy the throne of Damascus in an independent Kingdom of Greater Syria, which would include most of the region, except Arabia, Iraq and Egypt. Feisal had already established relations with some circles in Syria, but his problem was that most Syrian leaders were not eager to accept a monarchy. Independence for them meant a republican regime, and Feisal was seen as foreign to their old land, which was more sophisticated than his desert region of Northern Arabia. Another problem for the British and the Hashemite ruler was the fact that France was going to take over the Syrian region as a protecting power in accordance with the already mentioned Sykes-Picot agreement, which was signed between Britain and France in 1916, and that Paris had no wish to accept the Prince either.

The Sykes-Picot agreement, signed almost at the same time that the Arab revolt against the Turks broke out, did not take into consideration the notion that after the First World War and the expected fall of the Ottoman Empire, the Arabs might wish to become independent.

Hardly any single Arab national state except Egypt had been independent (at least for any substantial period of time), and the Allied governments easily agreed among themselves that these Arab entities needed protection, not independence. The Arabs generally saw — and still do see — this negative Allied decision as a treacherous turnaround from earlier promises given when the Allied cause needed Arab support. In the last decades of imperialism or colonialism this deceit of young national endeavours of independence was unfortunately not unique — far from it. But since the hopes of the Arab leaders had been so great based on official promises, the feelings of deceit and anger were all the more bitter.

Feisal did succeed in liberating his own important area of (Saudi) Arabia, around the holy cities Mecca and Medina and parts of what is today Jordan, and could eventually plan his liberation of Damascus. But the bulk of the allied forces were the British/Dominion troops under General Allenby, who had already successfully conquered Palestine and Western parts of Jordan and — following the common-sense advice of Lawrence of Arabia — could now afford to let the Arab leader, Feisal and his armed forces enter this important Arab capital. This took place on 3 October 1918, just a month before the armistice ending the First World War. Due to a mistake, some Australian troops had previously entered Damascus after the Turks had fled central Syria. Feisal's triumphal entry was carried out, however; but it did not have a long-lasting effect, since French troops followed and occupied Damascus on 6 October 1918, taking control of the city. The confusing situation was only rectified after two more years, when France could finally establish her claim to be the protecting force for Syria and Lebanon. Feisal, who with British support had established an interim administration in Syria, was defeated by the French in 1920, and the British — after having reconsidered the matter — would not set aside the Sykes-Picot agreement granting France supremacy in the area.

Feisal was compensated by receiving the throne of Baghdad in March 1921, which he managed to keep until his death in 1933. With regard to the administration of Palestine, the UK finally separated it from Syria in the same period, while the French eventually separated the Lebanese entity from that of Syria.

Feisal's elder brother, Abdullah, became Foreign Minister of the Kingdom of Hijaz, which his father established in 1917 after the Turkish defeat, and Abdullah tried to force the French troops out of Syria in 1921, assembling an army in Transjordan, where he had set up a government in Amman. But the British wanted to abide by the above-mentioned agreement with France and confirmed the two princes in their new monarchies of Iraq (Feisal) and Transjordan(Abdullah). The latter was first recognised as an Emirate, but Abdullah became *King* of Jordan in 1946, only five years before he was assassinated (1951).

Was the Arab revolt of 1916 a popular uprising against the Turks and the beginning of a Pan-Arab movement? This was hardly so, because the individuals involved in the liberation of the Ottoman Arab region were mostly soldiers. The feudal character of the Hashemite monarchy in the nineteenth century did not promote a really popular national movement. But it must be regarded as similar to some of the scattered Arab nationalist attempts in the early part of the twentieth century, which were directed mostly against the Ottoman Empire that was surely not a very liberal one, although the Istanbul regime could not isolate itself from liberal tendencies in other parts of the world. One of the ironic aspects of the Arab awakening during the First World War is that it went hand in hand, so to speak, with the Jewish awakening leading to the Balfour Declaration. But, as already mentioned, it was much weaker than the Zionist movement and a less popular one, since most of the Arab masses then were not very well-informed, lacking education and a modern upbringing in most places. And there was of course no Arab background similar to the Jewish diaspora, which makes it understandable that there was no strong popular urge to liberate the Arab world. Whether they were ruled by far-away Ottoman princes in their Islamic Empire or by distant Arab rulers of a similar feudal character did not seem that important to the masses, who were not used to freedom or democratic ways.

When the two Hashemite princes were established in their respective countries, neither of them paid much attention to *Pan-Arabism*, it seems. They probably had too many internal problems in their own Kingdoms to be able to promote the Arab cause as such. King Abdullah, who lived a good deal longer than his younger brother, continued to maintain a wish to expand his kingdom to Syria, a rather unrealistic dream. This intelligent prince is interesting in the context of our book because he showed some understanding of the Jews. His brother, Feisal, had held talks with the Zionist leader, Weizmann, as early as in 1919, stressing the promising aspects of the Balfour Declaration and "the goodwill and understanding between Arabs and Jews", as already mentioned — an optimistic vision that none of the parties could carry through. Abdullah engaged in similar talks at a much later stage, around Israel's independence. Then the Jordanian leader had positive talks with the leading Israeli politician (later Prime Minister) Golda Meir, but not much came out of these initial talks, because of nationalistic Arab opposition.[31]

We may conclude that the Hashemite rulers were ahead of their people with regard to a policy of understanding their new neighbours, the Jews. Or we may prefer to say that they went too far, without taking into consideration the opposition of the majority of their subjects. The first alternative represents logic, the second political realities. When the next Monarch, Abdullah's grandson Hussein, managed to carry through confidential talks with Israeli leaders, they eventually led to the peace agreement reached in 1994. But even this popular monarch had great difficulties obtaining sufficient backing from the majority of his people.

Another important Arab Kingdom was Saudi Arabia. Its first king, Ibn Saud, had to fight his way to the throne during the 1920s and 1930s, displacing first some minor competitors, then the Hashemite prince, Sharif Hussein, in 1924, and finally in 1932 establishing himself as king of the huge new nation, Saudi Arabia. This kingdom soon became the most important oil producer and remains so to-

---

31 It is a bit surprising to read that Benny Morris, in his op.cit., p. 83, talks of "Feisal's infidelity as characterising his attitude toward Zionism". How could one expect an Arab prince to show *fidelity* towards Jews penetrating an Arab area?

day. But Ibn Saud's long fight for supremacy and his expansionist dreams for his subcontinent did not make it possible for him to raise the banner of a Pan-Arabic movement. His influence in the Arab world, and that of his successors, increased over the years, but was never accepted in the same way as the final promoter of Pan-Arabism, President Nasser, who was hailed as the almost undisputed Arab leader. The Saudi banner was rather one of Islamic purity, in the sense that the kings purposely spoke of themselves as the defenders of the holy places, Mecca and Medina; they did not accept any religious tolerance, whether in the country itself or outside it, and this has remained part of the Saudi Arabian image since the kingdom was founded.

The 1936 – 39 Palestinian-Arab revolt against the Jews and the British, which shocked both, was a genuine Palestinian fight for national identity. Benny Morris calls it "the biggest and most protracted uprising against the British in any country in the Middle East and the most significant in Palestinian history until the *intifada*".[32] He also mentions that the revolt cost an estimated 3,000 – 6,000 rebels their lives (several of them were hanged), whereas the Jews had much fewer losses, of some hundreds, and the occupying British a similar number of casualties. The economic damages were substantial, and many of the local Arab leaders were either dead or in prison, while the majority of the Palestinians probably realised that their political lives were paralysed after the unsuccessful revolt.

As a result of this rebellion, which was fought on the Arab side under the motto "the English to the sea, the Jews to their graves", the British government, following the Peel Commissions recommendations, put its brakes on the Jewish march towards independence for a while.

For the Arabs it must have been a bitter consequence of their uprising that the Jewish defence capabilities were strengthened during the revolt and in its aftermath. Many arms factories were established by the Jewish armed movement, the *Haganah*, which had its roots in the first pioneer days, and the Jews had now learnt how to depend on themselves, in accordance with the teaching of Jabotinsky.

C. Pan-Arabism

Pan-Arabism is a doctrine which maintains that all Arabs belong to one and the same community or nation, wherever they live.

As we have seen above, there were various attempts at promoting freedom for the Arabs, but they were, generally speaking, vague and gave no indication as to how the *Arab Nation* was to be envisaged. The conditions were not helpful during the multi-ethnic/religious Ottoman regime, when the first attempts were

---

32   Op.cit., p. 129.

made. The same situation characterised the period between the two World Wars, when the Arabs were still very dependant on other nations, especially Britain and France.

The first concrete step towards creating some unity among the Arab states was taken — ironically enough — by Britain in its efforts to attract the Arabs into the Allied sphere of influence during the Second World War. As early as 1942, London declared that the UK favoured the idea of unity among the Arab World, and this led to the first meeting of the *League of Arab States*, held in Cairo in September – October 1944. On this occasion an appropriate pact was signed by the attending nations (not all independent yet) — Egypt, Iraq, Lebanon, North Yemen, Saudi Arabia, Syria and Transjordan — and by a Palestinian representative.

The League established its headquarters in Cairo and chose an Egyptian as its first Secretary General. In the following years, the other Arab countries that had become independent joined the League.

The member states decided to reject the UN resolution of November 1947 on the creation of two states in Palestine as "absurd and impracticable and unjust". They therefore decided to boycott Israeli goods as early as 1948 and launched an *attack*[33] on the new nation, Israel, when the latter declared its independence in May 1948. They signed a Joint Defence and Economic Co-operation Treaty in 1950, shortly after the first Arab-Israeli war, but many of the League's decisions had little effect.

It was only with the advent of the military leader of Egypt, Gamal Abdul Nasser, in the early 1950s that Pan-Arabism became an important movement in the Arab world and elsewhere. We shall later return to this forceful leader who managed to create hope among the downtrodden multitudes, first in his own country, and soon also in the entire Arab world. He knew how to raise the banner of Pan-Arabism and often exploited it to his own and Egypt's advantage. In 1958, he was the main party behind the establishment of the Arab Union of Egypt and Syria, and other countries joined this pact, which lasted only three years. Nasser did not manage, however, to keep a sound balance between Cairo's wishes for hegemony and the desire of the Syrian leadership to retain some influence. We may see this period of 1958 to 1961 as the peak of Pan-Arabism, which has never returned. In that period Nasser participated in the leadership of the third world countries, together with Prime Minister Nehru of India, President Sukarno of Indonesia and President Tito of Yugoslavia. Nasser was also the evident spokesman for the Arabs world-wide. Seen in retrospect, his voice was often more moderate than was believed by the West in those years; only in the immediate pre-1967 War period did he show more nationalistic and demagogue tendencies than previously, to the detriment, probably, of his own country's interests.

---

33   We shall explain, at a later stage, whether this term is correct.

It must surely have come as a great shock to Pan-Arabism and to the Arab world led by Nasser that the combined Arab forces suffered such a serious debacle in the 1967 War with Israel. In the 1956 war they had been able to use the British-French attack as an excuse for their defeat. Despite Nasser's dreams of eliminating the enemy or even Israel as a nation, which he made public just before the onslaught in June 1967, very little remained afterwards except shame, because the Israeli Defence Force (IDF) of the intruding small Jewish nation had again managed to defeat the much larger Egyptian army, despite the fact that the latter had allies. This defeat marked the beginning of the fall of Nasser, as the influence of this charismatic leader soon declined. He was eventually also struck by illness, which lead to his death in late 1970 at the fairly young age of 52. The state funeral was an obvious manifestation of his popularity among the masses.

The peculiar Libyan leader, Colonel Ghadafi, has often tried to promote himself in the image of Nasser's successor, wanting to carry Pan-Arabism further. But in his unpredictable ways, he lacks the solid charisma of the former Egyptian leader, and Ghadafi's country — despite its oil — does not carry the economic, historical or popular weight in the Arab world that would make it possible for him to have any serious impact as a successor to Nasser. His recent move in 2002, declaring that he wants to leave the Arab League because it lacks efficiency, in his view, confirms his unpredictability.

Was Pan-Arabism more than a hope, more than an unrealistic dream? We cannot easily judge, but my interpretation is as follows: Over the centuries, common Arabs had never had any political influence. Their leaders were often corrupt and remote from the people, and other powers established the framework that was decisive for their daily lives — first Arab feudal lords, followed by the Ottomans and then the British and the French. The Egyptian King ruling up to the time of Neguib and Nasser was corrupt and had no charisma or feeling for his subjects. Therefore the charismatic populism of Nasser was new and appealed to most Arabs. All Arabs are familiar with the holy book, the *Koran*, references to which would always appeal to the masses, because the book was (is) the cornerstone of Arab culture and tradition as early as the Arab empire established soon after Prophet Muhammed's death. But even that forgotten Islamic kingdom, based on conquest, soon broke up into smaller entities; it was simply too big.

In our own time, it was not realistic, either, to believe that a common regime could unite countries as far apart as Morocco and Iraq, Lebanon and Saudi Arabia. Traditions were utterly different, and Egypt in particular had many non-Arab/Islamic features that the common man felt were indirectly present in his daily life, even if he could not define them. Syria and Lebanon were even more mixed Christian-Muslim cultures, as opposed to Saudi Arabia, which was founded on Islamic purity and little tolerance. The example of the abortive union between Egypt and Syria finally illustrated the difficulties of uniting newly independent nations that jealously guarded their individual sovereignty.[34] Even if most Arabs understand each others' different dialects (and share the common, classical Arabic), it becomes difficult when their national geographical positions are as far apart as those of, say, Morocco and Saudi Arabia.

To give a parallel to our Scandinavian/Nordic countries, we have to admit that regional differences have been stronger than the wish to unite based on a common culture and very similar languages. On the other hand, in the northern regional area of Europe, political maturity and culture have been so highly developed over the last century that it has been possible to establish a tight cooperation — with great success in some fields — just as we now see the same developments within the European Union. It is exactly this developed political culture or maturity that is lacking in the Arab world, which is still composed mostly of authoritarian regimes that often ignore the wishes of their own subjects. Therefore it is so difficult to establish real political cooperation among the Arab nations and get beyond a certain point where not only words, but also deeds, matter.

It is also important to stress that within the various national entities, new national feelings have developed over the last fifty years to an extent that the rulers cannot ignore them, however artificial most of the original borders were at the outset when the colonial powers determined them.

D. The Creation of Israel, Born in War

1. Prelude

In the section on Zionism, we saw that serious difficulties arose because of the Jewish emigration to the Holy Land in the 1930s and in post-Second World War Palestine. It was understandable that the Arabs became extremely frustrated by the increasing pressure of immigration in the 1930s during the Nazi persecutions of Jews, which began in 1933, well before the Holocaust in the next decade. This was the background of the above-mentioned serious Arab uprising against the Jews and the British establishment in 1936 – 37, and the British government therefore eventually favoured a partition of Palestine. The Peel Commission recommended the partition in 1937, with the suggested creation of a very small Jewish state (5,000 square kilometres) and a larger Arab one. Ben-Gurion realised that

---

34 We may here recall how the Federal Union of Pakistan broke up in 1971 - 72, when Bangladesh was born out of East Pakistan, both because of the many differences between the Bengalis and the West Pakistanis and because of the enormous geographical distance separating them.

there was probably no way to avoid this proposed solution, even if he certainly regretted the limited scope of the decision favouring a Jewish state. He accepted it, however, but only as a starting point in order to obtain the desired recognition. Ben-Gurion carried so much weight in Jewish/Zionist circles that the Twentieth Zionist Congress in 1937, which was held in Zurich, accepted the Peel Commission's recommendations as a basis for negotiations with the British government. But the decision was not passed with an overwhelming majority; only 290 voted in favour, with 160 against and some abstentions. At the same time, Ben-Gurion was re-elected as Chairman of the Jewish Agency's Executive, thereby being assured of his leadership of the Jews. With this decision we have the starting point for the realisation of the State of Israel, and that is why it is discussed in more detail here than in the previous section on Zionism.

The road was still a difficult one, lasting some ten years more before the Zionists could become masters of the new nation of their dreams, Israel. In the meantime, London soon understood that there was a need to placate the Arabs because of the growing threat from the rising power of Nazi-Germany with which many Arab leaders sympathised.[35]

As early as 1939, the British government broke its promises to support even a small Jewish nation. A White Paper of May 1939 recommended that the Jews now be only a minority in a unified State of Palestine and that more restrictions would be imposed on Jewish purchase of land from the Arabs.

The reaction of the Zionists to the White Paper of May 1939 was understandably blunt and angry, and they decided to fight the new recommendations, which they naturally regarded with absolute frustration, as the old British promises now seemed forgotten. The Jews decided to fortify their old fighting units, the above-mentioned *Haganah*, against both the Arabs and the British. In Ben-Gurion's words: "the Zionists would fight with the British against Hitler as if there were no White Paper and fight the White Paper as if there were no war"[36]. The negative trend, as seen with the Zionists' eyes, was slowed to some extent shortly afterwards, when Winston Churchill was chosen as new British Prime Minister and insisted on keeping the promises of the Balfour Declaration.

I have referred above to the Zionists' ambitious *Biltmore Program* (adopted in New York in May 1942), which not only ignored the negative British plan from 1939, but also rejected the suggested partitioning of Palestine. This new Zionist

---

35 The Palestinian leader, Haajii Muhammed Amin al-Husseini, was one of them. He was establishing the *Arab Higher Committee* in 1936 and eventually fled the country after British punishments and a ban on his activities, and went to Germany during the World War. He even met Hitler there.

36 Shlaim, op.cit., p. 23.

The Zionist Congress in Vienna August 1939. In the front row from left to right: Moshe Sharett, David Ben-Gurion, Chaim Weizmann and Eliezer Kaplan.

plan was directly aiming at creating (only) a Jewish state in Palestine. It also implicitly referred to the necessity of transferring many Arab residents to neighbouring countries. The Biltmore Program was backed by Ben-Gurion and Weizmann, both present in New York then, and it may be seen as a cornerstone of the policies followed first by Jabotinsky and later by Begin and other right-wing politicians in Israel. Soon Weizmann openly discussed with a Russian representative the above-mentioned proposal for transferring Arab populations out of Palestine.

If the brakes on the progress of Zionism only operated for a while, it was because the tide soon turned in favour of the Allied forces and their defeat of the Nazis in 1943 – 45, at more or less the same time as knowledge of the Nazi Holocaust spread around the world. The 1939 plan therefore soon became abortive and even forgotten.

The after-war atmosphere completely changed the overall political picture, also in the Middle East, of course. There were still many difficulties ahead, and an unexpected setback came when elections in the summer of 1945, immediately after the war, enabled the British Labour party to form a government to replace the one led by Churchill. Its new Foreign Secretary, Aneurin Bevan, was known to be an anti-Zionist, and it was therefore logical that the British were met with increasing violence in Palestine that demonstrated the Zionists' impatience and frustration. The violence in Palestine culminated with the fierce and brutal attack on the King David Hotel in Jerusalem in July 1946, killing 91 people, Britons in particular, but also Arabs and Jews.

The British government soon decided to wash their hands of the impossible situation and turn over the problem of Palestine to the United Nations, the newly established world organisation in New York. This happened in February 1947, and Benny Morris tells us that "the political developments of 1947 were played out against a background of Jewish violence and reprisals spiralling almost out of control".[37]

A UN Special Committee on Palestine, UNSCOP, was created and sent to the area, almost at the same time as the dramatic affair of the *Exodus*.[38] After carefully considering the matter, including interviewing many Arabs and Jews, UNSCOP eventually decided in favour of a division of Palestine into a fairly small Israel and a neighbouring Palestinian/Arab state.

The UN resolution 181 of 28 November 1947 provided the starting point for the creation of Israel and a Palestinian state. It was passed by 33 states in favour, (including both the USA and the USSR) and 13 against, while ten had abstained, including the UK. But as we already know, there was certainly no agreement between the two main parties concerned. The Jews accepted the partition plan, albeit with a sad heart. Ben-Gurion and his team of realists could now work towards independence, if not safely so, at least with the important UN backing in mind. No date was yet fixed, but the British decided to leave the chaotic country in May 1948, earlier than originally planned.

The Arabs protested violently and after their immediate rejection of the UN resolution, the Arab League decided to provide arms to the Palestinians. It had already prepared Palestine for a fight through its decision to create a *Palestinian Liberation Army* in September 1947, even before the UN resolution.

What Shlaim terms *the Unofficial War*[39] and Morris *Civil War*[40] began soon after the UN decision to support an Israeli and an Arab state in the Palestinian area. Arab guerrillas fought against the Jews, and the latter decided on an offensive strategy, according to Shlaim.[41] Ben-Gurion had long ago understood the necessity of a strong force to protect Jewish interests, and he was not only the political leader but also became the head of the Jewish Agency's defence department (in

---

37 Op.cit., p. 181.
38 Benny Morris, op.cit., p. 183, gives an excellent picture of this tragic event of July 1947, which was later dramatised in the famous film *Exodus*.
39 Op.cit., p. 28.
40 Op.cit., p. 191.
41 Op.cit., p. 31.

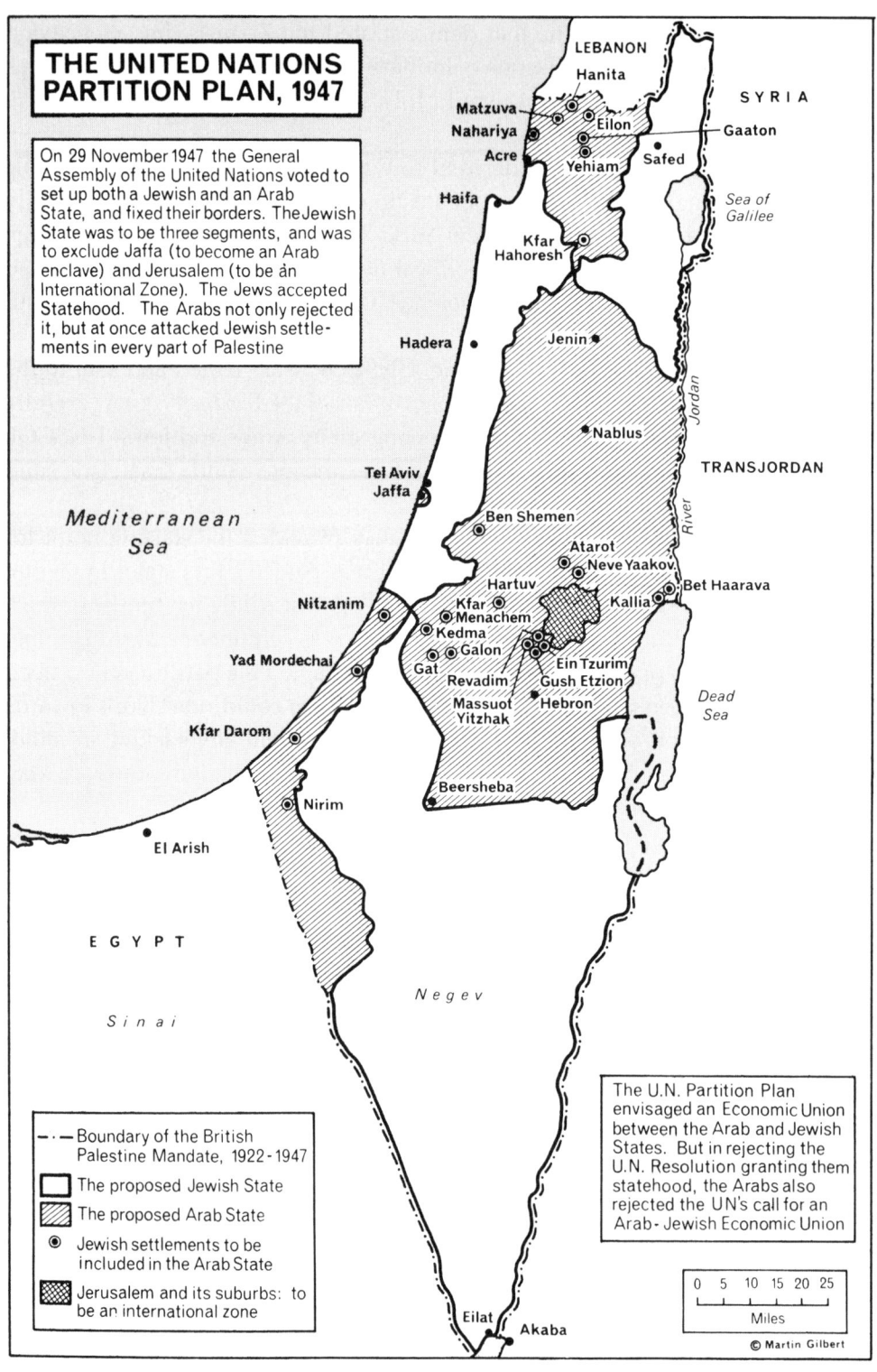

1946), controlling the *Haganah* forces. As such, he showed foresight and was a brilliant organiser. Upon several dangerous attacks by the Palestinian forces led by al-Husseini, who were cutting off the main roads, the *Haganah* launched a plan D that allowed for the eviction of Palestinian Arabs from villages in order to secure the Jewish state, which had been approved by the UN.

The last Jewish offensive took place in April and May, and according to Shlaim, the Palestinian society disintegrated under the impact of the Jewish military offensive; an exodus of Palestinian refugees was therefore set in motion.[42] One of the worst excesses took place when a strong force of several Jewish groups, IZL (Irgun Zvai Leumi or Stern) and LHI (Lehi group), assisted by the *Haganah* attacked the Arab village of *Deir Yassin* on April 9, 1948 and massacred hundreds of innocent men, women and children. Benny Morris writes that it is remembered "not as a military operation, but rather for the atrocities committed by the IZL and LHI troops"[43]. Although he corrects the original estimate of the death toll (given by observers in 1948) from 254 to some 110, the picture he draws is indeed a very brutal one, shocking all observers who were reminded of the (then) fairly recent Nazi excesses against the Jews. Many of the facts given by Morris derive from some of the participants in the massacre (Begin was one of the leaders of the operation). Morris asserts that it "seemed to push Jordan into the arms of those pressing for direct intervention by the Arab Stats"[44].

It was therefore not only an inhumane act in itself, but also to some extent counterproductive in political and military terms. On the other hand, it demoralised the Palestinian Arabs to the point of leaving the country, and that was certainly one of the most obvious aims of the Zionists behind their brutal onslaught.

We may accept or reject this interpretation of well-planned and brutal evictions of many Arabs from their ancestral land like the one just mentioned of Deir Yassin, but since the two often-quoted Israeli revisionist historians have only confirmed this account after careful studies, I think we can agree. Others will still prefer to stick to the more traditional Israeli view, according to which the flight of Arab refugees is interpreted as one of the unavoidable hazards of war. At any rate, there is probably no doubt that the ferocity of the Arab rebellion in the late 1930s and the Holocaust with all its horrors had convinced the Jews of the need to survive in a hostile surrounding, whatever the costs. The merciless onslaught against innocent village people must be seen in that light, but with the privilege of hindsight, it is easy to disapprove of what happened. We must feel compassion especially for the many lives lost, not only among the Palestinians, but also among the Jews in Arab attacks of revenge, and for the impossible

---

42   Ibid., p. 31.
43   Op.cit., p. 208.
44   Op.cit., p. 209.

situation that made the partitioning of Palestine such an unhappy event for the Arabs, and which is the main cause of the ensuing conflict that is still in the limelight today.

2. Independence and Open War

Whereas the Jewish/Zionist politicians generally accepted the UN plan for the partitioning of Palestine, the Arab leaders rejected it, as we have already seen. But initially the Arab states did not plan an attack on the new Jewish nation, and they decided to wait and see what was going to happen. They thought that providing arms to the Palestinians might be sufficient, but soon learned that the unofficial war in the winter of 1947 – 48 showed how greatly the strong Jewish military initiatives in the field were pressuring the Palestinians into defensive positions. This war confirmed the Jewish talent for good organisation, even if the Arab leaders would not admit it publicly. Diplomatically, too, the coming Israeli leaders were energetic in trying to obtain support or understanding from some of the Arab leaders. King Abdullah of Jordan was one of the few who could be expected to discuss any proposal from the Zionists, and talks were indeed held, as mentioned earlier, between the later Prime Minister, Golda Meir, and the monarch just before the outbreak of the war. Eventually, Abdullah, like his brother Feisal many years earlier, realised that he could not gain approval from his Arab subjects at a time when the Palestinians were being beaten in real military encounters in the unhappy land that was going to be divided. We have already mentioned that Abdullah might have been negatively influenced by what happened in Deir Yassin. He even told Golda Meir so, but she hardly understood his way of thinking.

It was this military preparedness of the Jews and the heavy casualties which the Palestinians suffered which forced the Arab intervention soon after Israel had declared its independence in May 1948. Despite foreign appeals for patience that might allow outside nations to find a compromise, Ben-Gurion had decided that Israel should declare her independence when the British publicised they were leaving the country.

3. Israel's Declaration of Independence on 14 May 1948

This unilateral declaration of Israel's independence came on 14 May 1948. Not only most Arabs, but also many outside powers opposed it fiercely, and even some cautious Jews were hesitant. They would have preferred to wait for outside mediation. However, the coming Prime Minister and founding father of Israel, Ben-Gurion, decided to act — despite all the risks. And as a born leader his advice was followed, if not enthusiastically by everybody. His declaration of independence in Tel Aviv was brief and issued against the background of all the risks

David Ben-Gurion reads the Israeli Declaration of Independence on the 14th of May 1948.

involved. His own diary shows his feelings: "In the country there is celebration and profound joy — and once again — I am a mourner among the celebrants, as on 29 November 1947 [the date of the UN resolution, my addition] "... Two days before, *Haganah* commanders had told him (Ben-Gurion) that the chances of victory were fifty-fifty.[45]

Shlaim writes that "the collapse of the Palestinian resistance prompted the Arab League to commit the regular armies of the member states to the struggle against partition, thus reversing an earlier decision merely to finance and arm the local Arabs".[46]

If we can trust this interpretation, as I think we can, the Arab *attack* on Israel must

---

45 Morris, op.cit., p. 215. Mrs. Golda Meir gives her account of the effect of the UN resolution in her memoirs, *My Life*, London, 1975 (revised edition by Futura, 1979) p. 172: "The crowd was drunk with happiness when they learnt about the voting at the UN". In her own speech on that occasion, she stressed that the "Partition Plan is a compromise, on what you [the Arabs], not what we wanted. But let us now live in peace".

46 Op.cit., p. 32.

be regarded in a different light than the one that has traditionally been seen: That of little Israel being attacked in order to reject a Jewish state or even to throw the Jews into the sea. It will never be known what would have happened to the Jews if the combined Arab forces had managed to beat the Jewish state. If one puts that hypothetical question to an Arab, as I have done several times, he will typically say that the Palestinians/Arabs would have accepted a secular state with Jews and Muslim and Christian Arabs living together in a sort of federation, perhaps. There was, therefore, according to many Arabs no question of wanting a forced exodus from Palestine of all Zionists, let alone mass killings, as the Jewish national philosophy, based on a wish for survival, has frequently maintained.

Here, two factors must be taken into consideration: First, that the Arabs had tolerated the Jewish intrusion in the 1920s and 1930s — up to a point. They were not anti-Semitic or anti-Jewish as such, as many Europeans had been, and the Holocaust was not their responsibility, which the Arabs often rightly point out. But they wanted an acceptance of the fact that they — the Arabs of Palestine — *also* had a right to continue to live in what they saw as their own country.[47]

The second point is that they could see no reason why Jews and Arabs should not be able to live together in a secular state with a population comprised of various religions, especially considering that Christian establishments had long been active in many parts of the country, especially in Jerusalem and Bethlehem. When they had carried out a serious revolt in 1936 – 39, it was in order to stress this fact and limit the growing immigration, which seemed to threaten their legitimate existence in their own country.

In light of the Zionist way of thinking that we have explained above, which aimed at the creation of a Jewish state whatever the costs, it is easy to recognise that these two contradictory ways of thinking could not be reconciled.

War was therefore unavoidable. It began on the day following the Israeli Declaration of Independence, 15 May 1948, when troops from Egypt, (Trans-)Jordan, Syria, Lebanon and Iraq invaded Palestine, primarily in order to reinforce the irregular Palestinian forces, according to Shlaim, as quoted above.[48] He adds that "on the Jewish side, the turn of the tide reinforced the conviction that military force offered the only solution to the Arab problem". But whatever the background, there was no clear-cut war aim uniting all the Arab leaders, as we shall soon see. They also ran a risk in attacking the new Jewish state, because of their weak forces and lack of motivation. King Abdullah's son, Talal, was among those who clearly foresaw an Arab defeat.

Even if the new Israeli leaders and most of the Jewish inhabitants surely also

---

47   When we think of contemporary European resistance to Muslim immigration, not least in Denmark, this protest may be better understood.
48   Op.cit., p. 32.

had their doubts about the outcome of the war and all the risks involved in any military encounter, the picture was not one of David against Goliath, as often suggested in the original tradition of the new nation. The fifty-fifty chance mentioned earlier may seem to have been more realistic, but the advantages soon increased on the Jewish side.

First of all, the Arab forces were not well-trained (except those of the Jordanian Arab Legion), they had no well-established uniform command nor any precise war aims, and their troops were far from being motivated in any way similar to the Israelis. Formally, the King of Jordan was the head of the Arab forces, but in reality there was no clear-cut command structure. It is worth repeating here that, unlike the image intended by Israeli propaganda, there was no discrepancy in favour of overwhelming Arab forces or war equipment. Morris tells us that on the contrary, at the beginning of the war, the number of soldiers on the Israeli side was a good deal higher than that of the Arab side (almost 40,000 men, as opposed to 28,000); it soon increased greatly in favour of the new nation, (65,000 as opposed to some 40,000 Arabs in June). The Jewish troops had received better training, and several soldiers had war experience from the World War or from the *Haganah's* fighting in the unofficial war with the Palestinians that had just ended; they also had better equipment, if not in heavy arms. But what was of course most important was the already mentioned high level of motivation of the Jewish troops. They realised instinctively — or were told — that this was a fight for their new homeland and was indeed a matter of life and death.

Most Arabs had no similar dramatic visions with regard to the conflict, and the Palestinian Arabs had already been utterly demoralised and partly defeated during the recent unofficial war, primarily because of their own weakness, but also because they had received little help from their fellow Arabs abroad. This negative treatment of Palestinian Arabs did not give them much hope for a better future. The Jordanian King wanted to secure for himself a larger kingdom at the expense of the Palestinians, and in this he was in agreement with the Zionists. He did not think in terms of securing any autonomous Palestinian state — quite the contrary, because he wanted to include the West Bank within the kingdom, which also happened. The other Arab leaders probably had more vague war aims. For Egypt, the aim was to secure its northern borders inside and beyond Gaza by occupying the Negev desert, which had been allocated to Israel. Egypt was also very sceptical of the Hashemite Kingdom and its ambitions. For Syria, the wish was to expand into Northern Israel to secure its own southwestern borders; and for Iraq, it was to secure its petroleum pipeline to Haifa. Lebanon barely took part in the war because it was weak; furthermore, there was strong opposition against joining the war from its large and still dominant Maronite population. We can easily see that there was a general lack of Arab solidarity, which of course helped Israel.

The largest Arab contingent was that of Egypt, which originally committed

7,000 soldiers, while Jordan supplied 5,000, Iraq 4,000, Syria 4,000, and Palestine 4,000 irregular fighters. Finally only 2,000 Lebanese soldiers joined the fight, mostly symbolically.

The Jews were favoured by the arms embargo imposed by the UN soon after the war broke out and respected by the Western powers of France, the USA and the UK. Since Egypt, Jordan and Iraq had been receiving mostly British arms, this embargo struck the Arab force much more strongly than the Jewish one. The Zionists had secured secret supply lines from Czechoslovakia, paid for by US Dollars provided by Jewish funds.

With regard to the Arab command and war aims, Morris tells us that "the Arabs had done no proper planning or intelligence work, logistics were in shambles, armaments and ammunition were in piteously short supply, and officers and soldiers were unprepared".[49] Shlaim adds that "it is true that the military experts of the Arab League had worked out a unified plan for the invasion, but King Abdullah, who was given nominal command over all the Arab forces in Palestine, wrecked this plan by making last minute changes".[50] Later he adds that "in the second half of the war, the special relationship between the Zionists and King Abdullah slowly began to assert itself".[51] If this is so, one reads with astonishment in Shlaim's and Morris' accounts that Ben-Gurion, in accordance with his offensive strategy, wanted to use the second half of the war to conquer the West Bank. He was, however, overruled by a majority of his Cabinet, upon the warnings of the generals who feared British support of the Jordanian Arab Legion. They also attached great importance to the fact that the Legion had respected the partition plan and not occupied any territory allocated to the Jewish nation, even if it had been able to.

It is not my intention to tell the story of this first war (or of any of the later ones) in great detail, but to give an idea of its developments and end. A first truce was reached in June, 1948, after a month of fighting that had given the Israeli forces some self-confidence which was soon fortified by the large supplies of arms pouring into Israel in the first months of the war. Morris writes that "the first four weeks showed a clear Israeli victory".[52] The truce lasted about a month, but when the battles were resumed, the Israeli army, confronting the Arabs on 8 July, was "radically different from, and far stronger than, the one they had met on 15 May".[53]

This was mostly due to the substantial arrival of armament supplies and trained recruits from abroad, and on this background it is surprising that the Arab pow-

---

49 Op.cit., p. 219.
50 Op.cit., p. 35.
51 Ibid., p. 38.
52 Ibid., p. 235.
53 Ibid., p. 236.

ers decided to ignore a UN appeal for an extension of the truce issued by Count Bernadotte, who was soon going to meet a sad fate as the UN mediator whom nobody seemed to want. His proposals were dismissed as unacceptable by both sides, and he was assassinated by extremist Israeli terrorists (under the command of the later Prime Minister, Shamir) on September 17, 1948.

4. Last Phase of the War

One remarkable aspect of this first war was the fact that the troops of Jordan, Iraq and Syria hardly engaged in hostilities with Israel when the second truce, which had begun on July 18, lapsed in October. Israel could therefore concentrate on the largest Arab power, Egypt, when hostilities were resumed, because the IDF broke the armistice, if we can trust Shlaim's account.[54] The first battles in May and June had not made any great changes and must rather be seen as consolidating the Israeli war aims in most parts, if not as the clear victory Morris terms it. The road to Jerusalem was thus kept open, but at high costs, and no other Jewish parts of the country, according to the division plan, had fallen into enemy hands. If western Jerusalem was still under Israeli control, the old Jewish quarter in the eastern parts of the city had been conquered in fierce and costly battles by the Arab Legion of Jordan, the only strong opponent that the Israelis feared. As already mentioned, this Arab force with many British officers in its ranks had respected the original division plan and did not try to conquer any of the Jewish parts.

The late 1948 campaign to secure the southern parts of Israel — including the Negev — which had initially been severely threatened by the Egyptians, was eventually successful, and the Egyptians had to accept that they were left with the control over only what was later known as the Gaza strip. The war ended with the Israeli conquest, in March 1949, of Eilat at the south end of the desert, thereby giving the new nation access to the Red Sea. This was an essential gain for Israel, because it gave the Israelis issue to the warm waters of the south.

The losses had been heavy on all sides — the Israeli losses of six thousand dead were frightening for the new nation and also confirmed that this was no easy battle like some of those in later wars, but the result gave Israel a new sense of security. Its defence forces had shown its capabilities, and the national existence now seemed guaranteed for a while.

The armistice agreements were signed in the early months of 1949, when Ralph Bunche, the new UN mediator, was helpful in organising the talks. The most difficult phases were those with Jordan and Syria. The first, because of the intricate question of Jerusalem, the second because of coups and counter-coups in Syria that showed the weakness of the country's leadership; the armistice with Syria was thus the last one to be signed, at the end of July, 1949.

54   Op.cit., p.39.

II. Fragile peace efforts, and widening conflict, 1949-55

In terms of land, Israel had obtained much more during this first war than the area allocated to it in the UN division plan. It now possessed 79%, instead of the 55% proposed and had a population of 716,000 Jews and 92,000 Arabs, after the substantial flight of some 700,000 Arabs to refugee camps in neighbouring countries, whether they had been forced to flee or done so by their free will. The truth probably lies somewhere in between, but surely none of the refugees had gone away because they preferred this solution.

The traditional wisdom among Israelis, including historians, has been to see the new nation surrounded by hostile Arab states that still wanted to eliminate Israel. If the Arabs had certainly been forced to admit defeat in the first round, 1948-49, they would most probably come back and attack again as they did in May 1948, it was said in Israel.

This version has been radically changed with the advent of the often quoted books by the most prominent among the revisionist historians, Benny Morris and Avi Shlaim. They write their new versions based on facts, and what is interesting about their work is that they have had access to the Israeli archives, which was not possible earlier. We have already underlined the difference in approach among the neighbouring Arab states before the outbreak of the war in 1948, and the significant understanding for the necessity of a Jewish-Jordanian *entente*, which at least the Hashemite King showed. The pragmatic regime of Ben-Gurion eventually accepted this, even if Gurion was always sceptical, often agreeing with those left-wing members of the Knesset who regarded the King as a feudal lord and a puppet of London. Shlaim calls the Israeli diplomacy facing Jordan "coercive, representing a major victory" for the new nation.[55]

There were other feelers from various sides: The Egyptian King, in the last phase of his government, instructed one of his diplomats to engage in secret talks with an Israeli representative in Paris before the final phase of the war, in order to propose a deal with the Zionists that would have left him with more territory than he acquired at the end. Gurion declined, because he realised that the IDF was

---

55 Op.cit., p. 44.

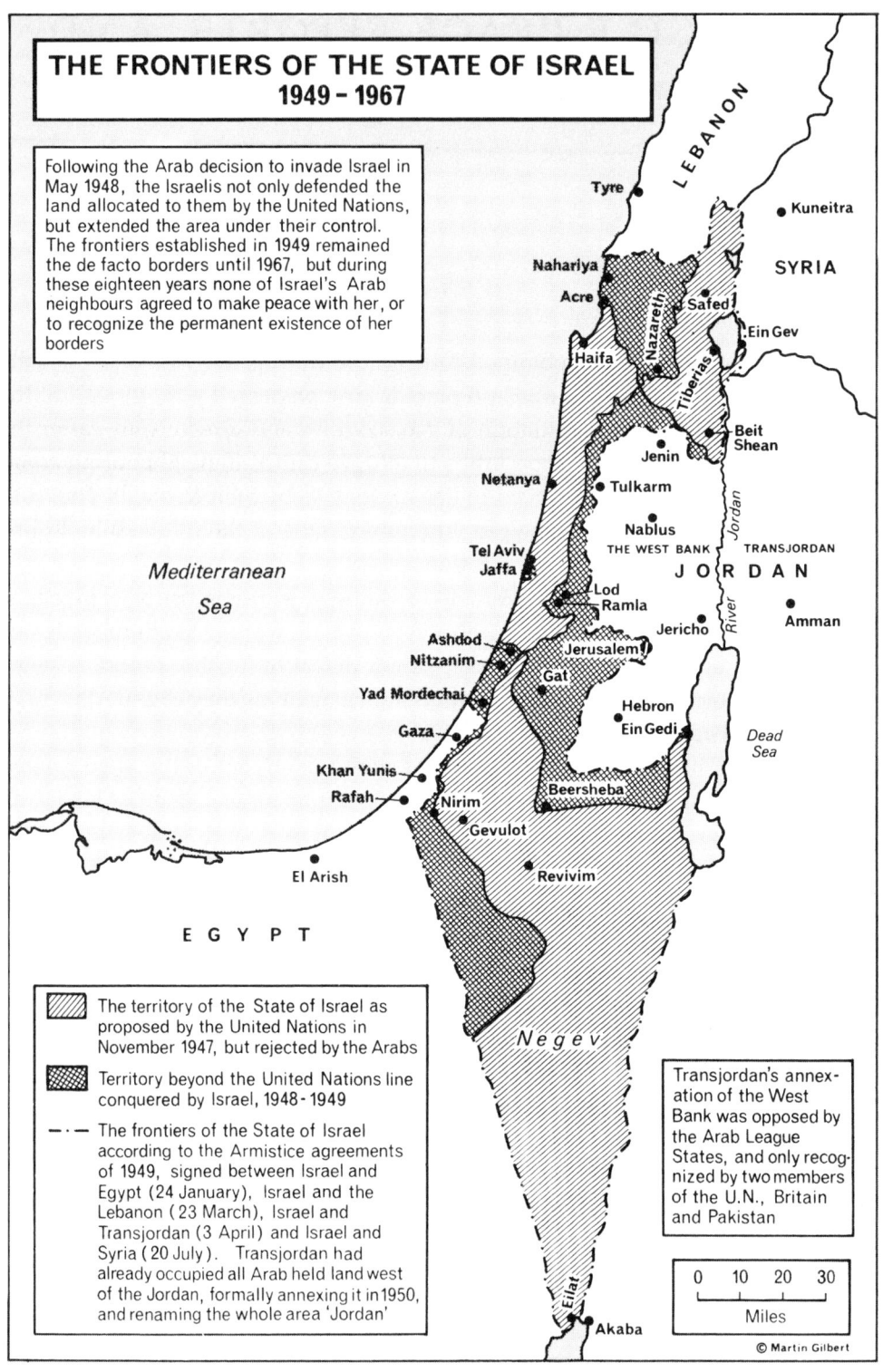

now in better shape than the Egyptian forces, weakened by the war far away from Cairo and the populated areas of Egypt and lacking ammunition and arms. Seen from the Jewish angle, this was the better policy, within a short time framework, but with regard to the long-term perspective, we may question this.

What is more surprising to learn is that even the Syrian government tried to placate the Israelis before the armistice agreement was finalised. A new President, the former Chief of Staff, Colonel Zaim, took power just before the talks began, and he offered to come to terms with Israel, even offering a peace treaty. But Ben-Gurion rejected this unusual offer, either because of the unbelievable new situation or because the Israelis did not expect this positive situation to last. In this estimate, they proved right because the regime of Zaim was indeed a very brief one, lasting only a few months.

With the Lebanese there were hardly any problems, so that the conclusion must be the following: With regard to practically all its neighbouring states, Israel had no insurmountable problems in the immediate aftermath of the 1948 – 49 war. The Egyptians wanted to end the hostilities that had been a total failure for Cairo, the Jordanians had some understanding for the new Jewish state, at least at the highest level, and in fragile Syria, a new opening showed that the war was now replaced by a positive situation, like the one Lebanon offered. The Iraqis, who were not direct neighbours of Israel, had already accepted that their troops be replaced by the Jordanians. Only the Palestinians were kept out of any agreement, both by the victorious Israelis and by their Arab brothers, who showed little or no solidarity at this stage.

All the armistice agreements declared that they should be seen as "facilitating the transition from the present truce to permanent peace in Palestine". But Shlaim talks of the following *elusive peace,* despite the promising start. He also mentions that he (and other modern historians) believe that Israel was more intransigent than the Arab states and therefore bore a larger share of responsibility for the political deadlock that followed the formal ending of the hostilities.[56]

In early 1949, Israel held its first elections, giving Ben-Gurion a mandate to form a coalition government that has remained the benchmark of Israeli politics since then. Soon after the last armistice agreement was signed, Israel entered into a period of consolidation; for Ben-Gurion, other things had higher priority than the proposal to enter into real peace negotiations, as his Foreign Minister, Sharett, wanted. The Prime Minister's main priorities, according to Shlaim, were building the state and assuring large-scale immigration, economic development and the consolidation of Israel's newly won independence.[57] Although a strong leader, Ben-Gurion wanted democracy to be established in the new nation, in continuation of

---

56 Ibid., p. 40.
57 Ibid., p. 51.

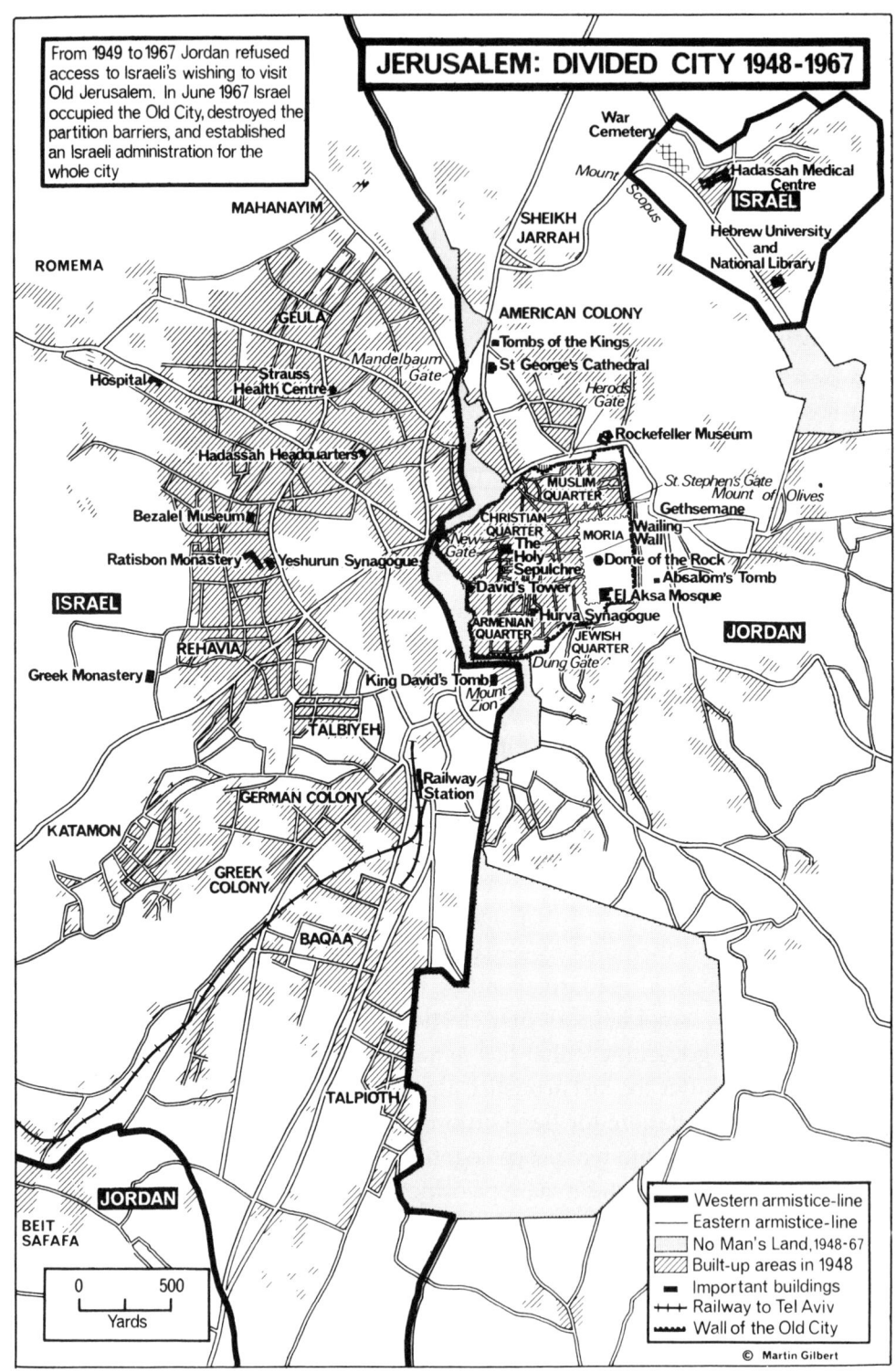

the system prevailing in Jewish/Zionist circles before Independence. Many Israeli leaders felt that time was on their side and that talks with the Arabs could wait until further notice. Here, we recognise Jabotinsky's idea of building a symbolic iron wall to fortify the new Jewish bastion of a nation.

Ben-Gurion's foreign minister, Moshe Sharett, on the other hand, believed that it was necessary to exploit any chance of a settlement with the Arab states, just at the time when the Israeli victory and all the armistice agreements had somewhat paralysed the Arab states. He did try to persuade the Prime Minister, but the latter was a stubborn leader, listening perhaps to his colleagues and advisers, but frequently deciding to follow his own first impressions. And these were often war-like, vis-à-vis the Arabs, not believing in their goodwill and preferring to ignore any offer of serious talks.

The armistice agreements were interpreted in strongly opposed ways by Israel and the other states, respectively. Whereas the former saw them as giving the new state all the rights with regard to the borders, a continuous cease-fire, which must be respected by irregular forces, and the right of Jews to settle everywhere within its borders, the Arabs did not see the agreements as synonymous with real peace arrangements. They maintained, on the other hand, that the borders were not recognised, international ones, that a state of war continued and that the Palestinian refugees had a right to return to their homeland from where they had been evicted. In this last interpretation, they were in accordance with the UN resolution 194, of December 1948.

There was hardly any compromise possible between these two versions. The UN tried, through the establishment of a *Palestinian Conciliation Commission*, to promote better understanding among the parties and aim at positive results. A conference was held at Lausanne between April and September 1949, in which Israel took part only reluctantly. It was referred to by one observer as "an exercise in futility".[58]

One stumbling block was the UN wish to internationalize Jerusalem, an idea which was anathema to the Jews, who held on to the Western parts and to the access route which had cost so many lives during the war. For the Zionists, this holy city was their main object in the conquest of their Jewish nation, and Ben-Gurion decided at this early stage that he would establish the capital of Israel in the holy city. In his diary he admitted the difficult challenge this decision involved, not only facing the UN, but also most Arabs and many Christians, both of whom regarded Jerusalem with the same religious fervour as the Jews. Israel's Foreign Minister, Sharett was adamantly opposed to this defiance of the Prime Minister and wanted to resign, although Ben-Gurion did not accept his resignation at this stage.

---

58 Ibid., p. 57.

Prime Minister David Ben-Gurion meets President of the United States, Harry S. Truman, during visit to Washington in May 1951. The third person is Abba Eban, Israeli ambassador and later Foreign Minister.

Relations with Jordan

Whatever the difficulties, secret talks were soon resumed with the Jordanian King and his ministers and lasted from November 1949 until the assassination of King Abdullah, in July 1951. Ben-Gurion remained sceptical and did not take part in them personally — they were held at civil-servant level on the Israeli side, whereas the King was the one who took the main decisions in Jordan, however difficult it was for him to get them approved by his ministers and advisers. But according to Shlaim, "it was mostly Ben- Gurion's lack of commitment to a political settlement with Jordan that was a major factor in the failure of the talks".[59] Ben-Gurion was more in agreement with one of his military advisers, Moshe Dayan, who participated in the talks, than with Moshe Sharett, his liberal-minded Foreign Minister.

One of the reasons for the assassination of the King was surely the fact that he was regarded as a traitor to the Arab cause by many Palestinians, especially those thinking in Pan-Arabist ways, even if the movement was hardly in existence yet.

---

59   Ibid., p. 67.

Relations with Syria

With Syria, relations soon fell back to a negative state, after the short interval with President Zaim, who, as we have seen, wanted peace. Israelis have generally taken the Syrians to be those most adamantly opposed to Israel, but also here, Shlaim questions a common assumption.

He writes that it is generally forgotten that relations were peaceful after the armistice agreement until the first military clash occurred in the spring of 1951; this was due to a Syrian reaction to an "Israeli provocation".[60] Shlaim adds that the "director of armistice control in the Israeli Foreign Ministry could always be relied upon to produce legal arguments to justify even the most outrageous Israeli actions". Moshe Dayan was also involved in the administration of the demilitarised zones, and both persons seem to have enjoyed the confidence of the Prime Minister. This militant policy finally led to the breakout of a limited military conflict, in which Israel used aircraft and the government did little to show any will to compromise. I shall not go into details here, but only conclude that after these clashes, the Syrian side proposed talks on the subject, which were refused by Israel.

When a new leader — Shishakli, who was pro-American — took power in Damascus in November 1951 there was an improved atmosphere and talks were finally resumed. Foreign Minister Sharett found that the Syrian side had shown more flexibility than his own civil servants (mostly military), but the Cabinet eventually declined the Syrian compromise proposals, because of a reference by an Israeli expert to the long-term water problems. Interestingly enough, this expert found that the ministers around Ben-Gurion "seemed like polite and frightened children in a kindergarten" (facing the strong leader).[61]

Relations with Egypt

After the assassination of King Abdullah, Israel decided to focus more attention on Egypt because — in the aftermath of the murder of the benevolent King of Jordan — relations with that country would surely be more difficult for a while. In Egypt, a new beginning started with the take-over of the Free Officers regime, which overthrew the monarchy in July 1952, partly because the King had engaged Egypt in the war with Israel without assuring that the armed forces were well prepared.

Ben-Gurion even congratulated the Free Officers in a speech in the Knesset in August 1952, and expressed the hope of a new beginning between the two countries. There were exchanges of goodwill messages from both sides in 1952 – 53, as well as some talks between diplomats in Paris, but no serious breakthrough occurred. One of the most positive Egyptian officers was — surprisingly enough

---

60 Ibid., p. 68. The Israelis tried to change the border by force.
61 Ibid., p. 75.

— Colonel Nasser, who would later become President but was not yet in full command. However, Nasser soon became frustrated over the negative attitudes of the Ben-Gurion government, despite the flexibility showed by Moshe Sharett.

Infiltrations

It is a fact that there began to be infiltrations into Israel from the neighbouring countries, but according to Shlaim most of those were due to social and economic problems of the more than 700,000 displaced persons who were often settled in the neighbourhood of Israel. It was therefore not a question of sabotage directed from above, by the Arab governments. The official policy of the Ben-Gurion government was what has been termed a *free fire* one implying several atrocities, some of which are mentioned by Shlaim: "gang rape, murder (of innocent civilians) and on one occasion the dumping of 120 suspected infiltrators in the Arab desert without water".[62] The policy might sometimes also involve military retaliations against the neighbouring state. This line of action, which has remained unchanged over many years, may of course have frightened possible infiltrators, and the neighbouring states as such, but it also created a very crude antagonism among the Arabs in general towards the new state and its leaders.

Benny Morris talks of the neighbouring policy of the Prime Minister, Ben-Gurion in the first post-war years in the following terms: "For decades, Ben-Gurion and successive administrations after his, lied to the Israeli public about the post 1948 peace overtures and about Arab interest in a deal […]. The recent opening of Israeli archives offers a far more complex picture".[63]

Here a personal note may be appropriate: In many democratic settings and even more so in other regimes, governments often do not give the full picture of a given difficult situation. The policy will generally follow the vague notion of *raison d'état*, which is more acute in war-like situations. *Liar* is a strong word that may easily be misused, I find. We may therefore try to understand that the Israeli government's reasoning (behind what Morris terms *lying*) could have been due to the general level of distrust in the country, after the serious first war, which had given most Jews a shock, because of the danger level, which was felt to be much higher than it turned out to be (fortunately, for them). Gurion was a strong personality and his leadership was accepted by most Israelis, because a majority felt that he could move things ahead while still respecting the new democratic institutions. He trusted his own strategy — based on his long experience as a Jewish pioneer in Palestine — which involved the building of the civil infrastructure of the new state, hand in hand with the increase in the defence capabilities of the

---

62 Ibid., p. 83. Quoted here in abbreviated form.
63 Op.cit., p. 268.

IDF, which had saved the new nation initially. But we must admit that inhumane brutality was part of the retaliation policies employed by the new government, and which were morally defended by one of its main officers, Moshe Dayan, in a letter to the foreign minister, who certainly did not agree. Dayan wrote that he knew of no other methods to protect the borders than the ones utilised; that was his *moral defence*.[64]

To sum up, we may try to explain the thinking of the government in Israel, when it reacted so violently to the first infiltrations, as follows: *We must impress on our neighbours that Israel is here as a reborn nation and that we want to remain in power in our new homeland, whatever the costs.*

Worsening Situation along the Borders

Ben-Gurion decided to resign in December 1953, when the situation along the borders had become worse than ever. He was tired because of his heavy responsibilities in a difficult environment; his resignation was probably also a result of the increasing and better-organised attacks from the *fedayeens* (meaning literally *self-sacrificers*, whether we term them *terrorists* or *guerrillas*) which had replaced the previous, more innocent infiltrations. The public was living under the impression of insecurity, even if, according to modern historians, they really had no need to feel afraid.

One affair which was particularly cruel involved *Qibya*, a border village of Jordan, in October 1953. Infiltrators, supposedly from Jordan, had killed a mother and two children in a small town near Tel Aviv, and the military set-up immediately decided to take revenge. Moshe Dayan, as already mentioned, was responsible for the border policies under the newly designated Minister of Defence, Pinchas Lavon, but Major Sharon (today Prime Minister) had the direct command over the retaliation act. The order said explicitly: "inflict heavy casualties on its [Qibya's] inhabitants".[65] Sharon's group took action in a manner recalling the worst excesses of the Nazi-SS entities. 45 houses were blown up in the village, which was left in ruins, and almost 70 people were killed, among them women and children, none of whom had any relation to the tragedy that had occurred in Israel.

This barbaric act gave rise to a storm of protests at home and abroad, including a condemnation of Israel by the UN Security Council. But the government denied any IDF involvement, despite the fact that the coming Prime Minister, Sharett, who was informed, wanted the government to express regret. The then ambassador at the UN, Abba Eban, wrote to his foreign minister: "No other government acts in

---

64 Ibid., pp. 273 - 275.
65 Shlaim, op.cit., p. 91.

this way".⁶⁶ According to Shlaim, the government's responsibility was evident and confirmed by several trustworthy sources mentioned in his book.⁶⁷ Thus we have here a neat example of a government denial that is equal to a direct lie, and even recognised as such by the Foreign Minister.

The negative aspects of this brutal onslaught may have influenced Ben-Gurion to give up the reins of leadership in December 1953. His resignation gave the public a shock, and many Israelis asked themselves the question: How can we cope without the founding father?

Another serious affair happened in Egypt somewhat later, when the IDF took an action that Shlaim characterises as a "sudden and totally unprovoked blow" against Egypt. The government in Cairo had made an agreement with Britain in July 1954, to the effect that the latter would withdraw its forces from Egypt. The Israeli military establishment under Lavon now thought that it would be an ideal moment to start actions in Egypt against this collaboration with the West and in order to destabilise the Egyptian regime. Bombing of cinemas showing British and American films, and of post offices and libraries were taking place in the late summer months of 1954 without doing much harm, except politically. This kind of strategy is difficult for a trained diplomat to follow, as it is, I think, for most reasonable people. Shlaim agrees and talks of this *disastrous action* that was even carried out in an "amateurish and incompetent way".⁶⁸ Some of the Jewish participants in the spy-ring were caught red-handed, and two of them were later sentenced to death and executed as terrorists.

Prime Minister Sharett, who always preferred diplomatic to military actions, was furious about this *disastrous action* and wanted it thoroughly investigated. The person who was directly responsible, Gibly, pointed to Defence Minister Lavon as the one who had given the orders. The new Chief of Staff, Dayan, had been away in the USA, and therefore had no part in the affair. A Commission was set up to investigate the entire matter, but it would neither condemn nor exonerate Lavon. The strange thing is that this affair was only termed *the mishap* in Israel, well in tune with the militant thinking of the government, with the exception of a few, such as Sharett. In the view of one expert, quoted here from Shlaim, "the problem was that it had become the practice of Israel's policymakers to find ways of accommodating the views of the military".⁶⁹

Soon after, Israeli strategists⁷⁰ decided to send a small merchant ship through the Suez Canal with the Jewish flag hoisted, and — as expected — it was seized

---

66   Ibid., p. 92.
67   Op.cit., pp. 92 - 93.
68   Ibid., p. 112.
69   Ibid., p. 111.
70   The term which Morris uses, op.cit., p. 281.

and the officers on board imprisoned and even beaten. This took place in September 1954, but Nasser, who was still in a fairly moderate mood, promised to release the ship soon.

The above-mentioned episodes involving Egypt were not the only negative ones in our conflict pattern. Another dramatic event occurred somewhat later, in December 1954, when five Israeli soldiers were captured inside Syria, where they had been on a secret, illegal mission. Lavon ordered a civilian Syrian airliner to be forced by the Israeli Air Force to land in Israel (a case of pure highjacking), with the intention of using its passengers and crew as hostages pending the release of the captured soldiers. An international uproar arose and Prime Minister Sharett was of course furious over this act of sheer piracy, about which he had not been informed beforehand. Israel therefore soon had to give in. Sharett sent Lavon a letter in which he accused the heads of the military of "stupidity and short-sightedness". We can easily agree.

Politically, Lavon's situation, facing an angry Prime Minister and a mostly negative opinion among the public, soon became an impossible one, and he therefore felt it necessary to resign, in February 1955. According to Shlaim, this minister was a very difficult personality who often presented *wild ideas* to the Prime Minister.

The sad thing about these affairs was that they took place when there was an interesting and positive secret dialogue in the correspondence between the two leaders, Nasser and Sharett. It lasted from October 1954 to February 1955 and began quite harmoniously with Sharett expressing admiration for the idealism and tenacity shown by Nasser in his struggle to liberate the country from foreign domination. Nasser obliged by promising an open dialogue between the two countries and thanked Sharett for his kind words. But Nasser refused the appeals of Sharett to show mercy towards those spies condemned to death in *the mishap*. He stressed the fact that it would be impossible for him to show leniency in this case, because he had just declined to do so in the case of some Muslim Brothers who had likewise been condemned and were indeed executed.

More or less in the same period (January 1955), Nasser had written an article in *Foreign Affairs* in which he termed Israel's policies as aggressive, but he had also promised "that Egypt did not want to start any conflict. War has no place in the constructive policy which we have designed to improve the lot of our people".[71]

The executions of the two Jews that took place in Cairo in early 1955 provoked an uproar in Israel and made things more difficult for Sharett. Most of his Cabinet members thought that he had not handled the affair in a sufficiently strong manner. They therefore appealed to Ben-Gurion to return to the government, which

---

71 Ibid., p. 267. Morris also confirms that "until 1955 the Arab states officially opposed military infiltration and generally attempted to curb it", p. 270.

he finally did, first as Defence Minister in February 1955. From the beginning, the former Prime Minister acted as if he were again the leader of the government, and he seemed to ignore Sharett, of whom he had never been a great admirer.

According to Michael Doran, Gurion "soon masterminded the aggressive border policies of Israel".[72] One of the worst episodes of this policy was the brutal Gaza Raid of 28 February 1955, soon after Gurion had returned to the government.

The background was the armed, but limited intrusion into Israel from Gaza, also involving the killing of a lone Israeli cyclist, and the retaliation was dramatic: Thirty- seven Egyptian soldiers were left dead and more than thirty wounded, and in addition, extensive destruction was done to Egyptian military installations. This action was also led by the brutal Ariel Sharon, and was seen as a devastating blow to the prestige of Nasser and his young regime. He no doubt used this onslaught as a turning point (and often said so to Western interlocutors), and a vicious circle began. Sharett had, under pressure, reluctantly approved the raid, but only on the condition that bloodshed be limited. Shlaim terms this massacre as the *summit of political folly* and thinks that Ben-Gurion purposely wanted to show his strong hand, not least as a demonstration to Sharett, whom he — like many others — considered a coward, or one desiring "to raise a generation of cowards. As opposed to this, we will be a fighting generation", he told his Cabinet secretary.[73]

The conflict between the former and the present Prime Ministers could not be concealed because it was evident inside the Cabinet and in some sectors of the open Israeli society; Moshe Sharett was therefore soon worn out by the constant struggle — as he saw it — to restrain Ben-Gurion and his officers, but he also felt that the old man's authority would still prevail in the Israeli pioneer society. A majority of the Cabinet eventually asked Ben-Gurion to take over again as Prime Minister. They found that after the Gaza Raid, the way of compromise was closed and agreed that the blunt policies of Gurion were necessary in order to overcome the crisis. The change at the top took place in early November 1955, but in the meantime, Gurion had seen his party leadership strengthened at the elections in mid-1955.

After he had assumed full responsibility again, Gurion ordered another of those dramatic actions that marked these years in a sad way. The episode, called *Operation Olive Leaves* or more straightforwardly, *Operation Lake Kinneret*, took place in December 1955 and was worse than the previous ones, since it was an "unprovoked act of aggression, carefully planned and brilliantly executed" by the well-known

---

72 *Diplomacy in the Middle East*, edited by Professor Brown, London-New York, Tauris, 2000; article by Professor Michael Doran, who uses these terms equivalently with those of Morris and Shlaim.

73 Op.cit., p. 124 and p. 128, respectively.

Sharon and his henchmen.⁷⁴ It took place near Lake Kinneret (Tiberias or Galilee) and cost more than fifty Syrian soldiers their lives, while thirty were taken prisoner. No serious incident had occurred to explain this act, and Shlaim even writes that the Syrians had generally been careful not to fire on civilian Israeli fishermen but only on military patrol boats. These were often used by the IDF, however, in order to provoke the Syrians, as on this occasion. Only the paint of a boat had been scratched by a Syrian warning shot in this case, and no one was hurt. The Israeli retaliation raid was soon condemned by the UN and caused serious damage to Israel's international standing, according to Shlaim.⁷⁵

While agreeing that Ben-Gurion and Dayan were "denied their war" (because they were entirely responsible for the provocative action) Benny Morris, however, in a more cynical mood, writes that the operation appeared to have its "fringe benefits" because it showed Syria and Egypt that they should not play with fire and try to start a war.⁷⁶

Moshe Sharett again became very upset, but he was now only Foreign Minister and no longer had the full responsibility for policy. In the Cabinet meeting, however, Sharett declared that "Satan himself could not have chosen a worse timing", because he had just negotiated an important arms deal with the Americans. The Foreign Minister feared that Foster Dulles, the Secretary of State in Washington, might now call off the deal, which was exactly what happened. Official American papers from that period confirm that Sharett was right in his assumptions.

After this negative result, which is a historical fact — unlike the speculation with regard to "fringe benefits" with which Morris concludes — there was open conflict in the Cabinet regarding where Israel should buy arms. Sharett would not give up his focus on Washington, but in those early Cold War years, the USA was not yet on the side of the Israelis. France, on the other hand, was offering an opening, and the Prime Minister was eventually persuaded by his generals, Dayan first among them, and the Defence Ministry's young representative, Simon Peres, that France would be a good source of arms for the IDF. The first important deal with Paris was signed as early as November 1955, providing Israel with new arms, including more tanks.

Egypt had for some time blocked the port of Eilat, and the episodes involving the Israeli boat that was arrested in late 1954 and the Gaza Raid in February 1955 had of course increased tension with Egypt. Some small islands at the south end of the Red Sea near Sharm-el Sheikh had been occupied by Egyptian troops, and Ben-Gurion now hoped that pressure from the world powers would force the Egyptian

---

74 This shows either that Sharett naively ignored his militant colleagues, or that the latter *purposely* ignored the Prime Minister.
75 Ibid., p. 153.
76 Op.cit., p. 286.

government to give way. If not, according to the Prime Minister's thinking, some more radical measures must be taken.

Sharett still preferred diplomatic solutions, but the warrior politician Ben-Gurion again at the centre of command, aimed at a confrontational line vis-à-vis Egypt, if foreign pressure was not forthcoming. Morris tells us that in the period 1954 – 56, the government members Gurion and Lavon and the supreme military chief, Dayan, often put forward plans of conquering the Golan Heights, Southern Lebanon, the Gaza Strip or parts of Sinai. "The Israeli government thus went a long way in 1955/56 to provoke the Egyptians into war".[77]

The UN Secretary General, Dag Hammarskjöld, went to the region in April 1956, in order to investigate the increasing tension along the Egyptian-Israel border. In his report to the UN, he was openly critical of Israel for violating the armistice agreements, which was not surprising since a strong bombing of Gaza City had occurred precisely on the eve of his arrival, costing more than sixty civilians their lives and more than a hundred wounded. This episode confirmed the escalation of the vicious circle of attacks and counter-attacks that had marked the Gaza strip since the dramatic raid in February 1955. The Secretary General found both Nasser and Gurion in an angry mood, and realised that the Israeli leader believed that the UN was biased against the Jewish nation. As I see it, this has unfortunately been a well-known aspect of official Israeli attitudes toward the World Organisation throughout the years.

With the withdrawal of Moshe Sharett from the Ministry of Foreign Affairs in June 1956, which followed soon after the final withdrawal of British troops from the Suez area, we enter into a new and more dramatic phase of the history of the conflict. Sharett was replaced by Golda Meir — a personality after the Prime Minister's own heart. Ben-Gurion was therefore freer to plan the aggressive actions that he had long had in mind, without the irritating complaints from his foreign minister.

---

77 Ibid., pp. 280 – 285.

III. The 1956 War

1. Collusion with Britain and France

When Golda Meir took over as Foreign Minister after Sharett had left the government in June 1956, Ben-Gurion found things easier, as we have just pointed out. Previously, a slight majority of Cabinet ministers had sometimes sided with Sharett when Ben-Gurion had presented various aggressive plans, with regard, for instance, to a limited war with Egypt, or concerning Gaza or Sharm-el-Sheikh respectively. Sharett and the majority had feared that it would not be possible to limit the scope of hostilities once a war had broken out.

Now, without this Minister advising restraint, Ben-Gurion could better plan the coming war, which he had always had in mind in various forms, even if he dropped it from time to time or replaced it with other ideas of aggression. His point of departure was a wish to enforce the young nation's will to survive and show the neighbouring countries that they could have a peaceful situation vis-à-vis Israel only if they accepted her existence unconditionally in the long run. So if he was a warrior politician, his ultimate aim was of course peace, but on Israel's conditions. His policy had been primarily expansion-oriented, as we have already seen, whereas Sharett had always tended to accommodate the other side, i.e. the Arabs, too, if at all possible, and would therefore try to find peaceful solutions that accepted the views of the other side. Sharett was a man of genuine compromise — too much, apparently, for the young nation.

The fact that both France and Israel had the same enemy — Egypt (France because of the war in Algeria, in which Cairo supported the revolutionaries) — made it natural for the Jerusalem government to intensify its efforts to procure arms from France, even more so because the Americans — as already mentioned above — had declined to provide arms after the brutal and unprovoked aggression near Lake Tiberias by the Israeli forces. Dayan told the French that he felt convinced that Nasser would eventually attack Israel. Because of the French secret plans already in existence, it was eventually easy to co-ordinate war efforts with Paris.

The nationalisation of the Suez Canal on 26 July 1956 was a dramatic blow, setting off a chain of events. In negotiations with the French on the new armament procurements that would give the Israelis breathing room and technical superiority over the Egyptians, the French Minister of Defence, Bourgès-Maunoury, asked Simon Peres, the representative of the Ministry of Defence in the Israeli delegation in Paris, how long it would take the IDF to reach the canal in a war. "Two weeks" was the answer. The minister then asked if Israel was prepared to take part in a tripartite military operation against Egypt. The two old colonial powers already had a plan to attack the Canal and now wanted Israeli collaboration in order to cross and occupy the Sinai. The British were yet undecided, but the French pressed the plan forward, and Peres found that this was a unique opportunity for the Ben-Gurion government. The Prime Minister was happy, because the plan seemed to underscore the fact that the West was no longer attempting an appeasement with Nasser. He therefore soon accepted an invitation to send government representatives to a conference at St. Germain on 30 September 1956. Golda Meir, Moshe Carmel and Dayan represented the Israeli government on this occasion. It was soon to be followed by the final conference at the highest level, in a villa at Sèvres near Paris on 22 – 24 October 1956, with Ben-Gurion, Peres and Dayan taking part together with the French leading ministers, including Prime Minister Guy Mollet and the British Foreign Secretary, who had the almost enthusiastic backing of Sir Anthony Eden, the British Prime Minister.

After the nationalisation of the Canal, the dominating shipping powers had established a *Suez Canal Users Association*, but a Soviet veto on 13 October, 1956 put an end to a plan intended to force this Association on unwilling Egypt.[78] We may say that this veto gave a new impetus to the joint British-French action, which turned into a tripartite one that included Israel. The conference at Sèvres ended with the signing of a formal, secret document, the *Protocol of Sèvres*, printed in only three copies. Shlaim writes that the British one was later destroyed by direct order of Anthony Eden.[79]

This most unusual agreement[80] involved an imminent and long planned military attack on Egypt, beginning with the Israeli onslaught in the Sinai on 29 October,

---

78 A Danish diplomat, ambassador Bartels, was appointed head of this association, which was never really put into practice.

79 Ibid., p. 177. The author is giving many details, including those about a secret deal made at the close of the talks between the French and the Israeli representatives, to provide Israel with a nuclear plant. See also Simon Peres' memoirs, *Battling For Peace*, Random House, New York, 1995, p. 130.

80 The always careful Israeli ambassador, Abba Eban, remarked in one of his books about this meeting: "At Sevres, the three groups of leaders decided on a grotesquely eccentric plan". Here this quoted from Shlaim, op.cit., p. 178.

to be followed by the occupation of the Canal area by the two European powers. It was of course under the strictest secrecy, so that the Israeli government had to find good arguments to explain the coming attack to the public at an appropriate moment. The propaganda to be used, such as the pretended Egyptian plans of aggression, already existed to some extent. The British and French would only intervene a few days later, according to the tripartite agreement, in order to protect their shipping and other interests.

Among the arguments eventually made public by the Israeli authorities — again the word *propaganda* comes to mind — were the following facts: Cairo had stepped up its retaliation attacks after the already mentioned Gaza Raid in February 1955, which killed 40 Egyptians and had been a shock to the Egyptian leadership as we know, and again after the attack on Gaza City in early April 1956. When the *fedayeens'* attacks consequently increased and they mortally struck a group of Jewish school children, inspiring a Cairo newspaper to write about the attackers "[t]he heroes are back from the battlefield", the majority in the Ben Gurion Cabinet felt that *enough was enough* and began to approve plans for a war. Their reaction was prompted all the more because the brutal attack followed soon after the Egyptian occupation of a small demilitarised zone, Nitzana, in October 1955.[81] In the collective memory to be exploited there were also such incidents as the execution of members of the Jewish spy/terrorist ring in early 1955, and the torture of Israeli seamen in late 1954 after the arrest of their ship when it tried to pass the Suez Canal, as already mentioned. The nationalistic propaganda easily omitted the reasons behind these events.

Looking in retrospect at the nationalisation of the Suez Canal in July 1956, it may surely be considered legal, because compensation was offered and good political and economic explanations could be found. It was, however, presented by Egypt as a defiance of the West because the American government had only a few days earlier (19 July) withdrawn an offer to finance the Aswan Dam. This act — probably not very rational in hindsight — was surely only the trigger that hastened the fateful developments. At any rate, the Egyptian nationalisation provoked an outcry in the old colonial countries, Britain and France; it was also seen as an excellent argument in favour of intervention, because the forced take-over of the Canal could be presented as an act of enmity against the Western shipping interests.

On 23 October 1956, Egypt concluded a military alliance with Jordan and Syria, which was presented in Israel as another serious warning. In the Jewish nation

---

81 According to Morris, op.cit., p. 285, this was not a one-sided Egyptian aggression, as the traditional opinion was in Israel. The quotation on the attack on Israeli school children is from Golda Meir´s memoirs (see her account pp. 245 - 248) and not referred to by either Morris or Shlaim.

General Moshe Dayan visits Israeli troops at Sharm-el-Sheikh, Sinai 1956.

it was easy to exploit this in the propaganda necessary to explain the war, with a reference to Israel's dangerous experience in the first war (of Independence), in which most Arab countries were united against it. In his memoirs, the later Prime Minister Yitzhak Rabin's writes that "the military commanders [he was one of them] were told that Israel would initiate an attack on Egypt. The reprisal raids had proved ineffective in dealing with the problem of terrorism, and the leading target of attention now became Egypt, since Nasser gave his full backing to the provocative actions by the *fedayeen*".[82]

When Ben-Gurion found that the time to act had come and that Israel must, at any rate, carry through her part of the secret tripartite aggression plan, he presented the agreement on military action to the Cabinet as late as 28 October, the eve of the fateful event, at the same time that he was issuing orders for a general mobilisation.

2. October 1956 War

Israel fell into this *dangerous trap,* as it is termed in the traditional version of events, because of the increasing concern for its national survival. In retrospect, however, many (in Israel, also) now find that the fear which the Jerusalem government used as the reason for the military conflict was not really well founded. We may also recall here the fact that many scholars, both in the USA and in Israel, now term the Israeli policies towards Egypt in 1955 – 56 as aggressive.[83] The two previously mentioned Israeli revisionist historians both clearly point out that it was Israel, not Egypt, which wanted (a pre-emptive) war. The word *pre-emptive* is in brackets because Dayan and Ben-Gurion actually wanted a war that could eliminate the Egyptian risk, as they saw it, once and for all. But we have to admit that they were probably genuinely worried about the increasing strength and aggressiveness of the Nasser regime.

Ben-Gurion and his Cabinet therefore made it clear to the public that it was (again) a matter of life and death for the young nation, but this time they knew — or should have known — that the government had all the reasons to be confident — unlike eight years earlier. Israel not only had the advantage of starting the war, but its military superiority was not much in doubt. What was of course most essential was the fact that Israel now had the support of two powerful European nations. The 1956 war became one of many examples of the eminent capabilities of the young nation's armed forces and their superiority on the battlefield and in the air.

---

82 Op.cit., p. 51.
83 *Diplomacy in the Middle East*, op.cit., p. 107.

The war started on 29 October 1956, but Ben-Gurion had issued orders that the air force not bomb Egyptian cities, so that the Egyptians would have no reason to retaliate. As their air force had been eliminated to a great extent in the early hours of the campaign, they surely did not have the means, and this deficiency in Egyptian air protection soon resulted in the swift advance of Israeli forces to the approaches of the Canal.[84]

On 30 – 31 October, the British and French sent ultimatums to both belligerents, warning them to keep a distance of at least ten miles from the Canal. Egypt, as expected, rejected the ultimatum, and this suited the Israelis well, since they knew the European plan in advance and had no wish to get directly involved in the fight for the Canal. Therefore they assented. Troops from the two European nations then occupied the Canal in early November, after having bombed Egyptian cities and destroyed what was left of the Egyptian air force.

Golda Meir, in her memoirs, *My Life*, from which I have quoted above, emphasises in strong terms that for Israel only one thing was important in the Suez strike against the Egyptians, and that was to prevent the destruction of the Jewish State.[85] Considering the above-mentioned documentation of Israeli provocative actions before the war and its secret collusion with the two foreign powers, it is not easy to follow her argument.

Benny Morris writes that several barbaric acts were committed by the IDF after the onslaught: "The Israeli conquest and its aftermath was characterised by a great deal of unwarranted killing, especially of retreating or captured Egyptian soldiers. In all, Israeli troops killed around five hundred Palestinian civilians [...] about two hundred of them in the massacres in Khan Yunis and in Rafa. Several dozen were summarily executed".[86]

Ben-Gurion was enthusiastic about the IDF's tremendous success on the battlefield, but his sense of almost unlimited victory was of short duration. Shlaim writes, "[t]he Prime Minister was drunk with victory [...] and in the Knesset on 7 November he hinted that Israel planned to annex the entire Sinai peninsula as well as the Straits of Tiran [...]. The arrogant tone of the speech caused much anger and antipathy outside Israel, not least among American Jews. Pride comes before the fall".[87]

Shlaim also states that "despite all the political miscalculations and failures of those who planned the Sinai campaign, it is their version that became firmly entrenched in the minds of the overwhelming majority of the Israelis [...]. However cherished, this version does not stand up to scrutiny in the light of the

---

84   Much faster indeed than Simon Peres had predicted.
85   "our survival was suddenly at stake", p. 299.
86   Op.cit., p. 295.
87   Op.cit., p. 179.

evidence now available. The official version is little more than the propaganda of the victors".[88]

The war was of very little cost to the IDF, because of its character of a *Blitzkrieg*: 190 lives and 15 aircraft lost, compared to 1650 killed Egyptian soldiers and 215 aircraft. The British-French losses were even much less than those of Israel.

When trying to give a historical verdict on this early period, I think one has to understand that the pioneer politicians still lived in a setting that often gave them the sense of Israel being the small and weak nation in threatening surroundings. Therefore, they often referred to this situation, both privately and publicly, despite the military facts. Golda Meir's opinion, as quoted above from *My Life,* is a good example of this attitude, still shared by many Israelis.

Knowing later history, it is strange to note that in 1956, Israel's best friends were the British and French, whereas their later supporters, the Americans, only intervened to stop the war, in collaboration with the Soviet Union at the UN — a strange and rare occurrence in the Cold War period.

But there was a distinct difference between the attitudes of the Soviet Prime Minister, Bulganin, and the American President, Eisenhower. Whereas the first sent a very angry letter to Ben-Gurion accusing his government of "playing criminally and irresponsibly with the fate of the world", the American President only expressed the hope that Israel would continue her friendly co-operation with Washington and no longer be of grave concern to the world.[89]

Under this heavy pressure from abroad, formalised in UN resolutions (which also demanded that the Anglo-British troops be withdrawn), Ben-Gurion was left with little choice. He had to relinquish any hope of annexation of the Sinai[90] and comply with the order to withdraw his troops, and did so in March 1957, after only months of occupation of most of the Sinai. Israel's UN ambassador, Abba Eban, was successful, however, in getting some reasonable guarantees, for instance with regard to open shipping, in exchange for the withdrawal. President Eisenhower sent Ben-Gurion a letter in which freedom of navigation was assured. A new UN force was established to control the borders on the Egyptian side, and all in all, the Israeli government had reached most of its targets, if not achieved its most ambitious plans.

Soon, however, the pride over the brilliant victory gave way to frustration in Israel, where many people again felt rather alone on the international scene. As a

---

88 Ibid., p. 185.
89 Golda Meir tells us that Eisenhower was furious to have been kept in the dark about the whole affair and even threatened sanctions against Israel if she did not withdraw. Ibid., p. 250. See also Morris, op.cit., p. 297 and Shlaim op.cit., p. 181.
90 The Israelis had tempted the French government with the prospect of being able to explore oil in Sinai.

matter of fact, Israel became fairly isolated internationally because of the combined American and Soviet anger, and in Britain and France scepticism also grew, with regard to how one ought to regard the war in retrospect. A realistic appraisal is that these two neo-colonial powers suffered irreparable harm in the Middle East for years to come, when their influence declined in favour of the USA. The French government that had hoped — through its collusion with the two other powers in their fight against the Pan-Arab leader, Nasser — to be able to maintain control over unruly Algeria, did surely not see its goal materialise.

Some restraint was imposed on all participants after the tripartite aggression, because of the threatening Soviet language in the immediate aftermath. It is obvious that relations with the Arab world became much more tense than ever before; the army of Egypt had only been defeated, after all, not fully destroyed. The pre-emptive strike had therefore proved to be a dangerous gamble for the young Jewish nation, as well as for Britain and France. On the other hand, however, it had again demonstrated the strength of the IDF. Israel's survival now seemed guaranteed for another decade or more, the Israeli leaders felt, if they soon had to give up the immediate euphoria of the victory. A further positive result was the opening up of international shipping through the Suez Canal and to Eilat, Israel's port at the Red Sea. One of the ugly pre-war episodes had, as we remember, been the above-mentioned arrest and torturing of Israeli seamen by Egyptians, when their ship was arrested in the Canal.

3. Aftermath

One clear result of the war was that Egypt (and the other Arab states) were now aware of the strength of the IDF and also of the strong will of the Prime Minister, Ben-Gurion, if they had ever been in doubt. Nasser faced the consequences and left the common borders in peace. This was of course an advantage for the Israeli government, but there was a new danger with respect to the even stronger Arab focus on the priority of the Pan-Arab movement and the Palestinian question, which Nasser now addressed. The Suez attack had confirmed his worst suspicions with regard to Israel's expansionist will; "the containment of Israel [now] became a Pan-Arab goal", writes Shlaim.[91] We shall soon return to the Arab world's political confrontation with Israel.

Because the two European powers which had joined Israel in the Suez Canal conflict had been forced to withdraw under the pressure in the UN of the two superpowers, USA and the USSR, Ben-Gurion — whose prestige and influence had reached a peak at home after the IDF victory — understood the signals from

---

91   Ibid., p. 187.

abroad. He now showed a greater interest in cultivating the Western superpower, but in the beginning, Washington was somewhat aloof to the new appeals from Israel. Both President Eisenhower and his Secretary of State, Foster Dulles, were cool and distant; but eventually, the world situation changed the picture little by little. The Cold War gave rise to the so-called *Eisenhower Doctrine* from January 1957, which was aimed at protecting the *free world* from military or other threats from the Communist countries. When Syria began its involvement with the USSR in mid-1957, this was a factor that some in the Israeli intelligence wanted to exploit. They maintained that there was the danger of a Soviet attack on Israel through Syria, a rather fantastic vision without much base in reality.

The CIA under Allen Dulles, therefore, did not buy the argument, but the alliance between Egypt and Syria in early 1958 was again taken as a new danger and consequently misused by the Jerusalem government. The new union was presented to the Americans as a dangerous *encirclement* by the Arab states around Israel. There was of course some truth in this, but it did not completely convince Washington at this stage. A new escalation soon resulted, however, with the advent of a new crisis in the Middle East in the summer of 1958, which presented a somewhat different picture. It occurred because of the brutal overthrow of the Hashemite King in Baghdad and the following American invasion of Beirut as a demonstration of force, at the same time that Western aircraft landed in Amman to reinforce the Jordanian King. Under American pressure, Israel granted permission for these aircraft to fly over its territory to reach Amman, but the hesitant Ben-Gurion's first reaction had been to decline because of warnings and threats from the Soviet Union. The Cold War, which had not been a decisive factor in the area around the time of the 1956 war, had become a hard reality in 1958.

Although these moments of crisis did not amount to much more than fairly isolated events, the Ben-Gurion government, in its search for allies, began a diplomatic campaign asking for an association of Israel with NATO. It was not taken very seriously among the Western powers, however, nor by the influential Israeli general and later politician, Moshe Dayan.

The friendship and continued collaboration with the French leaders lasted until the same decisive year, 1958, when it changed completely after de Gaulle came to power. It will be remembered how the then French President later accused the Israelis of being *an elitarian and dominant people*.[92] De Gaulle was certainly no anti-Semite, but looked for an improvement in his relationship with the Arabs, especially because he wanted to end the difficult war in Algeria soon after he came to power. This he eventually managed to do, as we know.

---

92   In his press conference on 28 November 1967, de Gaulle talked about ce "Peuple d´élite, sûr de lui même et dominateur", see Georges Corm, *Le Proche-Orient éclaté*, Paris 1999, p. 344.

With Western Germany, Ben-Gurion wanted to establish good relations at an early stage, realising that in the Federal Republic, there were new generations on the way, who wanted to let the world forget — as much as possible — the barbarism of the Nazis. Also the old anti-Nazi German Chancellor, Konrad Adenauer, realised that his government better consent to the establishment of a compensation system for the surviving Jews. Slowly, many Israelis could see that a new beginning might be round the corner in the Jewish-German relationship; but it was a difficult perspective initially, and surely not everyone rallied behind the Prime Minister in this delicate approach. Israel had already signed a reparations agreement with the Federal Republic of Germany in 1952, but it now asked for military assistance, and was successful also in this, even if modern Germany has always had a more cautious arms export policy than the two major ex-colonial powers that had helped Israel so far.

Finally, Israel invested in what Shlaim calls the *Alliance of the Periphery*,[93] which consisted in cultivating close relationships with such countries as Turkey (Islamic, but secular, and a member of NATO), Iran (equally Islamic, but with a Western-oriented Shah), and finally, and less importantly, with Ethiopia. Iran was going to be an essential supplier of oil to Israel, and until 1979, when the Shah fell, it was of great importance to the Israeli leaders. Turkey was always an important ally, and still is today.

Another clever move by Israel at an early stage was to cultivate relations with African and many other countries, to a greater extent than a country of its size normally would. This has given Israel a higher degree of influence in foreign politics and some valuable friendships around the world. It has also, generally speaking, helped the Jewish state to achieve more understanding than would otherwise have been the case.

One dramatic event led to much discussion in Israel and in many other places. This was the arrest in 1960 of Eichmann — one of the leading organisers of the incredible mass murder of Jews during the Nazi period — by Israeli agents in Argentina, followed by the transfer of him to Jerusalem. Ben-Gurion was perfectly willing to apologise to the Argentinean government for the infringement on its sovereignty, but insisted on carrying out the process against Eichmann, which ended in his death sentence and hanging.[94] Mrs. Golda Meir was for her own part, not very apologetic, writing in her memoirs that she felt angry when many accused the Israelis of a formal diplomatic infringement and forgot the abnormal crimes of the mass murderer who had escaped his just punishment in Argentina. Ben-Gurion's wish to carry out the trial was not for revenge, but

---

93 Op.cit., p. 192.
94 Eichmann´s own version, written while he was a prisoner in Israel, was published in 2002.

in order to teach the public in Israel and in the world at large about the mechanisms of the truly incomprehensibly murderous system of Nazi Germany. In the 1960's *Holocaust* was not yet a common phenomenon to speak about, as we have mentioned above.

I think that in the light of history, the world may now understand the Israeli way of thinking better than before and forget about the formal infringements on Argentinean national pride. (Some years later, Argentine gave the world another example of criminal thinking when its military government indulged in the killing of thousands of innocent victims.)

Israel and the Atomic Bomb

Despite the clear victory in 1956 over the most important Arab country, Egypt, Ben-Gurion told one of his aides that he could hardly sleep at night because of his fear of a combined Arab attack.[95] He therefore wanted to develop Israel as a nuclear power, and, as has been mentioned above, the French had shown their willingness to help the Israeli government during the talks on the tripartite agreement before the War of 1956. Even the Eisenhower government had agreed to give Israel assistance under the *Atoms for Peace Program* as early as 1955. Soon Israel had two Atomic research programs running, one with American, the other with French assistance, but Ben-Gurion emphasised in the Knesset in December 1959 that the reactors were designed exclusively for peaceful purposes. At the time this assurance was given, Israel was surely not producing atomic weapons, but Shlaim stresses that "Gurion gave no pledge of any kind about the future".[96] Later on, even the CIA warned that Israel's nuclear capacities would substantially damage the relationship between the USA and the West, on one hand, and the Arab countries on the other. Today, it is generally considered a fact that Israel has the capabilities and has probably also developed nuclear weapons already, in order to keep the upper hand in the fierce competition on arms supplies with its Arab neighbours. When Israel bombed the Iraqi nuclear installations in 1981, it was again in order to be assured of its military superiority, which only highly modern technology and better strategic capabilities, not manpower, can give Israel.

During the end of Ben-Gurion's period of government, he went to Washington and had a fruitful meeting with the young President, John F. Kennedy. According to Shlaim, the latter was the first US leader to tilt America's Middle East policy in favour of Israel, despite the inflexibility shown by the government in Jerusalem.[97]

---

95 Shlaim, op.cit. p. 205. This fear, if we can trust the witness, shows that the aggressiveness of Ben-Gurion was based on a real fear, rather than on expansionist dreams.
96 Ibid. p. 208.
97 Ibid., p. 211.

I agree, but we have to qualify this assessment with the fact that only much later did the American guarantees to Israel become evident. Regarded in retrospect, however, this tilt under Kennedy was a new development that — seen with Jewish-Israeli eyes — assured the Zionists of survival in their young nation, much more than modern arms, including nuclear ones, could ever do. But perhaps it was only because of its strong will to survive, combined with the strength of the IDF, that the Jewish nation was considered worth keeping secure in a difficult setting, seen with the eyes of *Realpolitik* in Washington. Even among nations we find something akin to Darwin's theory of the survival of the fittest.

The first years between the two wars of 1956 and 1967 were fairly uneventful in the Arab-Israeli relationship, and therefore the Israeli government, in Ben-Gurion's last phase, could carry out many internal reforms and a further strengthening of the armed forces. That these were still essential for national survival seemed evident, not only to Ben-Gurion and his government but to almost all Israelis, and at the same time, the armed forces could be regarded as an ideal melting pot for the incoming Jews and the *Sabra* generations.[98] No one was more certain of that than Ben-Gurion himself; we may say that at the end of his career he had come to fill the role of an old, highly respected patriarch.[99] Not a bad reflection on his character and on his influence in the young nation. Behind the scenes, the picture of the Prime Minister was surely a good deal less idyllic, as we shall now see.

His last years of government fell under the shadow of what he saw was the threat of the proposed Federation between Egypt, Syria and Iraq (which never materialised). Shlaim describes Ben-Gurion's "personal reaction as one of deep, almost irrational anxiety".[100] What also concerned Ben-Gurion was the pressure from the American side to open up for inspection of the nuclear facilities in Israel; Washington also demanded an assurance from the Ben-Gurion government that Israel had no intention of producing the atomic bomb. In his answers the Prime Minister referred to the West's ignorance of or disbelief in the early Nazi period, when threats of Holocaust were issued by the coming leader, Adolf Hitler, and were hardly taken seriously by anyone. He now reiterated his fears that the evil plans of the Arab states against Israel would mean the destruction of the Jewish state,

---

98 Those born in Israel.
99 The Danish author, P. Borchsenius, writes in his book on *Ben-Gurion*, Copenhagen, 1956, as follows:
    "Ben-Gurion is the captain at the helm on the bridge. He looks far ahead through fog, rain and mist and even stormy weather to find the right direction. That is his special strength". At the end of his lyrical praise Borchsenius tells us: "From Abraham to Ben-Gurion, that´s four thousand years. In this long period Ben-Gurion has become a modern Joshua. Just like the old time Joshua he led his people into the promised land" (my translation).
100 Op.cit., p. 214.

even more so because they were supported by their weapons program, especially involving sophisticated arms in Egypt through German assistance.

In one of his letters to President Kennedy, Gurion wrote a prophecy of gloom: "It may not happen today or tomorrow, but I am not sure whether the state will continue to exist after my life has come to an end".[101] These strange words of disbelief in the survival of the Zionist creation, which came at the end of his impressive career, shocked Golda Meir and other Israeli officials who were informed, but none of them could persuade Ben-Gurion or change his view on the content of his letter to the American President.

In the middle of this crisis, Ben-Gurion surprised the world and his own countrymen by resigning (for the second time) on 16 June 1963; actually, this was not so strange at his age of 77. He left the heavy responsibilities to his successor, Levi Eshkol, and as with his previous retirement from government in 1953, he made some important decisions with regard to the new government; for instance his persuasion of Eshkol to appoint Yitzhak Rabin, whom he had already promised this promotion, to the position of Chief of Staff, a post which is certainly more important in Israel than in many other countries.

---

101 Ibid., p. 214.

IV. The militant policies of the Arab League

It was previously mentioned how President Nasser changed his country's policy after the Egyptian defeat of 1956. He now decidedly gave up finding any compromise solution with Israel and wanted to focus more on Pan-Arabism and militant policies of the League. He also supported the Palestinians openly, even if the Arabs had so far seemed to ignore their interests after the first Arab defeat when facing the Israelis militarily, in 1948 – 49.

We have already referred to the first important step in creating a stronger Arab unity. The establishment in 1958 of the United Arab Union between Egypt and Syria, two Arab states that were both neighbours of Israel, could easily be seen as a new threat to the young Jewish state. It was one of those factors that contributed to Ben-Gurion's fears in the last phase of his government. He pointed to this new creation as part of the background for the establishment of a nuclear weapons program in Israel. Eventually, the new Arab Union showed its own weakness, due to the strongly hegemonic character of the dominant power, Egypt, which did not leave much influence to the Syrians. If the Union was dissolved only after three years, in 1961, a new plan of a federation between the two Arab powers, now also including Iraq, appeared in 1963 and worried Ben-Gurion in his last year of government, as previously mentioned. He could not know that it would never materialise.

1. Arab Summit of 1964

We may recall that the Arab League had been established as early as 1945, with its headquarters in Cairo; right from the outset, it appointed an Egyptian as its Secretary General, and with that, the strong Egyptian influence was stressed. Normally the Arab countries' foreign ministers held their regular meetings in the Egyptian capital, and only in January 1964 did Nasser organise the first Arab Summit of government leaders. It was at this meeting that the *Palestinian Liberation Organisation*, PLO, was formed, but it was not a very convincing occurrence, for many reasons. The first chairman of the PLO was a Palestinian, Ahmad Shuquiri, who had been director of the Palestinian Office, first in New York and later in Jerusalem. Several Palestinians, headed by the old leader, Hajii Amin al-Husseini of Jerusalem, were, however, sceptical, as was the case with George Habash and Yassir Arafat, leaders of the *Arab National Movement* (ANM) and the *Fatah*, respectively. Strangely enough, Arafat, who eventually became the PLO leader (in 1969), did not attend the Summit meeting in Cairo. Little by little, however, the strong influence of Nasser changed the picture, and the PLO gained increasing influence over the years. But strangely enough it was only after the next Arab defeat, the Six-Day War in 1967, that the PLO attained a more decisive influence.

The establishment of the PLO in 1964 is therefore an important historic event to recall, despite all the early weaknesses of the Organisation. One of its first initiatives was to create the *Palestinian Liberation Army*, which had its first encounter with the IDF in Gaza in 1967.

That the importance of the PLO was not evident at that moment went hand in hand with the fact that the Palestinian question — as seen from the Israeli perspective — had been solved through the division of the old British Palestinian mandate into two entities, that of Israel and that of Jordan, after the War of Independence, with the latter occupying most of those Arab parts that should have become a separate state but were now included into the kingdom, which Israel found comforting. Gaza was under Egyptian domination until 1967.

For many years, the Palestinians and their organisations were labelled *terrorist* by the Israeli government and it was even forbidden for Israelis to have official contacts with the PLO or any other similar *terrorist* organisation.

2. Terrorism

Was the PLO a terrorist organisation? No precise answer can be given to this delicate question, but as a liberation organisation aiming to create a new Palestinian state with a secular government that allowed Jews and Christians equal rights with the Muslims, the Palestinians thought that all methods could be employed, just as the Zionists had done in their fight for recognition before Independence. If Begin and Shamir should not be termed terrorists, then why should Yassir Arafat, it was argued.

In the first stage of the liberation campaign, it was the organisations like the oldest one, ANM, founded in 1952 by George Habash, or the more important one, Fatah (meaning conquest or victory) founded in 1958 by Yassir Arafat, which did the fighting or, to adopt the language of the other side, were responsible for the terrorist actions. ANM was more Pan-Arabic in its character, while Fatah's philosophy was that of allowing "revolutionary violence, practised by the masses, in order to liberate Palestine and eliminate Zionism" (not the same as eliminating

Jews, but seen from the Israeli perspective, the difference was insignificant and the aim fully unacceptable, of course). The first guerrilla acts were initiated by Fatah from Syria in early 1965, with the aim of blowing up a water pipeline. Morris tells us that in the period January 1965 to June 1967 there were 122 raids, but that most of them were "abortive".[102]

We might therefore have concluded that at this early stage, terrorism was not a significant or even very serious element in the Arab/Israeli Conflict. But regarded from the Israeli side in those early years, the trend of attacks from outside looked dangerous, since one neighbouring state, in particular, Syria, was known to give support to terrorist attacks from its territory. Even the fairly tolerant Prime Minister, Levi Eshkol, acknowledged in early 1967 that his government had to take drastic measures against Syria, for instance through the shooting down of military aircraft. His Chief of Staff, Rabin, later Prime Minister, had already publicly declared that it was necessary to distinguish between those states that did not favour acts of sabotage (Lebanon and Jordan) and Syria, which did.

But let us not think for a moment that Israeli retaliation attacks in the first two countries mentioned were soft-handed at all. In Jordan a regular army intrusion in the village of As Samu, in November 1966, became a brutal raid that was "rocking Hussein's Kingdom" according to Morris.[103]

---

102 Op.cit., p. 303.
103 Ibid., p. 303.

V. THE DECISIVE WAR OF 1967

1. The Background

As of the mid-sixties, the atmosphere had thus gradually become more tense between the conflicting parties, who, although never at peace, were now more and more on the alert against each other.

The continuing harassment, though often abortive, by the Palestinian movement, Fatah, against Israeli territory or settlements, in addition to the Syrian and Lebanese measures to prevent water from running into Israel, made things worse.[104] Morris writes that "ultimately it was the sputtering Syrian-Israeli border that triggered the process that led to the Six-Day War", but he also mentions later that "the road to the war had been lined by Israeli intelligence failures".[105]

The already tense situation intensified when Egypt — as of 22 May 1967 — again blocked the access of Israeli ships into the waterway leading to Israel's port of Eilat. Nasser must have known that this would be regarded as *casus belli* in Jerusalem. And his evil military intentions were accentuated— as seen with Israeli eyes — because the Egyptian government now asked the UN forces to leave the border area between Israel and Egypt, as if to prepare for a war against Israel. (The UNEF troops had been stationed on the Egyptian side of the border only.)

The Arab side pretends that tension had already arisen from the fact that the Israelis had threatened the Syrian Baath regime in 1966 with overthrow, because it gave assistance to terrorists attacking Israel. This was the main reason why the Damascus government felt compelled to sign a defence treaty with Egypt in November 1966 and open up for diplomatic relations with Cairo at ambassador level.

---

104 Officially, of course, the two Arab nations have denied this. A minister told me in November 2001 that Syria had done nothing more than what any upstream-country would do. Syria has a much more serious problem with Turkey, which is building huge dams and diverting the water. He also stressed that Israel had the means to get water from other sources (water treatment plants, etc.). Unofficially, however, some Syrians have admitted that diversion measures were undertaken or planned.

105 Op.cit., p. 304 and p. 310.

This happened only a few years after the break-up of the Egypt-Syrian Union in 1961, which had resulted in a very tense relationship, of course, between these former allies.

Syria had also informed Egypt that Israeli troops were congregating along its borders. The Arabs argue that this must be seen as the background for the urgent demand from Cairo that the UN withdraw its troops, to which the UN Secretary General agreed with undue haste, according to the Israelis and most outside observers. Jerusalem denied that the IDF had put any special pressure on the Syrians, and the Prime Minister said in the Knesset that "there was no shred of truth in talks of Israeli concentration of troops on the Syrian border". Abba Eban found that it was all due to Soviet misinformation.[106] Morris confirms that even Syrian intelligence could not produce evidence when the Egyptians asked for it.[107]

One of the more nasty preludes to the war, which frightened the public in Jordan and the Arab world, was the already mentioned brutal Israeli attack on the Jordanian village of As Samu in November 1966, which resulted in many casualties. Coming without any warning, if we trust Shlaim's account, this devastating attack resembles so many of those provocative acts that the IDF, usually with orders from the government, launched throughout this period, in order to frighten the Arabs.[108] This time the onslaught was one of those blunders by the IDF that almost unsettled the Hashemite throne and probably influenced King Hussein — who was particularly upset because the attack occurred on his birthday, 13 November — to align himself, though reluctantly, with Nasser, which he did only a few months later, in May 1967.

Whatever the reasons (and they may all be valid), the atmosphere became so tense that the Israeli government eventually took action. It relied again on its philosophy of pre-emptive strikes, and this time even more successfully than during the Suez War, 11 years earlier. Golda Meir in her memoirs stresses that there was severe criticism against Eshkol for not taking action earlier. "Eshkol seemed too uncertain, too reluctant to take action. These were heroic times, but where was the hero?" she asks in her blunt way. But in addition, she also honestly admits that the burden of decision-making was hard, as she herself was to learn later during the Yom Kippur War.[109] The later Prime Minister Rabin refers in his memoirs to Eshkol's "stammering speech to the nation that made a poor impression on the increasingly nervous Israeli population. The Prime Minister gave the impression that he could not control his tongue because of his state of terror".[110]

---

106 Op.cit., p. 303.
107 Ibid., p. 305.
108 Op.cit., p. 233, in which he mentions that no satisfactory explanation was ever given for the scale or ferocity of the attack.
109 Op.cit., p. 339.
110 Rabin, op.cit., p. 92.

He was not alone in this. Also the Chief of Staff himself, the same Yitzhak Rabin, experienced, as he admits in his memoirs,[111] some difficult moments of tension and exhaustion, and was out of circulation for a while just before the onslaught. He had been particularly depressed because Ben-Gurion himself had seen Rabin and warned him against any war action that he might take in his capacity of Chief of Staff. The old former Prime Minister (over 80 then) had finally had enough of wars, but never became weary of interfering. Why did Golda Meir forget this fact in her memoirs? She would normally listen to whatever came from Ben-Gurion, but this time she wanted the Prime Minister to be a warrior hero. We know from Foreign Minister Abba Eban that the first Prime Minister was never satisfied with Eshkol and even led a vendetta against his successor, not a particularly generous thing to do.[112]

Because of all this criticism, whether justified or not, in this period of trial, Eshkol had to admit some new members into his Cabinet, such as the later Prime Minister, Menachem Begin, and the efficient general, Dayan, who was appointed Minister of Defence just before the war.

If one reads Abba Eban's interesting account of his hectic diplomatic activity as Foreign Minister just before the outbreak of the war, it seems as if the Israeli government did not want to leave any stone unturned in the effort to find a peaceful settlement, until it decided to act militarily. The responsible leaders could eventually see no other way out of the dangerous isolation that the Egyptians, Syrians and Jordanians had imposed on Israel, on its shipping, in particular. And military action seemed all the more necessary because the building up of armed forces in the Sinai corroborated clear threats from Nasser and others to undo the establishment of the Jewish nation. Eban tells us in his book that these threats had a clear impact on the government. It was indeed difficult for the Cabinet to ignore the opinion of the public, especially now that it was becoming increasingly alert.

All this forced the Jerusalem government to take the initiative with regard to what was found to be legitimate self-defence, in order to avoid slow strangulation. Morris tells us that Meir Amit, the chief of the Israeli Intelligence, Mossad, was in Washington just before the June War was decided, and had got the clear understanding from the US authorities that "Washington would bless an operation if we succeed in shattering Nasser".[113]

Reading the Chief of Staff's account of the same pre-war situation in his memoirs, we learn that *Rabin waits for Nasser*, and later that *Nasser waits for Rabin*; thus the Israeli top general and later Prime Minister compares himself — and not without some assertiveness — with the Egyptian Head of State, and even uses these

---

111 Ibid., p. 81.
112 Op.cit., p. 301.
113 Op.cit., p. 310.

The victorious Israeli Generals. From left to right: General Uzi Narkiss, Moshe Dayan and Yitzak Rabin enter Old Jerusalem in 1967.

assertions as headlines of the two relevant chapters.[114] He paints a lively picture of how eager the top brass of the Israeli military was to enter into war with Egypt in these May days of 1967, not, of course, as warmongers, but because they thought that any delay would reduce the chances of certain victory. Eshkol was still hesitant and had to wait for Abba Eban's talks in Washington. Interestingly enough, Rabin also relates that he actively participated in the formulation of the instructions for Foreign Minister Abba Eban's visit to Washington, when they were worked out by the Directors General of the Ministry of Foreign Affairs and the Prime Minister's office, sitting together. This was a most unusual task for a Chief of Staff — unheard of in most countries.[115]

Israel always has limited possibilities for maintaining large military contingents in peacetime and is generally forced to act swiftly — a capacity it has learnt to explore fully. Exactly for that reason, Rabin — as Chief of Staff — was very eager not to delay further the making of decisions about the war, which he found unavoidable at any rate. As indicated above, he almost had a nervous breakdown just before the attack, mainly due to the government's internal disagreements and postponements of the final go-ahead order to the IDF, and because he was negatively impressed and worried by Ben-Gurion's unusually nervous attitude.

We learn from Eban's account that, as is normal for the head of diplomacy, he was among those who suggested patience and a further waiting period in late May, until Israel knew what the Western nations would do in order to support it. Since that support was only lukewarm, even the Foreign Minister (who was also Deputy Prime Minister) finally declared that he would no longer veto a decision to go to war.

During his last-effort journey to the Western powers, Eban first had long discussions with the French President, General de Gaulle, who in a polite, albeit aloof, way warned Israel against going alone. "Do not make war", he said. I have already mentioned the well-known anger of President de Gaulle after the brief war when the Israelis had ignored his advice.

In Washington, President Johnson did not speak in favour of war, as the Mossad Chief had reported based on other sources, but advised Israel against going alone in an attack on Egypt, saying, "Israel will not be alone, unless it decides to do it alone". But Johnson would not (he said he *could* not, without Congress) give any precise promises regarding the freedom of navigation to and from Eilat, which was the cardinal point for Israel. He therefore forgot or ignored the promises of free navigation given by one of his predecessors, President Eisenhower.[116]

---

114 Op.cit., Chapters Four and Five.
115 Ibid., p 87. In the instructions, it is emphasised that "Israel faces a grave danger of attack by Egypt and Syria".
116 In an interesting chapter in his *Peace Process,* Washington, 2001, William B. Quandt

Despite the warmer atmosphere in Washington than that in Paris and London, where Eban met Prime Minister Wilson, he felt that he did not get sufficient assurance, only polite promises that these two friendly nations would "try to do something". In the face of the hostile Soviet attitude, which among other things prevented the Security Council from acting, Eban came home almost empty-handed. He still used his influence in the Cabinet to persuade it of the necessity of postponing any military action for some time. Actually, after the Foreign Minister's talks in Washington on 26 May, the Cabinet decided on this postponement on 28 May, but a further negative development on the international scene, including an escalation of aggressive Egyptian statements, eventually convinced the Cabinet, including Eban, of the necessity to act.

Morris writes, "[t]he armies were extremely ill-matched. Israelis have tended, throughout their history, to regard themselves as *the weaker side*, their army smaller and less well armed than their Arab enemies. The truth in 1967, as at other times, was different".[117] He also asserts that "captured Egyptian documents show that Egypt's army was in fact preparing for a defensive battle, to absorb and repel an initial IDF blow".[118]

2. The Impressive Victory
(or Fatal Defeat)

On the morning of 5 June, the Israeli air force (most of the planes of French origin) bombed all the Egyptian airfields and destroyed 60% of the enemy's air force.[119] In the impressive *Blitzkrieg* that immediately followed, Egypt lost 550 tanks in the

---

gives a vivid account of the dramatic days, especially in Washington, just before the break out of the Six-Day War. See pp 24 - 41.

117 Op.cit., p. 311. One can surely argue that the number of planes, tanks, etc. was higher on the combined Arab front than on the IDF side. But what is much more important is that maintenance, skills and especially the much better co-ordinated command structures was to the advantage of the IDF. Even more, each and every soldier and officer in the IDF fought for his homeland in a way no Arab needed or would ever dream of. Their extremely high level of motivation decided this war, as it did the two former ones.

118 Ibid., p. 313.

119 Rabin tells us that the Commander of the Air Force had guaranteed "that our military position would be greatly improved within an hour of our air strike" but also gives an honest picture of the previous strong resistance to the war from political side, especially from the Minister of Interior. Op.cit., p. 79-80.

brief but violent battles in the Sinai. Later the same day, Israel struck the Jordanian forces that had attacked Israel first and now saw substantial parts of their equipment destroyed. On 9 June, the Israeli armoured regiments reached the Suez Canal after the retreat — flight — of most of the Egyptian forces. Israel also managed to occupy East Jerusalem and other parts of the West Bank plus most of the Syrian Golan Heights. They were under Israel's control already on 10 June, when a final cease-fire went into effect. Israel had not thought of attacking Jordan, but was itself attacked by the Arab Legion of Jordan, despite the fact that Jerusalem had warned Amman against participation in the war. This time even the best Royal Jordanian troops were no match for the IDF.

Rabin tells us that Dayan was the voice of prudence during the Six-Day War, and that an attack on the Golan Heights was not included in the original Israeli plans. They were attacked, however, when the other fronts seemed out of danger — the temptation was too great for the IDF. We also learn that Nasser lied at an early stage, when he told King Hussein that US and British aircraft had participated on the Israeli side. It also emerges from the Chief of Staff's memoirs that during the initial fighting, the Israelis were duly worried whether the Russians would intervene in order to save some of the lost honour of the Egyptians. This might of course have been a well-founded fear, explaining the eagerness of the IDF to show its strength immediately. Only because the onslaught was so decisive, no further complications arose for the Israeli government. Rabin also mentions that he specifically ordered his troops not to fire on soldiers surrendering themselves, thereby admitting indirectly that such excesses had taken place during the 1956 campaign.[120]

During the war, the Israelis attacked a US NSA ship, *Liberty*, which was near the coast of Gaza, fully equipped with various sorts of bugging and other surveillance instruments. According to Rabin, the attack was a mistake, because the ship was unidentified and suspected of being Egyptian or (later) Soviet. The Americans were of course furious, without being able to protest openly, since their naval presence was surely not in accordance with international law. But the two friendly nations went a long way to (mis-) use all methods in order to gain the upper hand in the conflict.[121] They were not alone, however, since the second superpower, the USSR, was also fishing in troubled waters. We should remember that this war took place

---

120 Ibid., p. 114.
121 James Bamford gives his account of this episode in his recent book, *Body of Secrets; Anatomy of the Ultra Secret National Agency from the Cold War*, New York, 2001. Rabin also gives many details in his memoirs, in a serious way. Op.cit., pp. 109 - 111. One of the fascinating things we learn is that both the USA and the Soviet leadership were, for a short while, confronted with a huge challenge: Whether to start ordering attacks on the Soviet fleet or the US fleet, respectively.

King Hussein inspects troops. On the left Hussein's uncle, Sherif Nasser and on the right Hussein's brother, Crown Prince Hassan.

during one of the most serious periods of the Cold War, when the US government was heavily engaged in the tragic Vietnam War, which made the American decision makers more nervous than before.

After the short war, Israel was in possession of much more than the old Palestinian territory, and there was a palpable feeling of relief in the nation, which could now see Eliat, its important gateway to the South, re-open, and a threatening border situation turned into one of evident superiority. Especially having all of Jerusalem within its control was the most impressive gain from this brief, but extremely successful war, if seen with Israeli eyes.[122] I happened to visit Israel, including Jerusalem, in May 1968, less than a year after the war and could sense the undisguised happiness of the Jewish population, whereas the Arab sentiments

---

122 When the Israeli Defence Minister, Moshe Dayan, saw that some of his soldiers had hoisted the Israeli flag over the holy Mosques in Jerusalem, he immediately ordered them to take the flags down. He realised that it would be seen as an unnecessary provocation to the Arabs. His later colleague, Sharon, could have learnt from that.

were those of the downtrodden and deceived. Once again they had been deceived by their own leaders and by the Western world, but also, we may presume, by their faraway friends, the Russians, had not intervened. Most of their opinions could not be expressed in a free way, anyhow.[123]

The new, armed conflict was of course brought before the UN, which had been hindered in advance by the Soviets from taking action to avoid the war. After prolonged discussions (under Danish chairmanship in the Security Council),[124] the Council passed resolution 242 of 22 November 1967, asking for the retreat of Israeli troops from *occupied territories*. This remains the key UN decision in the conflict, but so far it has still not been fully accepted or implemented by Israel. The government could not forget that when it previously decided to pull out of the Sinai, it was only to find itself blocked again a few years later from access to the port of Eilat. Unlike the English text, the one in French spoke of *les territoires occupés*, which implied a promise to the Arabs for the restitution of *all* occupied territories. Shlaim ironically terms the wording of the resolution "as a masterpiece of deliberate British ambiguity".[125]

The Arab side once again had to realise that the combination of Israel's national coherence, its modern war equipment and impressive knowledge in utilising it had led to this disastrous result for them. Whether the Arabs had provoked this war — as it seems likely to most non-Arab observers — or not, the frustration in the neighbouring countries towards the young Israeli nation became overwhelming and could not be ignored. It was soon to result in more terrorism, targeting Israeli civilians and foreigners as well.

I should like to quote once again from Rabin, who is one of the most impressive figures in Israel's modern political history. In his memoirs he stresses that even after the very overwhelming victory for which he was partly responsible as Chief of Staff, "the Israeli forces should never be regarded as *invincible*, as the mythmaking was now indicating. In a speech after the war, I emphasised that before June 5, I had repeatedly warned that […] it would be a difficult undertaking [.... T]he fact that our successes exceeded all expectations did not in any way disprove that prediction" [emphasis added].[126]

---

123 Once when I asked an Israeli Arab (bus driver) how he felt inside the Jewish state, the Jewish guide in the bus answered for him that he was "very happy".

124 The (then) soon to be Foreign Minister of Denmark, Hans Tabor, has written substantially about this event during the exciting period when he was chairman of the Security Council; see his memoirs, *Diplomat Blandt Poltikere,* [Diplomat among Politicians], Copenhagen 1995, pp. 164ff.

125 Op.cit., p. 260. He adds that only in August 1970 did Israel officially recognise the resolution 242.

126 Op.cit., p. 120.

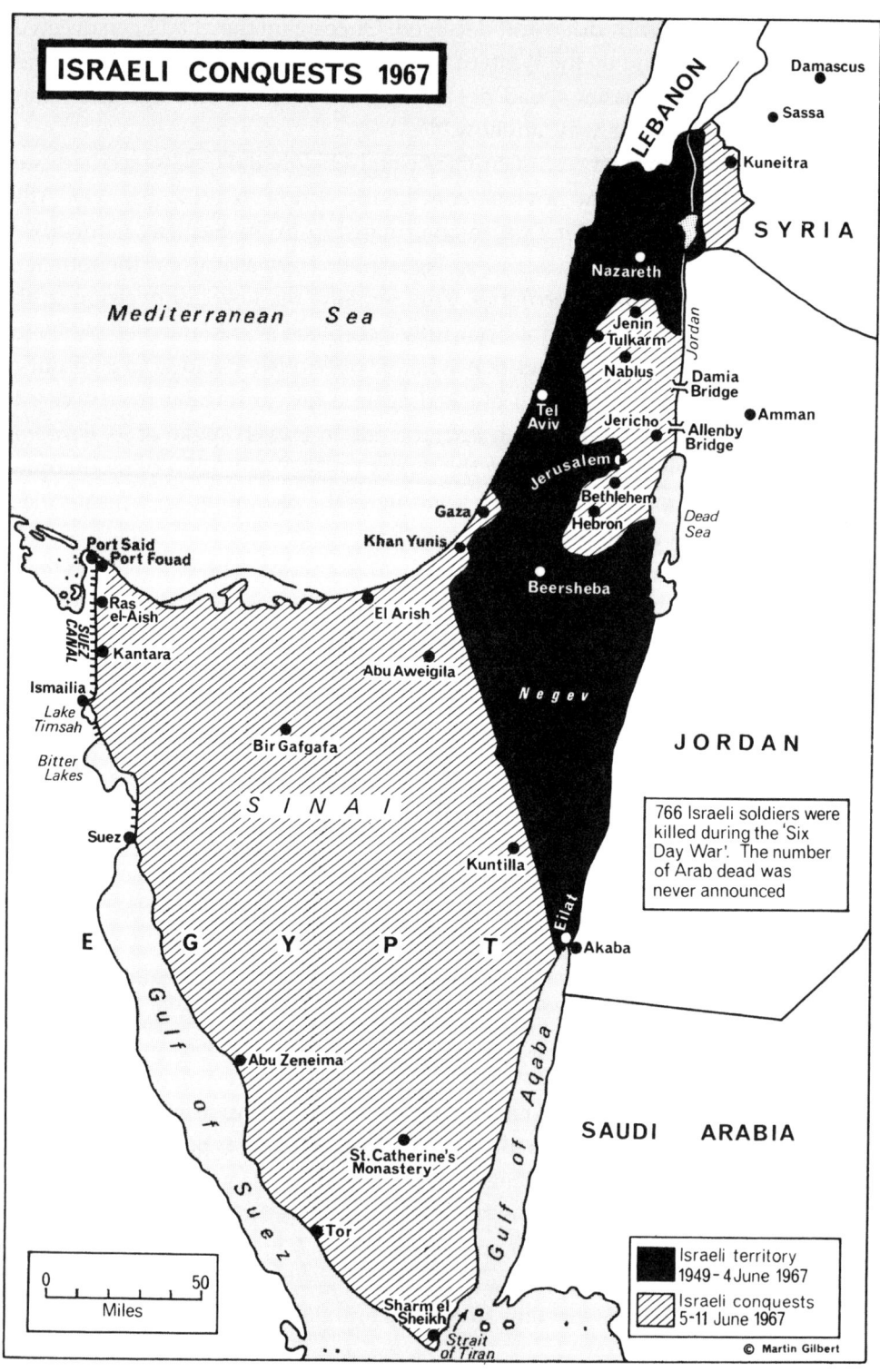

Rabin also writes in his memoirs that "Israel was now faced with three major problems: 1. Overnight we found ourselves in control of an enormous expanse of territory [...], 2. A million hostile Arabs [...] were now living under Israeli rule, 3. Finally, from the very start it was clear that Israel would not be left in peace to deal with the consequences of her territorial gains".[127]

This was the logical thinking of the brilliant general who was soon to become Israel's Ambassador to Washington (1968-73) and would later become a respected Prime Minister for two periods.

3. Aftermath

a. In Israel

No one could ignore the overwhelming victory of the June 1967 War, which had resulted in such tremendous changes on the map. Israel was now in possession of more land than it had ever dreamt of, especially because Jerusalem — with its sacred Wailing Wall — had come within its control. This was so important because Jews had not been able to pray at the old temple wall during the Jordanian period. The Arabs had been beaten on the battlefields for the third time and now had to reckon with the strength of the intruding nation. Israel no longer needed to fear the threat it had felt, especially from the Gaza and Sinai or the Golan Heights,[128] which dominated the Israeli plains. But even the most radical right-wing Israelis, including religious leaders, had up to that time not advanced any claim to take over this old Syrian land. If it was later annexed by Israel, it was because of its strategic value and perhaps as a political bargain when eventually facing Syria in negotiations.

Shlaim writes that the victory marked the beginning of a period of uncertainty, as foreboded by Rabin. There were of course lone voices of common sense, such as that of Prime Minister Levi Eshkol, and some of his more sensible colleagues, but they were sometimes lost in euphoric and nationalistic tones similar to those we heard when Ben-Gurion made all manner of expansionist declarations after the victory in 1956; now these were repeated by right-wing politicians such as Begin and others. I agree when Shlaim asserts that the result of the war reopened the old question among the Zionists about their territorial aims. Even the coalition govern-

---

127 Op.cit., pp. 118 - 119.
128 In posthumously published articles, Dayan has admitted that many of the Syrian attacks on Israeli positions were provoked by the Israeli side in order to be able to undertake an expansion and eventually the occupation of the Golan Heights. See also Shlaim, op.cit., p. 69 on "Dayan´s energetic and ruthless policy" in the DMZ.

ment could not agree on this, and all the more so because there was disagreement inside some of the participant parties themselves.

Those behind the Prime Minister, such as Dayan, Eban and Allon, met informally with Eshkol on 13 June 1967, and all agreed that Israel should present a peace offer to Egypt and Syria. The plan was later endorsed by the full Cabinet (19 June) and contained the important clause that some of the new acquisitions of Israel (Gaza and the West Bank) were not negotiable, while imposing a series of conditions on the Arab states, such as respecting the freedom of navigation to Israel (the prime *casus belli*), demilitarisation of the Golan and guarantee of free water flow into Israel. This proposal was sent to Abba Eban in the US so that he could transmit it to the American government, asking the latter to communicate the proposal to Egypt and Syria. The two main Arab states later informed the US that "this offer was not acceptable", because the IDF had to withdraw without making demands for conditions. This was still prior to the final resolution 242 from November 1967, which primarily granted what has later been called the *land for peace formula*, meaning that the IDF should withdraw from (all) the occupied territories in order to obtain peace.

The initial Israeli peace offer from June was never made public in Israel or globally, and soon even the Cabinet majority was no longer behind it, despite the fact that it did not seem very generous to the Arabs in general. It therefore had very little impact on the political negotiations that were to follow. What Shlaim calls a *creeping annexation* (of occupied land) was becoming the line of Israel, if not officially, then in the crude reality of politics. There was no consensus at all in the government regarding the future of the West Bank, and it seems as if the Jordanian option remained the most acceptable one, not least because of the Arab reaction.[129] When some apologists for Israel's policy point out that the Jerusalem government made a *generous peace offer* after the Arab 1967 debacle, it is therefore not in accordance with the historical facts.

One of the important Cabinet ministers (for Labour), Yigal Allon, proposed another plan that involved some form of negotiation with the Palestinian local leaders, but this element was later given up when the plan was changed to include negotiations with Jordan. The Cabinet neither approved nor rejected it, though it remained on the table for some time, like so many later abortive efforts to solve the problem. King Hussein, who had regular contact with the Israeli leaders, totally rejected the Allon Plan.

The aforementioned UN resolution 242, of 22 November 1967, which attempted to impose a final solution, did not provide any opening for Israel to acquire sovereignty over the conquered land, whatever its own feelings were. But the occupation became one of long duration and slow integration, and the situation, even

---

129 Op.cit., pp. 254 - 255.

more than 38 years later, has not changed substantially for the better (except for the Sinai) when seen with Arab eyes.

Jerusalem

The previously quoted Danish-Israeli journalist (himself a non-orthodox Jew), Herbert Pundik, wrote in *Politiken* not long ago: *Jerusalem makes people mad*.[130] He explained this by reporting how the various religious representatives in the holy city fight in order to obtain or retain influence, or even control, over the holy places, sometimes in the most absurd way. Jerusalem has certainly seen its share of violence, but in the first period after the occupation of the eastern parts of the city, the situation seemed peaceful and certainly euphoric from the Israeli point of view, because the Jews could again pray at their Wailing Wall.

It did not take long for the government to declare that the whole of Jerusalem was now an integrated part of Israel and that the holy city of the Jews would never be divided again. The sacred places of Islam (the two famous mosques) would be respected and free for all to visit (unlike the Wailing Wall under the Jordanian occupation). Where the real problem arose was in the Israeli policy of enlarging the municipal area of Jerusalem in order to get control over even more parts of the West Bank than the former city area, and that policy has been maintained until now, to the detriment of any solution for this intricate problem. The declaration of *Jerusalem as Capital of Israel* was not new but was now repeated for the united city, also in the hope that the embassies of foreign nations would move from Tel Aviv to Jerusalem. With a few exceptions, this has not occurred so far, however.[131]

Prime Minister Levi Eshkol died suddenly in early 1969, when the situation in the occupied areas and with regard to the Arab neighbours was still unsettled. Shlaim points out that a great deal of the criticism Eshkol had received was not really justified. He tried his best and wanted an opening for the Arab states, but "failed to communicate specific peace offers the them". Seen from the easy perspective of hindsight, Shlaim continues, and I agree: "[t]he real mistake was to occupy and stay in the West Bank".[132]

Eshkol was followed by a very different politician, Golda Meir; a true disciple of Ben-Gurion, blunt and militant, whereas Eshkol had some of the qualities of Sharett, with whom he shared a belief in diplomatic as opposed to military solutions.

---

130 *Politiken*, 31 December 1999. If the reader wants to get a lively impression of the atmosphere in Jerusalem, I can recommend the erudite novel by Robert Stone, *Damascus Gate*, New York, 1998.
131 The US Congress has voted in favour, but the Administration has not yet complied.
132 Ibid., p. 264. Rabin also praised *Eshkol as a warm, wise man*. Rabin, op.cit., p. 83.

b. In the Arab World

After the debacle of the war, the Arabs in general felt humiliated, especially because the defeat was so distant from the Pan-Arab promises heard from Cairo in the months leading to the war. The Palestinians, now under Israeli occupation, seemed paralysed and could not foresee any change in the near future. They knew that the Jews had gained the upper hand and — for a long time — it was felt. Any resistance appeared to be hopeless, and the Israelis could therefore initially enjoy peaceful conditions for the first time ever and hardly seen again since.

Clearly this 1967 debacle for the Arab cause had a great impact, not only on the Arab states, but especially among the Palestinians, who had to accept a change of masters from the former, monarchical, albeit Arab leader, King Hussein, to the detested and feared Israeli *warrior tribe*. Many of the Palestinians left the West Bank for Jordan soon after the war (the Israelis did not impede this flight), because they dreaded having to live under permanent occupation. If the majority initially seemed to accept their fate, as Arabs have done over centuries under the Ottoman Empire,[133] the daring opponents in the various Palestinian liberation movements soon turned into a decisive force willing to throw out the enemy by means other than those of classical warfare. This means guerrilla fighting, and the world was soon to learn about violent terrorist acts that shocked international opinion.

If the Arab states in general were humiliated, they were not paralysed, and the Arab League called a summit meeting in Khartoum in late August 1967, just after the Six-Day War, in order that the Israelis should take note that the Arab world was not accepting the defeat as a final *fait accompli*. The summit reaffirmed the rights of the Palestinians to their own country and now declared with the consensus of the leaders: "**No** negotiation with Israel, **no** recognition of Israel and **no** peace". Both President Nasser and King Hussein were present, and they were among the moderates, according to Shlaim. If they agreed to "the three **no's**", they did not interpret them as closing the door totally on confidential meetings with the enemy. King Hussein later wrote that he tried to avoid the "**no's**", but that most of his Arab friends turned against him, whereas Nasser — surprisingly enough — was on his (Hussein's) side. The President of Egypt even urged the King to explore the possibility of a peaceful settlement with Israel,[134] and there were indeed frequent meetings on and off between Israeli leaders and the apparently untiring King over the coming years. As I stress, it is surprising to learn about Nasser's will to compromise with the enemy at this meeting or at least about his suggestions to

---

133 The Arab nationalism which has been explained in some detail above, is a fairly new factor, rising in the wake of the Young Turks' movement in the early twentieth century. But we hardly know if there was a latent feeling of being subdued, at least seen in retrospect, in light of our modern knowledge.

134 Op.cit., pp. 258 - 259.

Hussein. As we know, he has generally been exposed as one of the most stubborn anti-Israel leaders among the Arabs, and the one who had set the defiant and threatening tune just before the June War. Probably the shock of the debacle had impressed him so much that he adopted a more flexible mood for a period.

The Knesset soon endorsed a government declaration closing the door on negotiations and thus cancelling the plan of 19 June, and it took as the basis for this negative stance the defiant Arab attitude at their summit meeting. The government and Knesset declared: "[t]he government notes with regret the fact that the Arab states adhere to their position of not recognising, not negotiating and not concluding peace treaties with Israel".[135] One can almost hear a sigh of relief in this negative declaration from the official Israeli side.

This apparent Arab unity was soon to dissolve, however, as will be seen from the following chapters, but initially the message was clear enough. We are in the days of the intensifying Vietnam conflict and the Cold War; the Arabs may therefore have hoped that the USA would soon be too preoccupied with Vietnam to go on supporting Israel. The still impressive Soviet Union continued to support the Arab cause, to an even larger extent than before, rearming the Egyptians for the second time and soon also the Syrians.

It is interesting to recall that the Arab defeat had a tremendous effect in Cairo. First the Pan-Arab leader, Nasser, offered to resign, but an immediate comeback was organised in response to public support. The unsettled situation in Egypt after the debacle, however, soon changed into a weakening of the President's position — even if it was not seen on the surface of events immediately — and in 1970, only three years after the debacle, Nasser became fatally ill and died.

In Jordan, the King had *miscalculated* (by not refraining from involvement in the war), according to the opinion among the chief politicians in Jerusalem, as represented by Golda Meir, who used that expression in her memoirs, and who was soon to take over in Israel.

Knowing the Arab mentality, I think it would have been difficult or impossible for the King to change his attitude and leave the Pan-Arab alliance, at least not as long as the Egyptian President was still the strong leader, enjoying great popular support. Jordan was soon going to suffer in the aftermath of the Israeli occupation of the West Bank.

In Syria, the 1967 War left the regime still more unsettled, but great political changes were soon going to be furthered by the defeat. The humiliation felt in Damascus opened the way for the ambitious military person, the already influential and somewhat enigmatic Hafez Assad. He assumed full power in 1970, the same year Nasser died. With him, a rising star was going to shine over Syria for thirty years, to use an eloquent Arabic way of expressing such glorious events.

---

135 Ibid., p. 259.

Lebanon had not been touched directly by the Six-Day War, but this fragile country was soon to feel the increased pressure from the PLO and other militant Palestinians who sought refuge in Lebanon — as they had already done in earlier periods — again after the debacle in June 1967, and finally after their expulsion from Jordan in 1970.

VI. The PLO and Inter-Arab Fights

PLO and Jordan

We have already mentioned that the establishment of the PLO in Cairo in 1964 was not an event that generated major headlines at the time, and also added that many Arab leaders remained sceptical about the new organisation. But little by little the PLO became more influential, not least after the 1967 debacle that weakened Nasser and his strong leadership. On the other hand it strengthened the Fatah leader, Yassir Arafat, who held a meeting with President Nasser in the aftermath of the war, at which Cairo promised political and moral support, but no funds for the Palestinian fight. Fatah had boycotted the PLO initially, but in 1968, under the impression of the need to fortify the resistance against the Israeli occupation of the West Bank, this boycott was given up. Therefore the Fatah leaders and other delegates attended the fifth session of the Palestinian National Council, PNC, in Cairo, in July 1968, only a year after the debacle. With an estimated guerrilla force of 15,000, Fatah became the most important element of the PLO and Arafat now became the Chairman of the Organisation, while remaining leader of the Fatah as well.

Fatah had established offices in Damascus and Algeria in earlier periods and now expanded into other Arab countries, particularly Jordan, under the banner of the PLO, because many Palestinians had sought refuge in the Kingdom after the occupation of the West Bank, thus continuing earlier settlements of Palestinians in Jordan. After this war, around half of the population of Jordan was composed of Palestinians (the others being of local Bedouin origin).

In 1968, when the Fatah joined the PLO, the Organisation decided that only through armed struggle could the Palestinian fight succeed and result in the liberation of the homeland. It is easy to understand that this direct aim of the PLO fight would create difficulties for the Hashemite regime. Even if the King showed Pan-Arab leanings and had to demonstrate solidarity with his Arab brothers, especially in wartime, there is no doubt that he was personally a pragmatist who wanted to find a solution with the Israelis.

What soon became dangerous for the King was the fact that the PLO and other Palestinian organisations were establishing themselves as a state within the state.

They had arms, they wanted to attack Israel from within Jordan's borders without consulting the King or his government; accordingly they soon began serious terrorist actions from their bases there. This was of course totally unacceptable to King Hussein, especially because he was aware of the risk of retaliation attacks. Little by little the latent conflict became a more open fight between Jordanian loyalists and revolutionaries, i.e. those behind the King or behind the PLO respectively. More and more often, the regime felt convinced that attacks on the King had only one source, the PLO or some of its affiliate organisations.

Groups like Fatah, PFLP and DFLP, all under the PLO umbrella, grew inside Jordan in the following years, and their combined forces soon posed a dangerous threat to the government order and indeed to the royal regime itself. They made several attacks on the King and his entourage, without ever entirely upsetting the regime, while the monarch became known as a survivor. It was surely not easy for King Hussein to keep these militant organisations under control without losing popular sympathy and support.

In March 1968, the guerrillas, strongly supported by elements of the Jordanian army,[136] managed to fight a military force of 15,000 invading Israeli soldiers with some success at al-Karameh. The Israelis wanted to eliminate a terrorist stronghold inside a refugee camp. The majority of Palestinians in Jordan found the guerrilla idea praiseworthy or at least understandable, and many other Jordanians often seemed to agree. In the same year, 1968, terrorism placed the Palestinian fight on the map of world conflicts. A *fedayeen* commando attacked an Israeli airliner at Athens airport, and this was the start of a series of such attacks in the same and following decade, shocking the world.

When the plan proposed by the US Secretary of State, William Rogers (see below) for settling the long conflict between Egypt and Israel following the 1967 war was approved by Nasser shortly before his death in September 1970 and endorsed by King Hussein, the Popular Front for the Liberation of Palestine (PFLP) demonstrated its opposition with violence. Their commandos hijacked and seized several aeroplanes and forced them to land in Jordan, where they were blown up.

These spectacular events were regarded as the last straw and finally convinced the King that it was time to intervene in order to save his throne. In addition to the most recent attack on the King's life, an American diplomat had also been killed in Amman, and a strike was called. Hussein therefore realised that if he did not act and

---

[136] Arafat' s version of this is that his forces fought alone, but in Jordan it is common knowledge that they certainly received good support from the army that joined the battle. See Adnan Abu-Odeh, *Jordanians, Palestinians and the Hashemite Kingdom*, United States Institute of Peace, Washington, 1999, 2000, p. 170. He adds that after "the Israeli troops had retreated, the two allies [the PLO and the Jordanian army] continued to fight among themselves".

eliminate the guerrilla — or terrorist — movements, he would soon lose all support and be overthrown. He formed a military government and gave the organisations an ultimatum, demanding that they come to a conference to discuss restrictions on their movements in Jordan. When they refused, the King gave orders to open the fight against them. Thus began the *Black September* crisis of 1970 that almost amounted to a civil war,[137] in which radical Palestinians opposed home-grown Trans-Jordanians or Bedouins supporting King Hussein and the armed forces. The latter were mostly of Bedouin origin, and had no desire to fight for the liberation of Palestine, and the King now had tight control over them.

In taking up arms against the PLO, the monarch won his gamble, as he had already won several similar actions before. Eventually, therefore, the PLO had to give up and leave the country. The main battle lasted ten days and was bloody, costing more than 4,000 lives. The PLA had posted tank units inside Syria with the aim of their coming to the assistance of the Palestinian units inside Jordan in case of open conflict, and in September 1970 they intervened. Despite (lukewarm) Syrian aid not involving the Syrian air force, these Palestinian units could not overcome the Jordanian armed forces, after the latter received an ample supply of arms flown in from western countries. The PLA only managed to prolong the war by capturing parts of Northern Jordan. Some of the Palestinian forces therefore survived for a time in this Northern region, near the border to Syria

Not until July 1971 were the last PLA commandos expelled from the hills around Jerash, a city near the Syrian border. Iraq did not come to the aid of the PLO, despite promises to do so. For the coming master of Syria, Hafez Assad, who was minister of defence at the time and came to power in Damascus only a little later in the same year, this conflict meant the beginning of his long rule in conflict with the neighbouring king. Their differences were not easily forgotten by Hussein,[138] according to the traditional wisdom. But this is contested by one of the King's close advisers and — seen from Damascus — many think that the ambitions of

---

137 Abu-Odeh writes that the foreign media termed it a *civil war*, but that it was not. See his interesting account, giving many details, in ibid., p. 169.

138 I was told this by the author of the already quoted book on *Jordanians and Palestinians* that the King was really grateful to Hafez Assad for not intervening more brutally in favour of the PLO troops. The later Syrian President might have considered, in the perspective of *Realpolitik,* that is was not advisable to fight a regime that now enjoyed decisive Western support. Hafez Assad was mostly a realist, not wanting too risky adventures. He attended the funeral of Hussein in February 1999, but kept away from the main group of visitors, because of his frailty; I was present but did not see him. He was too weak to move around and did not want to meet the Israeli Prime Minister, Netanyahu, we may assume. Only afterwards was a certain harmony attained with the new King Abdullah, especially under Bashar Assad.

Hussein's grandfather to expand power into Syria were initially a stumbling block in the relationship between the two countries, which were hardly ever on friendly terms. Arabs have long memories and it is likely that Syria felt that the smaller nation should not have demonstrated such animosity against the larger and more powerful neighbour.

One element behind the King's victory was, as already mentioned, the airlifting of arms from the UK and the USA to the Jordanian forces, and the knowledge that even Israel might intervene in order to save the King. Here the Eisenhower Doctrine was active, because at that time, Washington took the Marxist leanings of most of the Palestinian organisations as a challenge to the American way of thinking.

The King later told one of his close advisers, Adnan Abu-Odeh, that his decision to wage a war on the Palestinian groups was the most difficult he had ever taken in his life;[139] this of course sounds very credible.

After this serious defeat for the Palestinian cause, its leaders did not give up, however. They had lost a battle, but not the war, as the saying goes. They now moved to the neighbouring country of Lebanon, where they would create even more havoc in due course. We may say that the buck was passed from Jordan, whose regime could now breathe freely again, to smaller Lebanon, whose fate was soon at risk. But before we enter into the sad story of the Civil War in Lebanon, which is closely linked to the Middle East conflict, we shall look at the general picture of the conflict for a moment.

---

139 Op.cit., p. 180.

VII. WAR OF ATTRITION BETWEEN EGYPT AND ISRAEL, 1969-71

The situation of stagnation following the war was soon replaced by what has been called the *war of attrition* begun by the Egyptians under the slogan employed by President Nasser: "That which has been taken by force can only be recovered by force". Since Israel did not withdraw from the Sinai or present any serious peace proposals, and had also made a damaging air attack on some important installations, Egypt began a large-scale offensive around the Canal in March 1969, soon after Golda Meir had assumed power in Israel. Shlaim writes about her in the following manner: "Her assertiveness in relation to her civilian colleagues was matched by a curious subservience toward her military subordinates".[140] She would therefore blindly accept the views of her military advisers. Almost everything in the Israel-Arab post-war relationship was — or could be — seen in the perspective of a long-term military strategy. Nasser of course did not make matters easier, declaring that Egypt would ignore the cease-fire while continuing the heavy artillery fire on Israeli positions along the Canal. The Egyptian President was therefore able to blow both hot and cold, sometimes showing hard-line thinking, at other moments compromise, as we have seen above. The Israeli military set-up decided to establish what was called the Bar-Lev fortification along the Canal, named after the Chief of Staff who had proposed it. Israel also retaliated against the artillery fire with its efficient air force and made many successful attacks on the Egyptian infrastructure.

The fairly new American administration under Nixon wanted a more even-handed Middle East policy than that of the previous Johnson government — Nixon had taken over in Washington at almost the same time as Golda Meir in Jerusalem. It came as a surprise to her when the new Secretary of State, William Rogers, in December 1969, proposed a plan for a peaceful settlement, based on the UN resolution 242. If this proposal took the Israeli government by surprise, it was because Jerusalem saw it as part of a US-USSR arrangement to impose peace on Israel. When Golda Meir presented her new Cabinet to the Knesset soon afterwards, she

---

140 Op.cit., p. 289.

The newly elected leader of PLO, Yassir Arafat, and President Nasser at a meeting in 1969.

began by attacking *the Rogers Plan*, which she even termed "a disaster for Israel". The Prime Minister recalled the Israeli ambassador to the USA, Yitzhak Rabin, for consultations, and Jerusalem stepped up the military campaign against Egypt. Foreign Minister Abba Eban doubted whether Ambassador Rabin's view — that the Americans would agree to deep penetration bombing in Egypt — was true. But when at home, Rabin, with all his prestige as the former Chief of Staff who had been primarily responsible for the victory in 1967, managed to pass the militant policy through the Cabinet.

According to Golda Meir's own memoirs, Begin thought that the Israelis could *demand* that the Americans supply Israel with arms, whereas she more realistically found that Israel needed the USA more than Washington needed Israel; the government therefore had to be very careful —which was not in her nature, if we trust the views on her presented above by Shlaim. But on this occasion (when blaming Begin), she was in full agreement with the experienced diplomat, Abba Eban, and surely also with her ambassador in the USA, her later successor, Rabin. Eban had actively taken part in the drafting of Resolution 242 after the 1967 war, but apparently did not manage to make the French version correspond completely to the English one.

In her memoirs, Golda Meir accuses the Russians of arming not only the Egyptians but also the Syrians soon after the debacle of 1967, in a way that could only make the Israelis very nervous, fearing a new war. She decided "reluctantly", she says, in favour of in-depth retaliatory bombardments in Egypt. She calls this the "Egyptian War of Attrition" and saw it as a real one, even if no movements were registered on the ground. It was a question of knocking out as much modern equipment as possible in the enemy territory, and soon Israel was the more active of the two belligerents, showing all its military strength. If we can rely on Shlaim, Golda Meir's orders were not given *that* reluctantly, because she was generally under the influence of the military establishment, believing in a continuation of the aggressive policies from before the war.

She went on her first official visit to Washington in September 1969 — when this peculiar war was going on — specifically with the view to ensuring more arms deliveries from the USA in order to keep up Israel's military vigour. Rabin, as ambassador there, tells us how well received she was, especially by the new President, Richard Nixon, who had begun a much more pro-Israeli policy than his predecessor, Johnson. In his report to Jerusalem before Golda Meir's visit, Ambassador Rabin wrote that "[a] man would have to be blind, deaf and dumb not to sense how much the administration favours our military operations, and there is a growing likelihood that the US would be interested in an escalation of our military activity with the aim of undermining Nasser's standing".[141] He adds that Nixon

---

141 Op.cit., p. 151.

even told Golda Meir that "if he were an Israeli, he would find it truly difficult to give up the Golan Heights".[142]

Despite the many signals of goodwill from the President, Golda Meir's talks with high-level officials like Dr. Henry Kissinger and Secretary of State William Rogers were not always easy. Between the two American top officials there was no love lost, as will be recalled, and Kissinger eventually came to understand the Israeli position better than the Secretary of State, who preferred diplomatic ways to warlike actions. Ambassador Rabin, later considered a dove, went as far as to promote a campaign to persuade American politicians and other influential personalities to reject the original Rogers Plan, which contained a less than satisfactory solution to the Egyptian-Israeli problem, seen from the perspective of Jerusalem. But fortunately for the Israelis, the Egyptians rejected it, too.

Rogers later complained to Rabin about being made the scapegoat (for being anti-Israel) in Washington for the abortive American plan to balance Israeli and Egyptian wishes in the matter due to a deeper desire to accommodate the other superpower to some extent. Rogers added that there was nothing personal in his insistence, to which Rabin replied that he accepted that.[143]

Secretary of State Rogers, however, was ultimately successful in organising a cease-fire in June 1970, according to what was termed *Rogers Plan B*. It involved an armistice for three months and asked both sides to accept mediation by the UN. Even if Golda Meir's first reaction was to reject it, a letter from President Nixon strongly urged the Israeli government to comply, and this was finally understood as an *order* from the superpower, which normally helped Israel more than ever. Both sides had rejected the above-mentioned more comprehensive plan for a real peace arrangement, but now Nasser also accepted a cease-fire. It had been a very costly war that had led to some successes on both sides, but also to heavy losses and new risks. The war would probably have been especially dangerous for the Israelis — in the long run — even if they were unable to see this at the time. With Soviet assistance, the Egyptians had finally managed to build up a stronger defence line along the Canal, which involved SAM missile batteries — a potential danger to the IAF, if the war had continued. To some extent the Soviet aid — especially the supply of the missiles mentioned — eliminated the full air superiority that the Israeli Air Force had enjoyed for some time, even shooting down some Soviet aircraft manned with Russian pilots.

Rogers had not been able to organise a peace agreement, and the same negative result characterised Security Council President Gunnar Jarring's efforts in 1970 – 71. The Cold War resulted in serious disagreement between the two superpowers regarding the need to find a compromise. Israel would no longer accept anything

---

142 Ibid., p. 153.
143 Ibid., p. 164.

less than a secure and long-term peace settlement, desiring to avoid any risk of new threats to the country, which still had such fragile geographic and demographic structures.

Golda Meir decided again in 1970 to go to Washington, where she engaged in renewed and fruitful talks with President Nixon. She writes in this connection that the Russians were feeding and manipulating the entire Egyptian war effort. The French were now — according to her — almost as pro-Arab as the Russians, and the British were not far behind. Only the Americans were at all concerned with Israel's survival, and she could now thank them for finally bringing about the cease-fire in 1970, as mentioned earlier.[144]

Two other important events that influenced the conflict between Israel and the Arab states took place in the Middle East region in 1970: The first one was the above-mentioned *Black September* in Jordan, which led to the evacuation of the PLO forces from Jordan to Lebanon. While this event was certainly difficult to evaluate immediately from an Israeli perspective,[145] the second event — the death of President Nasser at almost the same time — must have come as a clear relief to Jerusalem and eventually led to an important change in Egyptian policies vis-à-vis Israel.

Golda Meir obtained promises of new fighter planes from the US government and states that "my meeting with the President was as warm as his initial welcome";[146] later she added: "I now felt sure that the US would stand by us and I really relaxed for the first time in months". Rabin writes that the American President, according to Kissinger, "would send a letter to Mrs. Meir in which his commitment to Israel's security be stressed, and at the same time assuring Israel of a supply of arms, sufficient to maintain the balance of forces between Israel and her neighbours".[147]

Here it seems as if we are at the beginning of the substantial and almost unconditional American support of Israel as a sort of *client state* of the US in the Middle East, as we have seen since then, counterbalancing and soon exceeding the support of the USSR for Egypt and eventually also for Syria. If the other Western nations were now more hesitant to support Israel fully, it was of course due to the feeling that the young Jewish nation had proved able to survive against many odds and had recently come under the protective wings of huge USA.

---

144 See above; accepting the cease-fire was one of Nasser's last political acts before his death .
145 Upon American request, Israel indirectly assisted the King so that he could have a better chance of surviving the desperate fight against him by the Palestinian forces.
146 Ibid., p. 327.
147 Rabin, op.cit., p. 169.

Golda Meir tried at the beginning of her period as Prime Minister to entice the Arab leaders into negotiations, but again without results. As one example of the many negative reactions, she quotes the following comment by a Jordanian newspaper, in June 1969: "Mrs. Meir is prepared to go to Cairo to hold discussions with President Nasser but, to her sorrow, has not been invited. She believes that one fine day a world without guns will emerge in the Middle East. Golda Meir is behaving like a grandmother telling bedtime stories to her children".[148]

Her blunt ways were generally not well received by the Arabs, whose mentality is so different from that of most Jews. "She rejected absolutely the possibility that some of the Arab demands might be justified", writes her biographer, Medzini, in his *Proud Jewess*.[149]

---

[148] Ibid., p. 321. We may comment that only a decade later, it was the other way round when Sadat came to Israel in order to negotiate a peace treaty.

[149] Here quoted from Shlaim, op.cit., p. 284.

VIII. The october 1973 war

1. Secret Preparations by the Arab Powers

We have just seen that the war of attrition had been a violent and dangerous confrontation between Israel and Egypt. Nevertheless, there were also some diplomatic developments between the enemies in the early seventies, however difficult they seemed. Eventually they came to a halt and were replaced by war as a result of Arab impatience and Israeli lack of flexibility. The government in Jerusalem and Golda Meir personally were involved in prolonged discussions with the Egyptians via the Washington administration, in order to find an agreement with the Cairo regime under President Sadat, who was a fairly unknown politician when he took over from Nasser in 1970. We can follow these discussions in detail in Yitzhak Rabin's already quoted memoirs. He carefully describes his involvement in these difficult negotiations, when he was ambassador in Washington. He admits that the Israeli position was not clear, and that this ambiguous attitude often annoyed the Americans, to put it mildly. That the Egyptians were even more frustrated is evident, of course. Rabin was asked by his government what exactly Kissinger meant, sometime in early 1972. The Ambassador wrote back to Jerusalem in his blunt way: "The problem (for me) is to explain what Israel means. Nobody outside Israel understands it. Our position is unclear". The Prime Minister replied, "Israel's policy aims toward a considerable change in our border with Egypt. That means a change of sovereignty, not just an Israeli presence. We do not employ the term *annexation* because of its negative connotation".

The Ambassador was not satisfied with the reply from Golda Meir and pleaded for more clarity, because, as he wrote, "[t]he Americans ask me simple questions and I am bound to give them straightforward answers". The answer Rabin received was still not very clear, however, although it referred to a Cabinet decision from March 1971 and emphasised the Israeli wish to retain the Gaza strip and control over Sharm- el -Sheikh, while admitting that "the Israeli position regarding the legal form of such control has yet to be formulated".[150] The atmosphere was therefore

---

150 Op.cit., pp. 210 – 211.

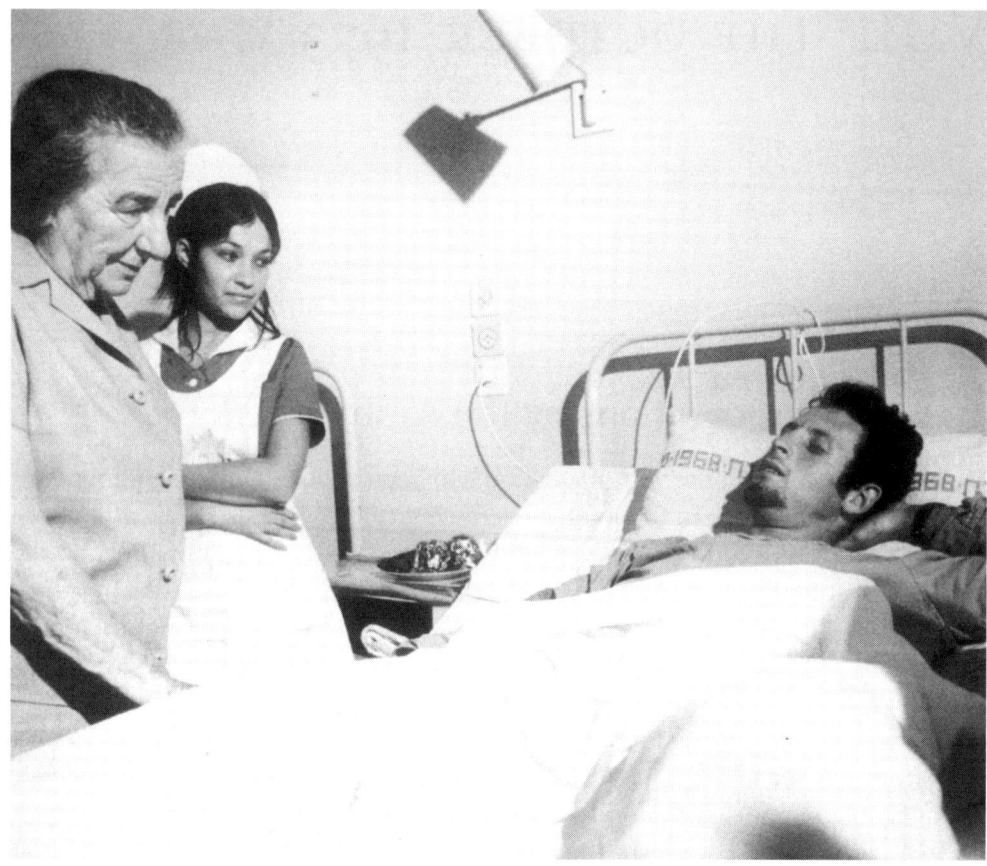
Prime Minister Golda Meir visits wounded soldier during the October War 1973

not relaxed when Golda Meir paid another visit to Washington at the end of Rabin's term in late February and early March 1972 and was told by Kissinger that "in the absence of any new ideas or proposals there will be no progress".[151]

The reason for the American frustration was the fact that Kissinger was then still trying to find a solution between Egypt and Israel and was engaged in useful talks with the Egyptian adviser, Hafez Ismail, who impressed him, and with the Soviet ambassador Dobrynin. The relationship between the two superpowers had its ups and downs in those Cold War days, but eventually the distance between them, as regards the Middle East, became too great, not least because the Vietnam War received most of the attention both in Washington and in Moscow. The US government could therefore propose no solution, which again made President Anwar Sadat more impatient. In the summer of 1972 he threw the Russian mili-

---

151 Ibid., p. 215.

tary experts out of Cairo, in a radical move that made the Egyptian President the focus of much attention. No one, however, realised that Sadat was preparing a new war and even the military expert, Rabin, admits that he was taken by complete surprise when the attack finally came on 6 October 1973.[152] Most observers simply did not believe the President when he declared, on many occasions, that a war would eventually be necessary to liberate the occupied land. Sadat saw to the preparation of secret political agreements with many Arab leaders, while his top generals were asked to prepare the offensive.

The Egyptian President had to improve the relationship with the Saudi King, in particular, which had always been delicate, especially after the Yemen war when Egypt had fought against the Royal government in Yemen that was supported by the Saudis. Now Sadat tried to improve relations by means of a secret journey in August 1973, during which he also saw the Jordanian King. With the latter he agreed to resume in September 1973 those diplomatic relations which had been broken off in April 1972 when the King had issued a declaration of the Joint *United Arab Kingdom*, including the West Bank area, for the time being under Israeli control. The Egyptian leader had inherited the old Egyptian suspicion of a Hashemite-Jordanian wish to dominate the whole area helped by their allies, the former British colonial masters. Sadat also visited the volatile leader in Tripoli, Colonel Ghadafi, who, because of his odd ways, did not have the same weight in the Arab world as the other two leaders. But the most important person was of course Hafez Assad, the Syrian President who had come to power almost at the same time as Sadat, in late 1970. The war could not be launched by either of the two countries alone but only in close collaboration, in order to free those territories which Israel had occupied in the 1967 war. While Sadat — as we know — had always openly declared that a new battle would be necessary, the more taciturn Syrian leader did not make such open pronouncements publicly. No one, however, could doubt Assad's will to fight, which was based on the humiliation felt by himself and in military circles about the defeat in 1967, which had caused the palpable loss of the Golan Heights, so important for the defence of Syria and its prestige.

Sadat had been particularly disappointed by the summit meeting between the two world leaders, Brezhnev and Nixon, some months earlier, in June 1973. The positive results of this summit proved to the Egyptian President that he could not expect much more than good wishes from the Soviet Union.

President Sadat also had to take into consideration the dramatic economic situation in Egypt. The country was deprived of its main sources of income, the oil fields in the Sinai, and especially the income from the Suez Canal, closed since the 1967 war. This was nothing new, of course, but became more and more evident as time passed without a solution to the warlike situation and the occupation of the

---

152 Op.cit., p. 235.

Sinai. Tourism had not yet developed into anything like its later significance, but it also suffered from the difficult situation in the area.

After the 1973 War, Anwar Sadat himself admitted that he had had to act because of this desperate economic situation. In a speech to the student leaders of Alexandria University in August 1974, he told his audience that the government income before the war was 200 million Egyptian pounds a year, while it spent 100 million monthly on the armed forces. "[t]here was [therefore] nothing left for us but to enter the battle", he stressed. This was certainly a dramatic gamble, also with regard to economics, since wars have rarely led to immediate prosperity; but in this case, Sadat probably turned out to be right. He might have guessed that the oil weapon was going to be used by the Arabs and thereby change the world economic situation a great deal, but at the same time he realised that all possibilities of a just and peaceful settlement with the Israelis had vanished into thin air. His war effort might eventually impress the Americans, who would therefore have to help in finding a solution, Sadat thought.

If we look at developments inside Syria, it was a picture similar to that of Egypt. What was uppermost in President Hafez Assad's mind was giving Syria an honourable place in the region. So far internal struggles and external defeats had characterised the young nation. The new leader now found it reasonable to approach his colleague in Cairo in order to combine their forces against Israel. They both had military backgrounds, were more or less the same age and had lived with the humiliating experience of the debacle of the 1967 war. Both presidents wanted not pure revenge but the restitution of their lost territories. While Sinai probably did not mean that much to ordinary Egyptians who lived along the Nile, the Golan Heights, only some 50 kilometres from the capital, are visible to millions of Syrians in and around the important city of Damascus, which comprises almost a quarter of the country's total population. In winter these snow-capped mountains, up to 3,000 metres high, are a beautiful and majestic sight. The fact that their peak, Mount Hermon, was almost visibly occupied by Israeli troops therefore caused, and still causes, the nation an added humiliation, felt by most Syrians.

Only ten days after his take-over in late 1970, Assad flew to Cairo to have a full discussion of all subjects with his counterpart. At the same time, he announced that Syria would join the proposed new federation of four countries, together with Libya and Sudan. Like so many other federal propositions this one was an abortive plan. Even if it never came into being, Hafez Assad was convinced that only through a close collaboration with Egypt could he realise his hope of recovering the Golan and building up common Arab prestige, lost after the 1967 debacle.

Sadat agreed, convinced that he needed a strong-willed ally in his first period, when he might appear to be weak to many observers — and even felt so himself — compared to the long time, charismatic former President, Nasser. Assad's biographer, Patrick Seale, explains that the Syrian President's eagerness to enter into an alliance with Egypt again — this time between equals — was based on Assad's assumption that the traditional Baathist call for a strong Arab Nation was still compelling and should take as its point of departure the fact that Egypt and Syria were the pivots of Arab history.[153]

Both Assad and Sadat knew that a two-front strategy against Israel was the prerequisite for victory, and Assad did not think that the Israeli strength was necessarily given or everlasting. But Patrick Seale calls the Egyptian President the *Unsound Ally*[154], referring to his view that Sadat was not to be fully trusted after his manoeuvrings against Moscow, throwing out the Russian military experts in 1972. Seale's epithet also refers to Sadat's secret dealings with the Americans at the same time, especially in the midst of the top-secret planning of a campaign to overcome the *unbeatable enemy* of Israel, which was supported by the USA. But Assad had no other choice than to collaborate with Sadat, and Seale's findings seem rather to belong to a very friendly biography of the Syrian President than to neutral writing of contemporary history.

Like his Egyptian colleague, President Assad realised that secrecy was of the greatest importance, and both leaders easily agreed that the attack should be one of complete surprise carried out jointly and co-ordinated at the highest command level.

The detailed war planning probably began in early 1971, when Assad still had full confidence in his ally. He combined this approach to Cairo with a similar one to Moscow, where he had to renew trust because his predecessors had somewhat frightened the Soviets with their radical opinions and style. The Syrian leader managed to win their support without giving in to the Soviet demand of a treaty of friendship. According to Seale, Assad had stated at some instance to the Russians that "friendship needed no treaty".[155] This first Presidential visit of Assad to Moscow was a success and made it possible for Syria to begin a thorough rearmament.

At the end of 1971, the two Arab leaders had agreed on the appointment of General Muhammed Sadiq as the supreme commander of both armies. They realised that only through a joint effort and a centralised command would there be a hope of winning the coming war.

According to Seale, it is obvious that the Russians must have realised that the two partners were preparing a war and even helped them with more than arms,

---

153 Patrick Seale, *Asad of Syria: The Struggle for the Middle East*, Tauris, London, 1988, p 189.
154 Ibid., p. 185.
155 Ibid., p. 192. In this respect he differed from President Sadat who did engage in such formal treaties with the USSR.

and this seems likely.[156] But the Soviet leaders feared a confrontation with Washington more and more and proposed a peaceful settlement in the Middle East along the lines of the UN SC resolution 242, when they were meeting with the American President and his Secretary of State, Dr. Kissinger, in California in June 1973. Henry Kissinger, who had recently taken over as Secretary of State, rejected the Soviet proposition that would implement the UN resolution from 1967, in order to avoid the threatening war about which Sadat had warned on many occasions. The Soviet proposal was based on the assumption that both superpowers would use their influence fully to persuade their Middle East partners to accept this settlement. The US Secretary of State, however, was not willing to accommodate the Soviets, in the light of the then dominating East-West Cold War.

According to Seale, the two leaders, Sadat and Assad, had different aims right from the beginning: The goal of Egypt's leader was to be able to continue his already begun peace diplomacy, after a necessary shock; Assad, on the contrary, wanted a seizure of land in order to begin a discussion on a settlement.[157]

In reality, I do not see a great difference between these two goals. Both leaders wanted to begin a war, not because they were warmongers, but in order to recover lost territory and to find a permanent settlement, granting them *land for peace*, as the UN resolution 242 already stipulated. As we have just learnt above, the American Secretary of State was not willing to grant what the Soviets suggested, also in order not to antagonise the Israelis. Neither of the two Arab Presidents wanted a long war, and they realised that the odds against them were great, especially since it was perfectly clear that the USA stood behind Israel. Even if Hafez Assad had declared that the Israelis were not invincible, he must have realised the dangerous gamble of this war. The two Arab powers thought they had no alternative, and could only hope for an honourable solution. The shock they were preparing was intended as an eye-opener, in the same way as the violent attacks against Israel or her friends which the Palestinians had already launched with some success since the beginning of the seventies and even before. It was only on that basis that the world had slowly begun to realise that the PLO and Arafat had been left out in the cold by Israel, especially after her total victory in 1967.

When Seale writes that "the fraud began at the Sadat-Assad summit at Burj-al-Arab in April 1973", he of course intends to stress that Sadat and not Assad was the villain. But he also admits somewhat later and more objectively that "Assad perhaps lacked the imagination to grasp that, seen from Cairo or Amman, the Arab-Israeli conflict did not have the clear-cut, black and white, good versus evil

---

156 Ibid., p. 193. Moscow was told of the imminent attack two days in advance. One reason for Sadat´s expulsion of the Soviet advisers in 1972 was probably that he wanted to protect the utter secrecy of the plans.

157 Op.cit., p. 195.

quality which was the traditional view from Damascus".[158] Assad may also have ignored the fact that the Egyptian generals had advised against a prolonged thrust into the Sinai, far away from the bases on the other side of the Canal, because it would leave the Egyptian lines utterly exposed to air attacks from Israel. Most likely, Sadat had never told Assad of these warnings, which he himself tended to ignore, making his own Chief of Staff angry and frustrated.

The two Arab states never managed to carry out pre-emptive strikes against the Israeli air force in any way comparable to the traditional Israeli attacks in 1956 and 1967, the first of which annihilated the Egyptian air force, and the second of which destroyed both the Egyptian and Syrian. And no massive Israeli air-strikes were carried out this time, when Israel learned about the attack very late, and for obvious political reasons (see below).

Benny Morris writes that according to one Israeli government aide, "Israel had missed a historic opportunity for peace in February – May 1971", but he also honestly stresses that this conclusion is very different from the way Golda Meir looked at these events.[159] She recognised that the war of attrition had been a costly fight in which Israel had not always managed to show its accustomed military superiority. But we also remember that she hardly ever trusted the Arab leaders.

The common background of the aggressors (as the Israelis saw them) was that both of the governments had felt humiliated by their losses in the Six-Day War, especially because they were Israel's two largest neighbours and much more populous than their enemy. When the two partners informed other important Arab leaders that a reaction was being prepared, and asked for solidarity and assistance, they evidently kept the exact magnitude and date secret, in order not to risk leaking any undue information to the Israelis. According to Morris, however, King Hussein (secretly visiting Israel) confidentially informed Golda Meir that some hidden plans were worked out and that the Syrian army was on alert, according to his own intelligence services. The King could not say whether Egypt was involved, but it would be surprising if he had chosen to inform the enemy as late as 25 September, some ten days before the onslaught, and thus betray his Arab neighbours.[160] At any rate, the Israeli side did not trust that there was any real threat. That the version of King Hussein's betrayal has often been denied by the Monarch or by his government goes without saying. I have personally heard his brother, the then Crown Prince Hassan, deny it vehemently.

One essential element of this war of October 1973 was of course the success of

---

158 Ibid., p. 201.
159 Op.cit., p. 390.
160 Ibid., p. 399. Morris's version does not indicate whether there was any real betrayal, but he emphasises that the King did talk about Syrian preparations and had reason, at any rate, to feel frustrated with Cairo.

the very secret military preparations undertaken by the two participant parties, Egypt and Syria. It seems as if the two leaders finally agreed on their common war effort only in April 1973,[161] and they soon reached a common understanding as to the detailed war preparations. At a top-secret meeting of the Syrian-Egyptian Armed Forces Supreme Council, lasting from 21 to 23 August 1973, the detailed planning was finalised, in order to have the two top leaders reach a final agreement during their meeting at Bludan, near Damascus, at the end of the same month. But the two Presidents gave the last green light only after their meeting in Cairo on 12 September 1973.

The hour of attack was set for 14.05 hours on 6 October. Until the end, the detailed planning remained secret, and even the otherwise efficient Israeli military intelligence did not detect anything unusual (except the preparation of what they thought was a large manoeuvre). Its leader informed Israel's Prime Minister, Golda Meir, that she need not worry about the Yom Kippur celebrations. Only on the very morning of 6 October, the day of the attack, did the Israelis detect that an onslaught was imminent, but then it was too late. Morris tells us that at the last minute, on 6 October, the Israeli Chief of Staff wanted to launch another pre-emptive strike, but that the responsible politicians (Golda Meir and Dayan) did not assent, because politically it would be disastrous for the government in Jerusalem, since the world had no knowledge of an imminent attack or even of any threat to Israel.[162]

Here we shall now turn to Golda Meir's own account of the war. She starts by emphasising that "of all the events upon which I have touched in this book, none is so hard for me to write about as the war of October 1973. I found myself in a position of ultimate responsibility at a time when the state faced the greatest threat it had known. The world in general and Israel's enemies in particular should know that the circumstances which took the lives of over 2500 Israelis who were killed in the Yom Kippur War will never ever recur".[163]

2. Surprise Attack

In May 1973, Israel had learned about reinforcement of Egyptian and Syrian troops at the borders, and again in September, about a build-up of Syrian forces near the Golan Heights. A serious air battle took place on 13 September, when the IAF downed 13 Syrian MIGs.

One could reasonably have expected the otherwise very capable Israeli Intelligence to give a serious warning to the government.

---

161 Different dates are given, and national secrecy does not yet allow a full picture.
162 Op.cit., p. 400.
163 Op.cit., p. 353.

Morris confirms that the Israeli authorities had indeed received substantial information that should have provided sufficient warning, and gives us his crude version of events: "Well before D-day, Israeli intelligence had most of the facts. But because of preconceptions, errors, and the Arabs' deliberate deception measures, it was unable to separate the telling signals from the background noise. The few who read them correctly went unheeded".[164]

On her side, Golda Meir tells us in *My Life* that on 5 October, "when I asked the Minister of Defence, the Chief-of-Staff and Head of Intelligence whether they thought the [last] piece of information [that Russian advisors in Syria were packing up and leaving, and which worried her] was very important. No, it had not in any way changed their assessment of the situation. I was assured that we would get adequate warning of any real trouble [...] everything that was necessary had been done, and the army was placed on high alert. Don't worry: There won't be a war [...]. Today, I know what I should have done: I should have overcome my hesitations and ordered full-scale mobilisation. I failed to make that decision".[165]

Understandably, she does not mention that during the severe crisis, she ordered Israel's entire stock of (ten) atomic bombs on specially adapted bombers.[166]

Nor does she mention her talks with King Hussein in September 1973, referred to above. The version by the historian Benny Morris probably gives a fairly accurate picture of the event, but Golda Meir has most likely not wanted to expose in her memoirs either the King, who was still very much alive and a possible future negotiating partner, or the Israeli Intelligence.

When the war eventually was won, the decision was made to set up a Commission of Enquiry in order to examine who was responsible for the fact that Israel was not prepared for the surprise attack. The Prime Minister was exonerated and the Chief of Staff received most of the blame. Eventually the crisis of the aftermath of the war led to the downfall of Golda Meir in 1974, when she felt worn out and resigned, being also fairly old, at 75 years of age. She survived only four more years.

Morris admits that Dayan was "one of the those who might have seen the writing on the wall, since he understood the depths of the Arabs' humiliation in 1967.[167] He agrees with the findings of the Inquiry Commission that the Chief of Staff was to receive most of the blame, adding that the failure must be seen against the background of the IDF's confidence after the victory in 1967.

Rabin's warnings to the IDF after the 1967 victory, against believing themselves to be invincible, mentioned above, had apparently fallen on deaf ears. The military establishment thus grossly underestimated the capabilities of the Arabs to attempt

---

164 Op.cit., p. 399.
165 Op.cit., p. 356-357.
166 Dilip Hiro, *Dictionary of the Middle East*, London, 1996, p. 194.
167 Op.cit., p. 398.

an open challenge to the IDF. We must take into account that this time, the Arabs not only managed to keep their plans secret until the last moment, but also in many ways arranged a successful policy of deceit beforehand, especially on the part of the Egyptians.

The attack came on Saturday, 6 October, during the most holy day for the Jews, *Yom Kippur*. Golda Meir was awakened at 4 AM and told that there was no longer any doubt: The attack from both sides (Syria and Egypt) was imminent and would be launched later in the day. This soon became cruel reality; a question of life and death for the young nation had arisen, since most of its soldiers were celebrating the holy day with their family members far away from the front along the Canal.

At the beginning, the Israelis were forced to withdraw because their stand-by forces were no match for the many attackers. Golda Meir was especially horrified, because her two closest military advisers, Dayan and David Elazar, almost panicking, and in disagreement about how to react, asked her to take some of the more crucial decisions about the war.

The following brief account of the Yom Kippur War will show how the Israelis turned the tide and eventually saved their country from an unknown, but surely disastrous fate, not least thanks to the American assistance. The Egyptians crossed the Suez Canal at its northern end during the first days and the Syrian troops captured Mount Hermon and other strategic areas. The otherwise dominant IAF no longer had the absolute air supremacy because of Egypt's better defence capabilities along the Canal; furthermore, the Syrian SAM missiles proved that the Arab armies were no longer a laughing stock as in earlier wars. This time they were a rather fearful enemy, and surely the soldiers did not run away, as in earlier wars. In many places the Arab forces fought bravely and even with dynamism, according to sources, including Jewish ones. The situation became so difficult for the IDF during the first two days of war that according to Morris, the Israeli government discussed the use of nuclear weapons.[168]

Fortunately this became unnecessary, mostly due to airlifted American armament that began to arrive on 8 October. Golda Meir appealed immediately to US President Nixon, with whom she had already established a good relationship, and asked for urgent assistance. In her memoirs she relates that she phoned the Israeli Ambassador in Washington at all hours of the day and even in the middle of the night, asking him to repeat her appeal. On the following day, the Israelis mobilised fully. (Dayan had thought that a partial mobilisation would suffice.) On 10 to 12 October, the Israelis launched a counterattack in the Golan and pressed back the Syrians, even going beyond the old armistice line, threatening Damascus. At the same time, the Egyptians mounted an offensive to relieve the Syrians. But as of 15 October, the Israelis succeeded in creating a wedge between two Egyptian armies

---

168 Ibid., p. 404. (see also above)

and establishing a bridgehead west of the Canal. Syrian counterattacks in the Golan did not change the picture substantially, and Damascus applied for assistance from other Arab states. On 16 October, the oil producing nations (in the OPEC block, including other than Arab nations) introduced an oil embargo, in order to dissuade the Americans and others from further assistance to Israel. It came as a shock to most of the Western world, not only to the USA.

Foreign Minister Eban was in New York on the day of the attack and had the opportunity to discuss it with the new US Secretary of State, Henry Kissinger, almost immediately upon its coming to his knowledge.[169] Kissinger intervened and soon initiated talks in Moscow, which led the way for UN resolution 338 of 22 October 1973, calling for a truce and mentioning the need for a just and durable peace in the Middle East. This resolution, calling for cease-fire within twelve hours, was not fully respected by the Israelis, who wanted to consolidate their conquest of the whole of Golan and reorganise the IDF troops along the Suez Canal; this they managed before a new UN resolution, 340 renewed a cease-fire call to all sides.

During the 20 days of military conflict, the Egyptians suffered 9,000 dead and 15,000 injured, the Syrians 3,500 dead and 9,000 injured and the Israelis 2,552 dead and 6,027 injured, to which were added the substantial losses of equipment on all sides.

3. Aftermath

One very important aspect of this brief but violent war was the fact that the two large Arab states had gained not a final victory but their self-confidence, and substantial respect from their long-time adversary, too. This is the reason why I have examined the war at some length and described the feelings on both sides before and during the battle. In the aftermath, to which I turn now, mixed feelings of pride and shock prevailed in Israel as well as in Egypt and Syria.

In Washington there was a genuine desire to try and find a better, more long-term settlement between the parties than had been reached after the previous wars. Henry Kissinger, who already knew the problem very well, had probably ignored the serious threat to Israel before the Yom Kippur War, just as the IDF and the Israeli politicians had themselves. He now began a *shuttle diplomacy* to reach cease-fire agreements between Israel on the one side and Egypt and Syria on the other. But it soon turned out that real peace was still not the issue. It is essential here, however, to emphasise that the Arabs now began to realise that Israel as a nation was a *fait accompli* and that it would not be possible to eliminate this state,

---

169 Strangely enough, Golda Meir does not mention this in her account of the dramatic events; see her *My Life*, op.cit., pp. 353 – 381.

however disliked it might be from the Arab point of view. The Arabs understood that other means than war must be put in the forefront in order to rescue as much land for themselves and the Palestinians as possible. The PLO had already been recognised by most of the neighbouring states, but of course not yet by Israel. As we know, *land for peace* was the formulation already established by UN resolution 242 from 1967 and then repeated in resolution 338 after the cease-fire in 1973; thus, this formula was also endorsed by the Arabs and eventually became the basis for the solutions that would be found in the following years or still pursued today.

I shall not go into detail here with regard to the talks, but only stress some of the features of the initial settlement.

Golda Meir describes the energetic efforts of Henry Kissinger as such: "At this point, the outstanding personality of the Middle East became not President Sadat, or President Assad, or King Feisal or even Mrs. Meir. It was the US Secretary of State, Dr. Henry Kissinger, whose efforts in the area can only be termed superhuman. I admired his intellectual gifts, and his patience and his perseverance were always limitless and in the end we became good friends".[170] Also President Anwar Sadat, who according to most observers had launched the war mainly in order to continue diplomatic efforts on a more respectful basis, felt that Henry Kissinger soon became his friend, just as the American Secretary of State began to respect Sadat, whom he initially had considered a sort of clown.

On the Egyptian side a new preliminary arrangement was soon reached. It was signed as early as 11 November 1973 and stipulated a general withdrawal of troops to the combat line of 22 October, but allowed Egypt to regain control over some small parts of the Sinai East of the Canal. UN troops were again to be stationed along the cease-fire-line in order to control the parties.

The Egyptian President played the American card to an extent that only few of his Arab colleagues could accept. Relations with most of the other powers in the region therefore became extremely difficult for Sadat. It has been said that Kissinger (himself a Jew) was the personality needed for this delicate task — intelligent, innovative and almost tireless. He is also regarded as the first Secretary of State to have developed a clear American policy toward the Arabs, which certainly seems accurate; yet it also characterises his role in creating a well-defined American foreign policy in general, in the sense of long-term strategic planning as opposed to the usual tactical strategies in use in much of the world.

In accordance with the Soviets, Kissinger also involved the UN, and its resolution 238 imposed a cease-fire which the Israelis did not accept at first, as mentioned above. At the time, the Russians were already threatening with military intervention and combined the threat with a strong supply of arms to the Egyptians. But Kissinger was equally capable of using his mighty military alert system in this

---

170 Ibid., p. 372.

Syrian president Hafez Assad during the Summit in Algiers, November 1973.

serious power game, probably the worst between the two superpowers since the Cuba conflict in 1962. At this stage, Nixon was becoming increasingly paralysed by the Watergate affair.

What was particularly difficult for the Egyptian President was his relationship with the Syrian President. They had launched this war in solidarity and had fought it against the same enemy, who was taken aback as a dwarf but soon woke up as the usual giant. As early as during the war, the Syrians probably felt deceived by Sadat, but the relationship became utterly difficult later when Sadat seemed to be lured, as the Syrians saw it, into the Western fold by Kissinger. The Egyptian President tried to escape the condemnation of the other Arabs, and especially Hafez Assad, by means of declarations of faith in their common cause. But Sadat's words never sounded like sweet music to his colleagues. He did, however, give his Syrian colleague the following assurance: "I owe President Assad a debt of honour until the Day of Judgement. I shall never forget it; we shall not sell him out".[171] But that was exactly how Hafez Assad and other leaders viewed Sadat's acceptance of a cease-fire at a time when the luck of the battle might still have turned round, they (very unrealistically) hoped.

There were really very few new developments in the Egyptian-Israeli relationship until Sadat suddenly turned into a dramatic person again, launching his idea of a visit to Jerusalem, to which we shall return later.

Kissinger soon realised that the Syrian President was a strong personality, and one of his well-known comments afterwards was as follows: "One cannot make

---

171 Op.cit., p. 171.

war in the Middle East without Egypt and not peace without Syria"[172]. Hafez Assad eventually began to acknowledge the existence of Israel, though, and was probably willing to negotiate an arrangement with the former enemy, if it could have taken place on the basis of resolution 242. But the mood in Israel surely did not yet allow the government to enter into negotiations, nor was the American government interested at this stage, as already mentioned. It took some years more for the climate to be ready for the overture from Sadat; only much later did even Assad finally accept the idea of bilateral negotiations with the enemy. And the general feeling in the West, including Israel, was that the Arab (OPEC) oil boycott, introduced in late October 1973 was unjust and led to havoc in the economies of the wealthy countries.[173]

Kissinger never managed to persuade the Syrian leader to come to Geneva, where negotiations were soon to take place on the withdrawal of the Israeli troops — and of the Egyptian — in a disengagement settlement after the cease-fire of late October 1973. The Israelis were not very flexible on their part, either. Only in the following year did Syria accept Kissinger's mediation efforts because it was no longer possible to believe in a resumed concerted action with Egypt or other Arab states. What was reached in Geneva was an agreement on disengagement that was to prevent the use of arms again in border incidents, but no real scheme for a peaceful settlement was within sight.

There was a marked difference between the two personalities of Sadat and Assad, who were responsible for the October 1973 attack. Whereas the first was flexible in a manner that might call to mind the term *opportunist*, the second was proud and stubborn, to the surprise of even Kissinger, who was an excellent and totally self-assured negotiator. He soon came to regard Hafez Assad as a respected partner, but in spite of this, Kissinger did not take the Syrian wishes into account, since they did not suit his own scheme for the area. For the American Secretary of State, Israel was seen as the foremost bastion of the USA in a troublesome region, and it was essential to respect its security interests. This was in keeping with President Nixon's feelings and has been the American policy ever since.

After the second disengagement agreement in the Sinai, Hafez Assad realised that he was left behind in the American political scheme, as organised by Kissinger. At the same time Syria's relationship with Iraq proved to be unfriendly, to say the

---

172 This quotation is common knowledge among diplomats, but I cannot tell when or where Kissinger said so.
173 Seen in the light of history, oil prices were very probably too low in the 60s and early 70s until the oil embargo in late 1973. Even after the recent increases in the prices, they are still not excessively high with regard to assuring the oil producers' buying power.

least. The Syrian President therefore wanted to upgrade the bilateral relationship with Moscow once again. He visited not only the weapon-rich country, Czechoslovakia, but also the Soviet Union, in the hope of getting more assistance from the socialist world. He managed to obtain some profitable assistance programmes, especially in the rearmament field, while the brief improvement vis-à-vis the USA soon turned into a cooler relationship that lasted until recently and was renewed during the Iraq war in 2003 and immediately afterwards.

Seale's somewhat cynical comment with regard to the missed opportunity for peace in 1973 – 75 is as follows: "The manipulative attitude towards the region which Israel had long had, took root in Washington also, as the two countries embarked on their strategic relationship from 1970 onwards".[174]

The arrangement that was eventually found for the Golan, where some fighting continued for a fairly long period, was not signed until 5 June 1974, almost the same time that the new Rabin Cabinet took over the government in Israel. The agreement had in fact long-lasting effects, still valid today. It returned to the Syrians the important city of Kuneitra, destroyed by the Israelis before their withdrawal, so that its desolate ruins are exposed to the world to see even today, as one of many relics of a lost war. The agreed settlement included deployment of UN troops in a border disengagement zone between the parties in the Golan, and the stationing of Israeli troops on the Western parts of the mountains, with the Syrians allowed to occupy the lower hills on the Eastern side. Since then peaceful conditions have reigned to a surprising degree in the Golan. If there is still no question of any real peace, this cease-fire agreement has at least been fully respected by both sides over the many years.

Despite repeated Syrian and Egyptian celebrations of what they felt was their brave and successful war, Damascus and Cairo could not persuade any but their most stubborn pro-regime citizens that they finally *won* the war of 1973. But as we have already emphasised, they won self-esteem and the respect of fellow Arabs and others. We may refer again to Golda Meir's memoirs, which relate that Syrian and Egyptian forces managed to enact a frightening scenario for the hitherto self-confident and unruffled Israel. And the initial surprise effect meant an important step forward and a comfort for the Syrian President, Hafez Assad, just as for his Egyptian colleague, Anwar Sadat. They had both come to power only three years before the war and needed some success to consolidate their hold on the public in both countries. Dayan writes in his account of the war that this time, the enemy soldiers did not run as they had before (especially the Egyptians). Generally speaking, the Syrians were considered fairly good warriors.

---

174 Ibid., p. 265.

IX. Lebanon's war, 1975-90, Spillover of the conflict

A. Background and Interference from Abroad in the Civil Wars

1. The First Civil War of 1958

Even if this first Civil War was not a direct consequence of the general Middle East conflict, it had its roots in it, almost as much as the later and much longer civil war from 1975 to 1990.

The prelude to the brief, but violent civil war of 1958 was the assassination of a Christian newspaper publisher, which led to anti-government rioting in Tripoli and the introduction of a state of emergency. President Chamoun (a Maronite Christian) had already become isolated from and utterly dissatisfied with the opposition and was under increasing pressure from it. The large Muslim minority of the population (perhaps 40% then) had seen the *light* coming from the important signal provided by the rising Pan-Arabism. Especially the establishment of the United Arab Republic between Egypt and Syria in early 1958 had tremendous repercussions. This new union could easily be seen as part of an Arab movement to fortify the opposition to the intruding nation, Israel, especially after the Egyptian defeat in the 1956 War. President Nasser of course wanted to include other Arab nations in this new Union, created in the name of Pan-Arabism, whereas President Chamoun was adamantly opposed to this idea, seeing the risk that his small country might be absorbed into a very large and predominantly Muslim union.

One of the leading opposition groups was the Muslim Socialist Front, led by the *Druze*[175] chief, Kamal Jumblatt. He initiated protest marches against the dominant Maronites that soon degenerated into riots, resulting in several deaths. This led to the brief civil war of May to July 1958, with Chamoun's militiamen and the *gendarmerie* fighting the Jumblatt supporters while the army remained neutral for some

---

175 The Druze people are members of a secret Muslim sect living mainly in the mountains of Lebanon, but also in Syria.

time. When the Druze and other opposition forces had occupied almost a third of the country, however, the President ordered the army to intervene. Chamoun also found it necessary to appeal to the US government to apply the *Eisenhower Doctrine*. (France, which normally had — and still has — close relations with Lebanon was already engaged in the War in Algeria and had internal problems at home, leading to the advent of General de Gaulle's presidency.) This Cold War doctrine permitted US interventions abroad whenever a pro-Western regime was in danger. The Lebanese President had realised that the fall of his friend, the King of Iraq, who had just been assassinated in Baghdad on 14 July 1958, could be seen as a danger signal not to be ignored. Chamoun could not withstand this Pan-Arabist pressure without help from abroad, he thought.

Washington agreed to come to the rescue of the President and the Christians. It therefore sent several warships (the Sixth Fleet) with a force of 14,300 Marines and air-borne troops to the Lebanese coast. This American intervention meant that the civil war was internationalized, but also that the conflict, after some initial intensification, soon came to a halt at the end of July, when a compromise between the fighting elements was reached. It involved among other things the acceptance of the army commander, the Christian General Chenab, as sole presidential candidate, elected in 1958. The American troops were withdrawn as early as October 1958.

Thousands of Lebanese civilians (estimates vary between 1,500 and 4,000) and others were killed in this brief, first civil war. It was brutal enough, but very limited compared to the following, much more serious conflict, seventeen years later. It confirmed the beginning of the unsettled society in Lebanon, which felt the dangerous repercussions of the regional conflict.

2. The Long Civil War

Initially I want to try to penetrate the background of this apparently internal strife, which was actually due not only to the spillover from the larger conflict between Israel and its Arab neighbours that is our main topic here, but eventually also to direct interventions from several foreign powers.

It seems essential to evaluate all elements of this war — which has marked almost a third of the life span of Lebanon as a free and independent nation — especially because it had enormous influence, not only on the fate of the nation, but also on the wider regional conflict in a sort of reciprocal reaction. As so often in history, there is no singular or simple cause or explanation for a serious conflict, and this was certainly also the case in Lebanon.

Many Lebanese people will tell you that it was all due to foreign interference into "poor little Lebanon", whereas others — foreigners and more objective Lebanese observers — tend to admit that some of the reasons for the increasing conflict derived from the divisions within the nation itself. Of course both factors throw some light on the background of the conflict, but I shall try to elaborate as follows.

The establishment of Israel in 1948 is of course one of the basic, albeit remote roots of the two Civil Wars, just as it is the dominant factor in all the bones of contention studied in the present book on the Middle East conflict.

When we look into the matter in more detail, however, the most obvious reason for the Civil War was the fact that the Palestinian cause had already been involving Lebanon to an increasing degree at an early stage of the conflict. Officially this multi-religious nation had shown understanding for the liberation movement through the signing of the so-called *Cairo Agreement* in 1969, which granted the PLO special rights inside Lebanon. But this understanding, which came just one year before the PLO expulsion from Jordan, was never wholehearted, especially when the regional conflict continued beyond the first years of Israel's independence. The defeat of the PLO during the *Black September* 1970 conflict, or war with the Hashemite kingdom of Jordan, was an important step that not only fortified the presence of the radical Palestinian groups in Lebanon, but also led to a substantial increase in the presence of Palestinians in the nation on the whole, as they eventually comprised almost ten percent of the total population.

When the PLO's natural backyard in Jordan had been banned to the important Palestinian politicians or militias, Lebanon was of course felt to be attractive by the PLO and other liberation movements as another small country neighbouring Israel. The increase in Palestinian presence occurred whether the Lebanese population agreed or not. Most of them did not, eventually, despite the above-mentioned controversial agreement that granted the PLO special privileges. As we remember, when the old West Bank territory was lost and taken over by the IDF after the 1967 defeat, there was hardly any possibility for the Palestinians to continue the fight against the intruding nation from their own territory; they were therefore forced either to find another refuge from which to operate or to give up their fight passively.

The various resistance groups had initially tried hard to continue operations inside occupied Palestine (the West Bank and Gaza), but the harsh suppressive methods of the Israelis practically stopped these attacks within a year. There is no doubt that "the overwhelming majority of the West Bank and Gaza Arabs from the first hated the occupation", if we are able to trust Morris, which I believe we can.[176]

If initially there was much more sympathy for the Palestinian cause in Lebanon than later, this is quite natural. Whenever a just rebellion is far away and does not involve one's own national interests, sympathy is easy. When one's own security becomes involved, the sympathy will soon evaporate and change into antagonism and even strong opposition.

Among those Lebanese showing most sympathy for the PLO problems were the above-mentioned Druzes, present not only in Lebanon but also in Syria and Israel (in

---

176 Op.cit., p. 342, on the "Israeli quick and brutal repression".

the occupied Golan, especially); some left-wing politicians and militias also showed understanding and wanted to collaborate with the Palestinian cause. This tolerant attitude waned little by little, however, when it became clear how disastrous the results of the dangerous intrusion were for Lebanon as an independent nation.

The slogan *One Arab Nation* — pronounced especially by Pan-Arabist politicians — may superficially sound beautiful in many Arab ears, but when it comes to the more deep-rooted popular feeling, it has much less value now as then. Only few Lebanese nationals were eventually willing to fight for a Palestinian/Arab cause, which was felt alien to most, especially to the Christian majority.[177] And that was surely the case when the dramatic events of the Civil War developed into chaos.

The Palestinian influence grew especially in the late sixties and early seventies, increasing up to the 1973 war between Israel on the one hand and Egypt and Syria on the other, and also during its aftermath, which meant a rethinking of Arab policies. In the period during and after the wars with Israel, almost 300,000 Palestinian refugees arrived and settled inside Lebanon, which at the time had less than three million inhabitants; today, they still number around ten percent of the total population.

The 1970s were characterised not only by the dramatic events in unsettled Lebanon, but also by many terrorist attacks in Sudan, Vienna and Madrid, to mention only a few for which Palestinian movements were responsible. These attacks frightened not only world opinion, but even more so the traditional Christian upper class and probably also a large majority of people in Lebanon. The leaders lived in a dangerous setting, and the nation was dominated by feudal lords, while the democratic system was weak and rested on fragile pillars, that is, existed mostly in surface appearance.

After the 1946 independence of Lebanon, many foreign observers regarded the new nation as a haven of tolerance and tranquillity in an otherwise dramatic and restless region. But this view is only partially true. If we listen to the well-known Lebanese observer, Georges Corm, he tells us that this picture was an entirely false one. In the 1950s and 60s, the ruling class of Maronites had seen the danger signals from Cairo during the peak influence of Nasser's expansive Pan-Arabism and also later from the increasing influence of Islamic fundamentalists. The other minority groups had similar fears of their own, vis-à-vis the new challenges. Corm writes: "The crazy Lebanon that starts burning in 1975 is a country dying because of a minority complex". He also states that "facing the increase in fundamentalism, the *Phalange* [the Maronite militia] became a more muscular form of Christian self-assurance".[178]

---

177 Before the civil war there was still a slight majority of Maronites and other Christians in Lebanon, but this is no longer the case.

178 Ibid., p. 420.

Here we are at the core of the initial conflict, since the Phalange, with its roots in fascist thinking and inspired by German uniformed movements in the 1930's, was the group that fired the first shots. This happened when Phalange members attacked a bus in the initial, terrible massacre of 13 April 1975, which resulted in 27 dead, mostly Palestinians, some of them innocent refugees. Surely the Phalange saw this Palestinian presence as a confirmation of the dangerous foreign infiltration into Lebanon, until then dominated politically and economically by the old upper class, the Maronites. The latter, from which the Phalange recruited most of its members, were naturally afraid of a new dominant influence by the Palestinians in Lebanon, since they had seen the dangerous *state within the state* situation in Jordan only a few years earlier. The Phalange was also influenced by the fear created not only by the influx of refugees and the increasing aspirations of hard-line Palestinians, but also by Beirut's being, in early 1975, a point of "rendez-vous of Marx, Lenin, Che Guevara, Mao and Nasser who wanted to oppose the imperialist plot", according to Corm.[179] Another Lebanese intellectual, Samir Kassir, expresses the same idea: "All Lebanon had become a secure base for the Palestinian resistance in the late Sixties and up to 1975 (in some cases up to 1982)".[180]

Corm adds that the more conservative Arab regimes — and there were many — were afraid of the radical thinking among the Palestinians and their supporters in Lebanon. They surely did not want to support these radical movements, but rather see them disappear, just as the King of Jordan had found it necessary to eliminate the Palestinian fighters when they became increasingly dominant and threatened the fragile national identity and his throne. In his peculiar way, writing sarcastically about the famous (dead) radicals meeting in Beirut, as we have seen in the quote above, Corm wants to stress how the local political sector had come under a dangerous influence from outsiders. Despite his own profession today as a politician (recently as a minister), he does not want to exonerate his own class of any guilt, quite the contrary.[181] One of his critical points against the politicians before and during the Civil War is that they allowed the national army to be so weak, probably because it was split into several fractions, just like the Lebanese society. The army had only 15,000 soldiers, and if it was unable to put up any substantial resistance when the Israelis intruded massively in 1978 and 1982, it could at least have put up defensive action against most of the militias before they became too strong, Corm finds. But the armed forces did not even make any serious attempts.

The tense atmosphere in the Arab world that was due to the many terrorist attacks especially before and in the aftermath of the Black September tragedy was

---

179 Ibid., p. 427.
180 See his book *La guerre au Liban*, Paris, 2000, p. 64.
181 Ibid., p. 429. But born in 1940, his own responsibility as a young man of 35 when the war started must at any rate have been limited. He is an economist by education.

probably felt more in Lebanon than in other Arab countries. It is easy to understand why, because this nation was utterly exposed to political and military risks. Not only vis-à-vis Israel, but also in facing the refugee problem that was fortified by the many heavily armed fighting groups building up their militias in the country. After the influx of many Palestinians over the years, including representatives of several radical organisations who hardly represented their interests in a neutral way, this needs no further elaboration. Often these foreign organisations found easy support among representatives of the lower classes in Lebanon, especially the Shia-Muslims, who could use them to exploit their own sad situation.

We may therefore agree that it should not have come as a complete surprise that the *muscular Phalange* — representing primarily the formerly unchallenged masters of Lebanon, the Maronites — took up a fight against the PLO and its supporters, because they were afraid of losing their national identity as it was before the war — or in cruder terms, losing their old privileges. The Phalange had probably originally underestimated the sympathy for the PLO among various, especially left-wing, groups of the country; again, this is easy to understand because the latter had been frustrated by the Maronite dominance of former years.

We have to admit, however, when commenting further on the violence, which is always difficult to compare or classify, that *initially* most of the meaningless killings, such as the massacres of April and December 1975, were the responsibility of the Christian Phalange. Later on none of the parties put on kid gloves when fighting the enemy.

The Syrian interventions became one of the most important elements of the Civil War, almost right from the beginning. They began as early as the first period of the war, when Foreign Minister Khaddam (later Vice-President of Syria) intervened. He did so in May 1975 (because of the first chaotic situation after the April massacre), in order to persuade President Frangie to dismiss his newly appointed military Cabinet, setting aside a government led by a Sunni-Muslim Prime Minister as was traditionally the case.[182] This effort of political persuasion by Syria was successful. It is noteworthy, by the way, that the first Syrian military intervention happened to ease the pressure by Palestinian and leftist groups against the Maronites.

Initially, of course, the Syrian intervention in favour of the Maronites surprised and to some extent antagonised the other Arab states. Eventually, however, the Arab/Islamic world as a general rule tolerated Syrian interference, because most of the countries had no intention of mediating or helping militarily themselves. Those who did, such as Iraq and Iran, were soon occupied by their own dramatic war, starting in the middle of the Lebanese one.

---

182 According to Lebanese political tradition, a Maronite was chosen as President of the Republic, a Sunni Muslim as Prime Minister and a Shia Muslim as Chairman of Parliament. See also Samir Kassir, op.cit., p. 109.

For the Syrian leader it felt natural to intervene. His country had just then (at the beginning of the Civil War in 1975) come out of the 1973 War with more self-confidence than before, because it had fought what was considered to be a brave war, and Hafez Assad was a master of long-term planning. His main interest was of course to increase the Syrian influence in the region in the long run. But in addition, he wanted to establish a better political balance inside Lebanon so that this neighbouring country could resist those attacks by the Palestinians and Israel (which was always seen by Damascus as the potential attacker and permanent enemy) that were ongoing or could be expected. Hafez Assad eventually realised that what the Israelis, especially a figure like General Sharon, wanted was a further splitting up of their Northern neighbouring country, so that Israel could easily create small Christian enclaves or protectorates there. If the rest of the country's inhabitants would continue their internecine fights, so much the better, it was felt in Jerusalem, at least in those right-wing circles that Sharon represented.

All in all, we may conclude that if Syria certainly did not interfere for the sake of the Lebanese nation as such, its actions were not devoid of realistic thinking, which could be said eventually to benefit the very fragile Lebanese system, even if many Lebanese will never admit it. Some of the Syrian deeds during the Civil War were of course brutal; there was, for example, the assassination of President-Elect Gemayel, which involved the killing of many people other than the main target, and the killing of the Druze leader, Kamal Jumblatt, probably decided by a Machiavellian member of the military in Damascus. But in a sea of violence throughout the War, the Syrian actions were not always the worst.

Israel was the second power to interfere in the Lebanese War. It had been quite happy when the Syrians helped the Maronites at the beginning of the war when Rabin was in power in Israel. In March 1978, when a right-wing government under Begin was at the helm of affairs, it gave orders to intervene in Lebanon. A bus had been hijacked by a group of Fatah terrorists/fighters landing near Haifa, and 39 Israeli civilians were killed. The IDF was therefore authorised by the Begin government to retaliate and invade the south of Lebanon in order to fight the terrorists. It was a brutal affair when the Israeli forces, using three brigades and heavy fire by artillery and aircraft, soon occupied a zone south of the Litani River (excluding the city and environs of Tyre). This onslaught was an extremely violent one, in which orders given to the IDF were to kill and not to take prisoners, despite the fact that only a few PLO fighters were active in the area, according to Birgitte Rahbek.[183] The Israeli intrusion was soon stopped and the IDF forced to withdraw by means of the UN Security Council's resolution 425 of 19 March 1978, which also ordered the deployment of 6,000 UN soldiers in this border area.

---

183 *En Stat for Enhver Pris,* Fremad, 2000, p. 216 (quotation from Odd Karsten Tveit, *Nederlag*).

The second and much worse IDF intervention came four years later with the onslaught in 1982. The Israeli government had been impatiently waiting for a *casus belli* in order to launch a big invasion of Lebanon to combat and preferably eliminate the Palestinian influence. At the funeral of Sadat in October 1981, Prime Minister Begin had informed the American Secretary of State, General Haig, that Israel was preparing such a venture.[184] The Secretary of State had only warned Begin in general terms but not clearly attempted to dissuade the Israeli government from taking such action. Jerusalem found its desired *casus belli* in the assassination attempt against the Israeli ambassador in London on 3 June 1982, although this attack had not been ordered by the PLO but independently by one of the more radical Palestinian groups. The declared reason for the Israeli attack and occupation was to *secure peace in Galilee* by eliminating PLO and other resistance/terrorist attacks from Lebanon into Israel. Prime Minister Begin emphasised this in a message he sent President Reagan when the invasion took place under that slogan.

The attack began on 6 June 1982 and was a massive operation, surprising even the US and large parts of the Israeli public. In the UN, Secretary of State General Haig first accepted a resolution, 509, asking for a cease-fire. The resolution, demanding the immediate withdrawal of troops from Lebanon, was passed on the same evening, the sixth of June. When Israel continued its thrust against the PLO, the US Secretary of State vetoed a resolution condemning the Israeli government, despite the fact that others in the US administration had recommended a vote in its favour.

The Palestinian fighters fought bravely but were no match for the heavily armed IDF, which used tanks and modern aircraft. The utterly weakened Lebanese army kept out of the battles, once again.

The IDF advanced as far as the capital, and President Sarkis was literally ousted from his Beirut Palace by the invading troops in June 1982. This of course created havoc in the Lebanese political situation, already very confused. The chosen candidate for the presidency, Bashir Gemayel, had been the leading figure among the Christians as head of the Lebanese forces, the military arm of the Lebanese Front, and he had managed to create a fairly peaceful and well-organised zone out of East Beirut for some years. He has been accused of being a long-term agent of the CIA,[185] recruited when he worked for a law firm in Washington, and he then collaborated almost openly with the Israelis, not only militarily, but also in order to achieve some form of official relationship between the two countries. At an early point during the invasion (11 June), Gemayel had even made an unofficial agreement with Sharon regarding their common interests after the invasion, especially as to how the link-up between the IDF and his own forces should operate. He per-

---

184 George W. Ball, *Error and Betrayal in Lebanon*, Washington, 1984, p. 34.
185 See Dilip Hiro, op.cit., p. 89.

General Ariel Sharon explains the Israeli troops movements into Lebanon in June 1982.

sonally had to suffer humiliation because of the arrogance of this Israeli politician and military leader, supported almost without restraint by Prime Minister Begin. When Gemayel was elected President inside a military camp on 23 August, by 57 out of 65 Parliamentarians, the Israeli occupation was still going on. He had not yet taken over his high post, however, when he secretly met with Israeli Prime Minister Begin on 1 September. He must then have realised how impossible his situation had become. There was no doubt that most Muslims regarded him as a traitor,[186] but according to some Lebanese observers he had given many Lebanese new hope in an otherwise hopeless situation, because of his personal charisma and qualities. His life, however, soon came to a dramatic end when he was assassinated on 14 September in a bomb explosion that killed 30 people and destroyed the Phalange

---

186 Corm, in his op.cit., praises Bashir Gemayel and names him a possible hero of those days, because of his open talks to the population on TV, giving it some sort of hope and understanding in a difficult time, see pp. 506 - 507. This verdict could seem to come from a fairly lone Maronite voice, in favour of Lebanon´s unhappy president, who never took power. But I have heard other witnesses who confirm that indeed Gemayel was seen at the time as a promising figure, even outside the Christian/Maronite group. His charisma and the population´s feeling of being lost in a dreadful war gave him special support. The Lebanese might also have seen that the pro-Syrian President, Sarkis, had not been able to save the country from the fate of a new invasion.

headquarters. Traitor or not, this attack should not have come as a surprise, given his lenient — even Quisling-like — attitude toward the Israeli invaders.

The Parliament in disarray chose Bashir Gemayel's elder brother, Amin, as the new President; he received almost all votes in the election, since the country was still in shock after the occupation and Bashir Gemayel's assassination. Amin was not as openly pro-Israeli as his brother, but could of course not change directions completely, not only because of Israeli pressure, but also because he was compelled by other Phalange leaders, and therefore had to follow a policy similar to his brother's to begin with.

The Syrians were, without much doubt, behind the assassination of what they saw as a shamelessly pro-Israeli president. The Israeli Defence Minister, Sharon, used the opportunity to invade West Beirut, normally a Muslim stronghold, in spite of American warnings against such a dangerous move. The assassination was soon followed by cruel attacks in revenge, in the same pattern as seen so often before. They were aimed especially against PLO refugee camps and organised by the Phalange with the implicit understanding of the IDF. Altogether more than 1,000 — some sources say 2,000 — most of them innocent refugees, were murdered in a bloodbath in the Sabra and Shatila refugee camps, practically under the very eyes of the IDF. We may recall the American diplomat Ambassador Habib who, as a witness to the dramatic situation in Lebanon then, described this massacre, the worst of its kind in the Middle East, asserting that "Sharon was a killer, obsessed by hatred of Palestinians".[187]

Today, now that human rights have a higher priority than previously, even heads of state like Pinochet and Milosovic and, most recently, Saddam Hussein are or have been accused. Sharon, too, was put in the dock by a Belgian court, in the course of 2002 – 2003, although the matter was later dismissed because of his status.

The American diplomat quoted above, George W. Ball, writes that Sharon's long-term dream of having the PLO troops sent back to Jordan to unsettle the monarchy there represented "Opium dreams" or "Napoleonic ambitions".[188] Shlaim tells us of Sharon's ambitious *Big Plan*, aiming at an expansionist Israeli nation,[189] eventually also comprising Jordan. Today we may conclude that Sharon, just like Shamir before him, has neither forgotten nor learnt anything from the past.

---

187 Ball, op.cit., p. 176. An Israeli special court criticised Sharon so much in the aftermath that he had to leave his post in the government. One of the important Christian militia leaders in the Civil War, Hobeika, was brutally murdered in Beirut on 24 January 2002, just before going as a witness to the Belgian court considering a case against Sharon that was later given up because of his position today. Many would not preclude Israeli responsibility, even if the government itself — as could be expected — said it was absurd.
188 Ibid., p. 29.
189 Op.cit., p. 405, p. 406 and p. 413.

One of the main results of this phase of the Civil War was the establishment of the new resistance movement, *Hisbollah,* which today is still one of the important factors of the conflict between Lebanon and Syria on one side and Israel on the other. It was of Iranian inspiration and came under the leadership of a Shia-Muslim cleric, Sheikh Muhammed Hussein Fadlallah. The organisation's aim was to engage in resistance against the occupation army and later also to participate in the political life of Lebanon. It initially worked together with an Iranian contingent of 2,000 Revolutionary Guards who had been sent to Lebanon in mid-1982 to fight the Israelis.

According to Morris, the week-long IDF 1982 *campaign* (a chosen euphemism for *invasion*) in Lebanon had split the country into four quarters, controlled by the following forces: 1) The Syrians (whom the IDF attacked despite promises not to, *my addition*) occupying the Bekaa in the east and parts of the north: 2) the Israelis who were in the south up to Beirut and the important Beirut – Damascus road; 3) the Christians that controlled East Beirut and the mountainous hinterland to its east and northeast; 4) Syrian units and the PLO, holding West Beirut, surrounded on three sides by the IDF and Christian forces. He adds that the Mediterranean coastal area was controlled by the Israeli navy.[190]

The US administration had become increasingly concerned by developments and now told the Israeli government that it would be necessary to have a Western multinational force to keep order in Lebanon and see to it that the PLO left the country in a controlled way. This new force was composed of troops from Britain, France, Italy and the US and was deployed on 20 September, just before the election of Amin Gemayel. The Israelis left Beirut soon afterwards, on 29 September 1982, their dirty job done. The goal of the right-wing government had not changed, however, and Jerusalem was aiming at an agreement with the new Lebanese President, which would grant the IDF continued influence in the war-torn country. A *Lebanese-Israeli Peace Treaty* was finally signed by both sides on 17 May 1983 and was also approved by the Parliaments.[191]

During the Civil War, no new elections had taken place so the Lebanese Parliament was composed of old, frightened men and was therefore of little representa-

---

190 Morris, op.cit., pp. 531 – 32.
191 Whereas on an earlier occasion in 1982 before the agreement was finalised, Sharon had boasted to Ambassador Habib that he had already reached such an agreement with the Lebanese President, Amin Gemayel, later facing Habib, denied that he ever signed it; see Seale, op.cit., p. 404. Corm tells us that the agreement was only *initialled*. One has to be a diplomat to understand the difference. A treaty is only final when *signed and ratified* (normally by Parliament). The *initialling* by the negotiating diplomats is only a preliminary, albeit important step, as a first confirmation by them of the agreement they have made.

tive value. Georges Corm heavily criticises the Americans for forcing the Lebanese government to enter into this agreement. "It was very short-sighted to impose such a treaty on an exhausted population", he writes.[192]

The unusual treaty had only limited validity and hardly any repercussions in actuality, except that of further antagonising the Muslim parts of the population, the Syrians and other Arab states opposed to the Maronite President. He had come under US pressure to enter such an agreement as soon as he assumed office, and talks were begun under US auspices in late December 1982. They dragged on for many months until the President yielded and even Parliament endorsed it, as mentioned above. Under influence of the other side, primarily pressure from Hafez Assad, however, the President withheld his own signature for a long time, although there seems to be some uncertainty about whether he actually did sign it or not. At any rate, President Amin Gemayel finally abrogated the short-lived treaty as early as March 1984. In the meantime, other dramatic episodes had influenced this war-stricken country and the region.

Because of the Western intervention that included the bombing of various areas, the foreign troops soon became the target of revenge attacks, and a violent bomb explosion in Beirut on 23 October 1983 killed 241 Americans, mostly soldiers, just as the French lost 59 soldiers in a similar way, almost at the same time. The first-mentioned catastrophe of course shocked the USA and eventually led to a withdrawal of the American force, in keeping with the US policy (at the time) of not becoming too involved abroad whenever there was a high level of danger. The taking of foreign hostages also became a feature of the civil war that sent a permanent warning to foreigners who tried to interfere, whether from the West or from Arab nations. But before their withdrawal, the Americans intervened in early February 1984 against the Shia-Muslim *Amal*-militia that had concluded an alliance with the Druze forces. The US did this in order to support the Lebanese government, which was still under heavy pressure from these left-wing militias.

The Muslim elements of the Lebanese army had long since defected, and the Amal-Druze alliance expelled the Christians from West Beirut. Soon afterwards, on 7 February 1984, the Americans and eventually all the Western troops left the war-stricken country, which was then again at the mercy of the warring fractions, more angry than ever and continuously exposed to Israel and Syria on each side of it.

When the IDF withdrew from Beirut, it established a *security zone* in the south of Lebanon which was controlled by the IDF's own soldiers and by their Lebanese henchmen. But it was eventually realised that it was too costly an affair, when the Israeli losses became politically unacceptable. The IDF was inside hostile territory, and in recent years losses of up to 50 young lives a year were creating a difficult

---

192 Op.cit., p. 524.

situation for the Jerusalem government which therefore decided to withdraw the IDF in May 2000.

We have seen that the fragile political system of Lebanon disintegrated almost totally under these foreign interventions, especially that of the IDF in 1982 and the following long-time occupation of almost ten percent of the Lebanese territory in the south. Not only did the Begin government interfere directly in Lebanese politics but it also permitted brutal repressive measures against the Palestinians inside the country. If the main goal of the Israeli government — that of expelling the PLO and all the militant Palestinians from Lebanon — was achieved, the *Big Plan* of Sharon was, however, not implemented. The serious impact of the IDF occupation and the Israeli political intrigues almost paralysed the nation and still cause side effects in the country today, especially with regard to the difficult Lebanese-Syrian relationship. After impressive diplomatic efforts in 1989 – 1990 by several Arab countries, such as Saudi Arabia and Syria, together with Lebanese political representatives meeting in Taif, Saudi Arabia and supported by the USA was a cease-fire or peace accord achieved in 1990, finally stopping the war. Despite the tragedy of the Civil War that often saw sights of *surrealistic carnage* (a description Corms uses several times), we may conclude here that Lebanon emerged from the civil war with a more balanced political system than before. It is still no Western democracy, but the nearest one comes to it in the Arab world. This new system, according to which the President has to share power with the other pillars of the political society, the Prime Minister and Parliament, will hopefully enable the nation to survive better in the still troubled region. Many Lebanese remain frustrated because their freedom is not as unlimited as before the war, but at least no interreligious hatred dominates the political life of the nation today, and the inter-ethnic or religious fighting has come to a halt. The future of Lebanon will depend on general developments with regard to the peace process, which is practically knocked out at the moment.

B. Essence of the Civil War

The War took place, as we know, in an area where the expression "an eye for an eye and a tooth for a tooth" is well known, not only as an old Jewish saying but also as something palpable in the entire region. Retaliation is therefore a factor to be reckoned with; no one finds it necessary to show much restraint when an act of retaliation is planned or carried out. Personal vendettas also characterise this area and became an important factor during the civil war. Whenever the enemy created havoc, the response could easily include such acts of personal revenge. The physical elimination of even a future politician (such as a President's son) in order to avoid his possible election is such a far cry from our modern democratic thinking that it is difficult for us in the West to understand. Money, prestige and clan mentality were involved in these acts more than politics as we practice them. But we have to put on record that such actions took place, if not often, then certainly fairly frequently.

The history of civil wars shows many examples of bitter brutality, including a lack of respect for human lives in general. Most foreign observers were taken aback by the sheer brutality exhibited during the war. The conflict was often felt to be utterly futile because violence was so overwhelming and often meaningless.[193] If a leader had to be eliminated in Lebanon, the militia involved, or any other irresponsible body, could easily have him assassinated or disappear, in some cases along with many people who just happened to be near him. The fact that almost a tenth of the pre-war population in Lebanon was killed or disappeared is an indication of the huge loss of lives in this war, reckoned to amount to 200,000 dead or seriously wounded. This number does not even include those who had come under such mental strain that they hardly ever recovered.

Corm again comments on these observations by rejecting the inaccurate idyllic picture that most foreigners had of Lebanon before the civil war. He sees his own country rather as a microcosm of the Arab world or of the old Ottoman system and far from the Western democracies with which Lebanon was often compared, but resembled only superficially. He is both right and wrong, in my opinion. Right, because the idyllic picture some had of pre-War Lebanon was of course not a realistic one; but wrong today, because with time Lebanon has been influenced in the right direction, especially through the experience of the civil war. The war presented such bitter examples of brutality that it probably vaccinated the population against similar ventures in the future, just as has been seen in Spain or the USA after the civil wars there.

We may ask if the war was fought along primarily religious lines, as is normally thought by those who have only a superficial view of the conflict. The answer is both yes and no. The initial conflict was of course basically due to the old Maronite (Christian) order's defence against the intruding Palestinians, the latter supported by local left-wing and Muslim opposition to the old order. But it soon became much more complicated. What many in the West often ignore is the fact that the Palestinians are not all Muslims; quite a few of them are Christians, so this is a deviation from the "Christian versus Muslim" pattern. We may also remember that the Syrians intervened militarily in the early phase of the war in favour of the Christians and not the Muslim groups. At the end of the war,

---

193 That some Lebanese do not necessarily regard the civil war only in a horrible light in hindsight can be seen from the observation I got from a well-known lawyer in Beirut. She said that the atmosphere during the war years was not characterised only by negative factors. There were many positive ones as well, she pointed out to me. Life was even worth living then, she continued.

Muslim groups often fought other Muslim groups, and some Christian groups fought among themselves.

It is sufficient here to state that basically the Lebanese population was and still is aware of its *uniqueness* as a small, diversified nation, part Arab-Christian, part Arab-Muslim, and more developed than most other nations in the Arab world, regardless of what the self-critical Corm would say. No other society in the region (not even Israel to some extent) can show such a developed press, almost free, such lively cultural activity, such fine arts and such a rich and varied literature, for instance, as we see in Lebanon.[194] It is an essential element of the civil war that the different religious groups such as Christians, Druzes, and Shia – or Sunni Muslims did not, generally speaking, hate each other, and still do not, as mentioned above, even after fifteen long years of brutal fighting. They again collaborate in government and many other sectors of modern life and can easily stand to be in the same room together, unlike the situation seen in the recent Balkan wars.

The American writer Thomas Friedman, who worked as a journalist for the *New York Times* in Beirut (and later in Jerusalem) during the civil war, relates that he was hardly ever harassed by any group in the Lebanese population, despite the fact that he is a Jew.

The civil war was more a conflict between militias or *warlords*, as they could also be called, than between the different popular factions (religious or other) in the Republic itself. Before the war the various religious groups lived peacefully together in many places, as they still do, for instance, in Damascus, where 20 percent of its large population of three million inhabitants are Christians. These groups even continue to cohabitate in many places in Lebanon, though of course some changes took place during the war, when many Christian enclaves were moved from the south of Lebanon to the north in order to avoid the fighting. Many Christians also fled Lebanon during the war years, so that their relative number declined. Likewise, numerous inhabitants of Beirut moved northwards to protect themselves during the War and have remained there; the whole coastal zone is now one long urban development — not a very pretty sight, compared with the former beauty of the Lebanese coastline.[195] In few places can one still be lucky enough to find beautiful, unspoilt settings.

An unusual aspect of the Lebanese civil war is the fact that a single government remained in power during most of the fighting years. Thus there were not two against each other, as in the American civil war in the nineteenth century or the one

---

194 According to a list of the twenty most sold books in Lebanon in 2003, twelve were in French, eight in English and NONE in Arabic, see *Arabisk Rejse*, p. 40, *Det Udenrigspolitiske Selskab*, Copenhagen, December 2003.

195 I can compare, since I visited Beirut in 1964 for the first time and in 1994 for the second, and many times later.

in Spain in the 1930s. It was a fight between the various militias, and the impotent government often refrained from interfering, as we gathered from Corm's criticism, mentioned above, of the passivity of the Lebanese armed forces. The government was threatened not only by the internal fighting groups but even more so by the militant Palestinians and other intervening forces from outside, such as the Syrians at the beginning and the end of the war and the Israelis in the middle of it and until, and even after, its end. The Parliament was composed of politicians getting older and older, because their mandates could not be renewed, since no general elections were possible in the chaotic war years.

Outside Beirut, with its bloody *Green Line* dividing the city into East and West, there was hardly any frontline, and during many phases of the war only parts of the territory, not all of Lebanon, was touched by open conflict.

Only in the last phase of the civil war did chaos penetrate as far as into government, and two command lines functioned side by side: one under the almost self-appointed President and supreme commander (over militia groups and remnants of a practically non-existent army), General Aoun, and the other under the long-time Prime Minister, Selim Hoss. The latter had carried on when the last generally accepted President, Amin Gemayel, had stepped down when his function lapsed in 1988. No new president could be elected then because of the war, and Gemayel therefore appointed Aoun as his successor and stopgap head of state (until further notice), which only a few accepted.

Prime Minister Selim Hoss, however, felt that he had the mandate to carry on and therefore controlled a good deal of the traditional administration. Strangely enough, Corm assures us that "the two governments, both pretending to represent the sovereignty of the nation, co-existed fairly well and got the administration to work better than in normal circumstances".[196] I take this in the Gallic, ironical spirit in which Corm normally likes to express himself, because to most observers, it seems evident that the absurd split into two competing administrations, both of whom were only controlling smaller or larger parts of the nation, could not continue for long. Fortunately the end of the war was in sight. As already mentioned, the cease-fire and peace agreement came with the *Taif-Accord* in 1990 and was due to a joint Arab effort, supported by the USA and others.

Because the main element of the War, as we know, was the foreign interference and threat, especially due to the Palestinian exodus into Lebanon from Israel or the West Bank, there is, generally speaking, a common understanding among Lebanese today that the country cannot absorb the many refugees who remain in the nation; they are still unintegrated and amount to almost ten percent of the entire population, or 300,000 — an unhappy lot, fed and assisted only by the UN special agency, the UNRWA. In contrast to the Jordanians, in whose country many

---

196 Ibid., p. 562.

have been completely integrated (and a beautiful young woman has even become Queen), the Lebanese are adamantly against such absorption.[197] Some say that the difficult balance between the religious groups would be upset if they had to be absorbed; others will point to the different traditions of the Palestinians which make it impossible to grant them access to or continued residence in Lebanon. The country is very mountainous and already heavily populated (more than three million inhabitants in a country only a quarter of the size of Denmark) and has no large unused areas like Syria or Jordan. The former of these two countries has been fairly tolerant, and Jordan even very tolerant, of the Palestinians, from the first arrivals of refugees from Palestine.

All in all, we can conclude once again that the civil war was partly — and increasingly — due to foreign interventions which sprang from the broader Middle East conflict. It was a cruel experience for Lebanon, probably worse than many other civil wars in the world. It lasted fifteen long years, it split the country into a multitude of fighting militias and it cost ten percent of the population their lives or their health. Many Lebanese emigrated, to the point that millions now live outside the nation,[198] often as influential businessmen or in professional jobs, especially in West Africa and Latin America. The old Phoenician spirit has not completely died out, and it is to be hoped that eventually it might be used for reforms within the country, so that it could become what it appears to be at first glance: A modern, efficient state with a lively and well-informed population, now living mostly in harmony and enjoying a sort of democracy seen hardly anywhere else in the region.

When promising the wonders of Jerusalem, the Prophet Isaiah referred to Lebanon as *the promised land* (Isa. 35:2 and 60:13), but he would not have been able to recognise it in the period from 1975 to 1990.

---

197 When the (then) Danish Minister for Overseas Development visited Beirut in 1998 and saw the (then) Foreign Minister — in my presence — the latter emphasised how much all Lebanese were in agreement with regard to not being able to absorb all the refugees inside Lebanon. They must therefore have to go back to Israel, he stressed.

198 No official figures exist. But my Brazilian colleague in Beirut once told me that in his country alone he reckoned that there were over eight million Lebanese immigrants.

X. THE EGYPTIAN PEACE OPENING, 1977-78

A. Sadat's Great Plan

1. The Initiative

We recall that although it was unsuccessful in the end, the joint Egyptian-Syrian war effort in October 1973 had given the attackers prestige and self-confidence. In the aftermath, Sadat had shown his will to enter into peace negotiations on the basis of UN resolution 242, granting *land for peace*. His good relationship with the American Secretary of State, Henry Kissinger, had gradually helped him to prepare the way and convince Washington to help Egypt, but the Israelis had perhaps not understood this new situation fully.

President Sadat spoke to the Egyptian Parliament on 9 November 1977 and launched his ambitious plan. "I am ready", he said, "to go to the end of this earth […]. Israel will be astonished to hear that I am ready to go to their own house, the Knesset itself, to talk to them". Strangely enough, few paid attention to Sadat's proposal to go to Jerusalem, and even in Israel hardly anyone took note of the Egyptian President's declaration; maybe because, as we must always keep in mind, he was a very talkative man, putting forward new ideas fairly frequently.

The new Israeli Prime Minister, at the time, Menachem Begin, who had suggested such an opening beforehand, probably without believing in it at all, was also sceptical at first and thought the Sadat declaration was one of his "usual tricks". But the following day, when a team of American Congressmen were in Israel and asked Begin about the Egyptian President's proposal, the Prime Minister said that if Sadat really meant what he declared, he would be welcome. The President would be received with all the honours befitting a president, and Begin soon realised that this was a godsend for himself. Sadat had expressed his willingness to come to Jerusalem without any preconditions, it seemed. What more could the new Likud Prime Minister ask for? Begin therefore accepted, addressing the Egyptian people on TV and stressing the hope that the two neighbouring peoples could live together in peace.

The cornerstone was then laid for the most momentous event in the history of the conflict.

2. The Extraordinary Journey

The matter soon gained momentum and the visit took place only ten days after the idea was launched and accepted, on 20 November 1977. Most Arabs would not believe it, and for the Israelis, it was almost a miracle that it took place. One Israeli TV commentator expressed what millions probably felt, when saying: "I see the Egyptian President being received by our top politicians and inspecting a guard of honour — and I *still* don't believe it". The world press focused on this most unusual event when the leader of the largest Arab country on his own free will appeared in Jerusalem to deliver a speech to the Knesset. Some of the Arab leaders regarded this episode, the way we now regard the journey of the then British Prime Minister, Chamberlain, to Germany, in order to meet the sabre-rattling leader and coming war-maker, Chancellor Adolf Hitler.

The somewhat new President of the USA, Jimmy Carter, had expressed the hope that 1977 would be the year of peace in the Middle East, and this good piece of news seemed a fine omen of success. Sadat had already invested a great deal in his friendship with Washington in Kissinger's time, and it would therefore be difficult to go back to the old Arab solidarity pattern. But as always, things were not that easy, and a long diplomatic struggle lay ahead of the three leaders concerned, Begin, Sadat and Carter, before a treaty could be signed in Washington in the following year. Not only was the visit itself a great historical event, but also the speech delivered before the Knesset by the courageous Egyptian President was of the utmost importance. Whatever one thinks of Sadat's policies, we have to admit that civil courage was one element of his character that must be recorded by history.

"All war is vanity", he began, and said that he had no ill will towards those who received the message of his journey with surprise and amazement. He had consulted none before taking this momentous decision, and it constituted a great risk. Then he stressed the sadness of war, the fate of the families and widows and then continued, "[f]or the sake of them all. For a smile, for a smile on the face of every child born in our land [...] for all that, I have taken my decision to come to you".

This warm and sentimental tone went down well with the astonished Israelis but was followed by a more somber tone when Sadat emphasised that he had not come to ask for a separate or partial peace. But he also said, "you [Israelis] want to live in this part of the world. We welcome you among us. We used to reject you but now today, I tell you, and I declare to the whole world that we accept to live with you in permanent peace based on justice".

Analysing Sadat's opening speech, we find that it had its high points and low ones, as did all of Sadat's undertakings. There was a special warning against the inclusion of the whole of Jerusalem under Israeli sovereignty and a reminder to the former enemy that Israel should not behave like the crusaders of their time (the latter were disliked equally by Jews and Arabs, of course).

When he stressed that he did not want a separate peace, it was in keeping with the usual Egyptian-Arab policy of not entering into agreements with Israel that pertained only to one's individual country and ignored a more comprehensive arrangement.

Generally speaking the President's address to the Knesset was what the Israelis had dreamt of hearing, but had hardly expected in their own lifetime.

The Egyptian President found the visit successful and could at any rate travel home with the impression he wanted to carry with him, because he had opened up a fruitful and overdue dialogue between Israel and Egypt, who were now on speaking terms. We may add that the warmth of the reception from many sides in Israel impressed Sadat and other Egyptians.

Surely the self-respect that Sadat, and Egypt as a whole, had gained in the October 1973 war helped the President to take this daring initiative. Inside the framework of the general Egyptian political setting, Sadat had met with strong opposition to his economic liberalism, leading to inflation and discontent. Because of the President's final failure as the supreme commander in 1973, he had become unpopular with most of the officers and perhaps within the army in general, so that he could never feel completely at ease at the top. Muhammed H. Heikal, the famous journalist and editor-in-chief of the highly respected newspaper *al Ahram* in Cairo, and a personal friend of Nasser, had criticised some of Sadat's policies and was removed from the newspaper in 1974. He later came under arrest (in 1981, just before the assassination of Sadat).

It was not the first time in history that a leader took new initiatives abroad, in order to draw attention away from unpopular measures at home. However, this is a negative explanation, and I prefer the following positive one: That Sadat was a far-sighted statesman and had the vision of a long-term peaceful settlement with Israel. As a competent officer and in light of his experience of the debacle after the Arab initial gains in the 1973 war just four years earlier, he was certainly aware that the Arabs could never, or at least for a very long time to come, emerge victorious in wars with Israel. At any rate, he had decided to go to Jerusalem in order to suggest a settlement with the former enemy.

As a typically negative comment with regard to Sadat's initiative, we may quote Dilip Hiro's *Dictionary of the Middle East*, in which he sarcastically writes: "In November, in a dramatic move, Sadat addressed the Israeli Knesset, and this made him something of a hero in the Western world, a factor that paved the way for the commercial success of his autobiography, *In Search of Identity* (1978). Washington began to provide military aid to Egypt".[199]

A directly opposed — and much more correct — picture was painted by Yitzhak Rabin, who in his memoirs describes the Egyptian President's speech to the Knesset as "a stroke of genius" or a political coup, and he praises Sadat's behaviour

---

199 Op.cit., p. 281.

in Jerusalem with these words: "I was enormously impressed by the poise with which the President handled himself in a unique situation [...;] he has an enviable talent for saying just the right thing at the right time".[200]

Begin, on his part, did not fully rise to the atmosphere of this memorable day, because in his answer, he preferred to show mainly a restrictive and sceptical mood. Israel was not to be lured into an easy and costly settlement, he said in his usual blunt way, not following a manuscript and not mitigating his words much for the sake of preserving the friendly atmosphere. He did not even applaud at first, when Sadat had finished his speech, and such displays will always be regarded as a slight to Arabs.

The Israeli Prime Minister also pointed out that the two sides had different ideas about the borders and that some of the positions of the Israelis (for instance on Jerusalem) were not negotiable. But Begin was in agreement with Sadat when he conceded that the dialogue must continue. It was for this reason that Begin accepted this important opening to a much-needed dialogue, which he had indirectly suggested himself, probably without believing in it. The Prime Minister could therefore hardly have declined such an offer, not least because it had always been a well-established policy in Israel to profit from any opportunity to be accepted by the neighbouring states. Begin began his term showing that he meant business with regard to peaceful arrangements with the Arab states, but it was made clear from the outset that this would be based on Israeli conditions.

Begin, all in all, received little praise for his "unimaginative speech" after Sadat's. According to Shlaim, "his tone was hectoring and his reply notable for its harshness and lack of generosity [...]. His speech contained nothing to encourage optimism".[201]

After his first disbelief and later unimpressive reaction in the Knesset, the still fairly new Prime Minister of Israel was happy to see the largest neighbouring state come to the conference table, and a prospect for real peace now seemed within reach. For the first time a faint light could be observed at the end of the tunnel, but difficult negotiations lay ahead, in particular because Begin's character was generally nothing but inflexible. He shared the hope of most Israelis, however, that it would be possible to live in peace; nevertheless, he was also ambitious with regard to the demands of Israel, which he saw in the light of his own dreams of a greater Israel.

Altogether, I think we have to see this important move by the Egyptian President in a very positive light, as a brave effort to persuade his population and fellow Arabs that time had come for a change. Sadat had just abrogated the friendship treaty with the Soviet Union; he had done so in anger, because the USSR did not

---

200 Op.cit., p. 323.
201 Op.cit., p. 361.

want to forgive Egypt's large debts. He had already negotiated with the USA regarding all kinds of aid, a move that has certainly led to an increase in prosperity for the Egyptians, especially in the light of the decline in importance and dissolution of the USSR that followed some ten years later.

3. The Follow-Up

The first bilateral meetings after the opening in Jerusalem took part in Egypt and Israel, respectively and went very badly, especially because of Begin's stubbornness[202] and antipathy towards any real concessions with regard to the Palestinians. Egypt wanted what was soon termed *the linkage*, that is, that the Palestinian question be included in an agreement. Sadat even began to talk of "a Palestinian State" that should be established in the West Bank and Gaza.

The first bilateral meeting between the two former enemies to follow the one in Jerusalem was organised as early as December 1977, when Begin came to Ismailia in Egypt. Sadat had also invited most other Arab leaders, but they, including the PLO leader, Arafat, refused — not unexpectedly. Even the moderate states of Jordan and Morocco declined the invitation to participate in a follow-up conference in Cairo in December 1977. On the other hand, Libya invited the Arab states to a meeting of protest at the same time in Tripoli, where what we could call the *rejectionist states*, Algeria, Libya, Syria and South Yemen, met and "denounced Sadat's initiative that amounted to great treason", it was said. They promoted a break with Egypt at this early stage, and this proposal was also endorsed by Arafat, who participated in this negative setting.

Those who had hoped for an easy continuation were soon disappointed, because the bilateral talks at Ismailia did not go well. The Egyptian leader tried to get a common Declaration of Principles on the Palestinian question passed by the two sides, but Begin declined, because the very mention of autonomy for the Palestinians was still anathema to him. For Sadat it was important to include some agreement on the Palestinian question in order to avoid the accusation from other Arab leaders that he was going it alone in his peace efforts and forgetting about the other nations in their group.

It was evident that only very few Arab leaders approved of Sadat's opening up of this new dialogue. The fact that they were taken completely aback by his

---

202 Shlaim tells us that Boutros Boutros-Ghali, who was the Egyptian Minister of State for Foreign Affairs then, has described "Begin´s stony personality that was apparent in every word he uttered and every movement he made [...] he was bellicose and struck me as a danger to peace. On the other hand, Weizmann [...] charmed us with his light-hearted style, and his presence eased the atmosphere. Dayan was more unpredictable", op.cit., p. 367.

initiative was worrisome to many Egyptians, but not so to the President. He had invested in the American card and now in the Israeli one as well, in order to create a new situation in which he set the agenda along with his American friends. But Sadat had utilised the change of government in Washington, where his "friend Henry" was no longer responsible for the US foreign policy, to make it crystal clear that he, *Sadat*, was the one who took the initiatives. *He*, as the President of old Egypt, was the central figure, since none of the other Arab leaders had similar influence or prestige, he found, whether or not they had oil. He was a proud man and often used the ancient culture of the Nile area as proof of the soundness — the historical right, so to speak — of the Egyptian government's policies.

Sadat thought of breaking off diplomatic relations with several Arab states, in order not to be the insulted party that had to withdraw his ambassadors on the demand of the others. Sadat understood protocol and prestige, so important to many in his part of the world, very well. But because the other nations felt they ought to be first to take such a dramatic step, Sadat's initiative to go to Israel led to a serious break-up in the united Arab front, in favour of which Sadat had spoken out so many times. At this stage the President had come to the conclusion that a bilateral settlement with Israel, backed by the USA, was to be preferred, instead of continuing the Arab-solidarity line upon which he and his predecessor previously had put so much emphasis.

When, in his proud way, Sadat considered breaking off diplomatic relations with many Arab countries,[203] he was of course aware of the threatening isolation of Egypt. If he did not act, he knew that the others would take the initiative. Before his trip to Jerusalem he had learnt that only three countries, Morocco, Oman and the Sudan, supported his idea. Whether he realised that the impact of his initiative would be as serious as it proved to be, we do not know. In today's Cairo, there is very little willingness to talk openly about the division in the Arab world following Sadat's Jerusalem opening and the Camp David Agreement, because it has been almost fully healed in the last decade or more.

Sadat pretended that the other Arab states needed Egypt more than it needed them. The President had especially hoped that the Jordanian King would, in his usual pro-Western way, see the good reasoning behind the Egyptian action. But the sometimes unpredictable King had had enough of Egyptian manoeuvrings and now let Sadat down, in favour of the Arab League agreement in Baghdad in November 1978 (see below). The most important reason, however, was that Jordan had a special relationship with Iraq, popular with the masses, which the King could not ignore at this stage.

---

203 In the biography of Sadat by David Hirst and Irene Beeson, London 1981, it is mentioned that he did break off these relations, whereas in today's Egypt this is denied.

Prime Minister Menachem Begin, President Anwar Sadat and Vicepresident Hosni Mubarak during the Cairo talks.

In Cairo public opinion was not free, and the media were hiding any serious form of dissent. "The degradation of the Egyptian press, once the most vigorous and respected in the Arab world, began under Nasser, but Sadat completed the process", write Hirst and Beeson.[204] It is certainly a fact that many, including members of Sadat's entourage, did not agree with his way of thinking. Even his Foreign Minister, Ismail Fahmi, was one of those who were opposed to the new opening and therefore resigned. But the President knew his people, he said, and passed a referendum with 99 percent approving his policies. We may rest assured that democratic rules were not highly respected in the counting of results. But, in his authoritarian system, Sadat could easily step forward as the victorious gentleman of peace, which was the same picture that the international media, except in the Arab world, now gave the public.

Today, many Egyptians say that there was indeed popular backing behind Sadat's initiative to start a peace process with Israel. Some officials in Cairo told me as recently as in March 2002 that probably up to 85% supported the new visionary policies of the President in 1977.

---

204 Op.cit., p. 278.

4. The Camp David Meeting and Peace Agreement

The Carter government was very eager to explore all possibilities of pursuing the initial opening between the two leaders in order to promote a peaceful settlement. As we remember, a peace conference had been arranged in Geneva in the aftermath of the 1973 war but had led only to a cease-fire between Egypt and Israel; a bilateral arrangement with Syria was also achieved with regard to the Golan, even if it took more time. The bilateral talks between Egypt and Israel after Sadat's visit to Jerusalem were only a beginning, and the final peace agreement was still something distant and had to be carefully worked out.

The US President, Jimmy Carter, therefore invited the two parties to serious talks in Camp David, and Washington eventually announced that the two leaders would join the US President in Camp David on 5 September 1978, "in order to seek a common framework for peace in the Middle East". It had not been easy to convene the opposing sides, and particularly Begin remained suspicious of the outcome of what was expected to become an American-imposed arrangement. Even many American observers admitted that it was a dangerous gamble for Carter, who was investing tremendous prestige in the project. His personal role in this venture was impressive and "his views proved to be partly correct and partly wrong" as qualified by Quandt in his book on the peace process.[205] "Partly right because he sensed that the best avenue for real progress lay in getting a detailed understanding between Begin and Sadat on Sinai [...] partly wrong in believing that the talks could be concluded quickly". In his conclusive remarks, Quandt somewhat euphemistically mentions that "[t]his remarkable adventure in summit diplomacy achieved more than its detractors had been willing to acknowledge".[206]

We may therefore conclude that the tenacity of the morally high-standing President of the USA succeeded, and the White House could triumphantly announce on 17 September 1978 that the parties had reached an agreement in Camp David. It was indeed a great surprise to the world, but the final agreements still had to be worked out and could only be signed after yet another round of talks and heavy pressure from President Carter.

One of the difficult questions had again been the *linkage* of the Palestinian problem. For the Israeli Prime Minister, Begin, it was important to exclude any commitment in this regard — for Sadat equally essential that the problem *should* be discussed with a view to the opening up of later negotiations. In this way he hoped to avoid Arab criticism that he had abandoned the Palestinians. He had not had any preliminary discussion on the subject with the PLO leader, probably because of a lack of time on both sides; in the case of Sadat, since he seems to

---

205 Op.cit., p. 199.
206 Ibid., p. 204.

have acted very suddenly, and in the case of the PLO leader, since he had his hands full inside war-torn Lebanon, in order merely to survive. But we have to stress that Arafat was, at any rate, very sceptical with regard to any accommodation of the enemy, the Israeli government. Sadat certainly did not avoid criticism, however, and his primary aim was of course the Egyptian national interest that — in the President's final consideration — concerned first and foremost his own country.

All the participants in Camp David were exhausted afterwards, especially Sadat, whose Foreign Minister, Ibrahim Kadil, had decided to resign (like several others) before the final result was announced. So Sadat was a solitary man but would not give up before the agreement was realised. He had perhaps less reason to be happy than the other two leaders, according to Sadat's main biographers. And he openly admitted that Carter had won, because the latter showed more persistent patience than the other two participants. But while the American President won political prestige, Begin and Sadat reached a peaceful solution to a long drawn-out conflict; for Egypt, there were the very tangible results that the Sinai (including its oil revenue) would return to Egypt after more than ten years, and that the control over and opening of the Suez Canal could finally be realised. The Camp David Agreement — which ought in fact to be written in the plural — stipulated that the final texts would have be signed within a three-month period, but here again, new hurdles arose.

Announcing *the battle of liberation is over*, the Egyptian President returned home to a hero's welcome. The volatile masses probably felt relieved, as their leader did, because of the positive result, but in many ways the triumph was orchestrated by the government press and by Sadat's collaborators. No free opinion polls to express the truth of public feelings were permitted. The reaction of the remaining Arab world was utterly negative in general, and the long-term isolation of Egypt would soon begin.

The Camp David Agreement involved a later signing ceremony, but it was no easy task to persuade the parties, especially Begin, to come to Washington. According to the agreed-upon document, the deadline was 17 December 1978, but the date passed without rapprochement. Begin had just a week before collected his share of the Nobel Peace Prize in Oslo, while Sadat had refused to go. The Egyptian press indicated that he alone should have had the prize, not sharing it with anyone, least of all Begin, who had not been very forthcoming. President Carter tried to persuade Begin to come to Washington for the final signing ceremony, but had to make many attempts in vain before finally attaining Israel's acceptance. In order to get it, Carter personally visited both Jerusalem and Cairo in March 1979, and only after a dramatic last minute intervention by the American delegation, (promising oil guarantees to the Israeli government to smooth the way) did Israel's Prime Minister agree to come to Washington and sign the treaty. The signing took place on a wintry afternoon, 26 March 1979, in front of the White House, where both leaders signed, as did Carter, in his capacity as witness. His government's and especially his own personal diplomatic efforts and skills had finally broken the ice and proven to be fruitful.

A new chapter in the Arab-Israeli relationship could begin after so many wars and almost permanent crisis up to that time. The peace treaty followed the main lines of the Security Council resolution 242 mentioned above, which established the formula *land for peace*. It thus stipulated that the Israeli forces must be withdrawn from the Sinai, and that almost the entire occupied zone should be returned.[207] Egypt must then recognise Israel and establish normal diplomatic relations with Jerusalem, as the first Arab power to do so — no small concession to the right-wing government in Israel.

As already pointed out, one of the odd aspects of the Camp David agreements was the fact that they tried to include an arrangement for the Palestinians without consulting the PLO leader, already recognised by most Arab nations as the sole representative of the Palestinians. But the agreements envisaged an autonomous status for the West Bank and Jerusalem, and if this did not work, Sadat promised that a solution to these issues could begin with Gaza, formerly under Egyptian administration.

Since these elements had never been discussed with the PLO leader, whom Begin had not met and would never consider meeting, it was to be expected that Arafat would reject any solution for which he had not taken part in preparation, and this was indeed the result. Even the Americans, who tried to persuade the Israelis to be more forthcoming, were disgusted by the negative reactions displayed by Begin concerning this issue. Zbigniew Brzezinski, President Carter's National Security Adviser, exclaimed: "It's like in South Africa. You are taking away the right to vote from the people".[208] He also used the word *Bantustan*[209] in referring to what the PLO was likely to get. As recently as 2002, a South African delegation declared that the conditions inside occupied Palestine were worse than those in former Bantustan.

---

207 Israel tried to obtain a small piece of land around Taba, but eventually lost the legal battle on the issue at the International Court at the Hague.
208 Morris, op.cit., pp. 444 - 477 gives a full picture.
209 The white *Apartheid* regime of South Africa carved out some areas with black populations, which were granted autonomy. But in reality the local governments in these Bantustans had very little say with regard to administrative measures and surely no influence in important matters such as foreign affairs, military or police matters.

B. The Isolation of Egypt

After the first meetings in September 1978 at Camp David, the Americans tried to *sell* the arrangements to the so-called moderate Arab nations. Secretary of State Cyrus Vance was sent to Jordan and Saudi Arabia in this matter. But it was already too late, because no self-respecting Arab state would accept the fact that Egypt had run its own course, forgetting all former engagements of solidarity dictating that no individual Arab nation have separate negotiations with Israel. When Sadat tried to claim that he was not negotiating on behalf of Egypt alone and referred to the inclusion of the Palestine areas in the agreements, his claim was not accepted as a relevant excuse by any of the neighbouring nations, least of all by Arafat and his people.

In order to lure Sadat away from the Israeli-American triangle, the other Arab nations held — for the first time ever — a summit without including Egypt. The venue was Baghdad in November 1978, and the meeting ended with an agreement comprising a mixture of promises and threats. With regard to the first category, those Arab states that were leading oil producers *promised* more oil money to the fast-growing population of Egypt. A high-level delegation was sent to Cairo to inform the Egyptian government that the oil states would provide assistance of $2.5 billion a year to Egypt, if it abandoned the Camp David agreements. But on the negative side, these Arab states also *threatened* Cairo with *excommunication* from the League if it continued along the wrong path, and this involved severe economic reprisals. Sadat became angry, probably even more so because he already had serious difficulties at home, under an apparently smooth surface. The President would not even receive the Arab emissaries and began insulting his former brothers of the Arab world that had often acted as paymasters. Sadat stressed that he could not be bought for oil money, emphasising that his neighbours were using *Jewish Banks* to control their money. He called many of the heads of state "dwarves" and bragged that the others could never isolate Egypt. He, on the other hand, had already isolated the Arab neighbours, he boasted.

Despite his pretending that no separate peace was concluded, since the agreements also included promises of a better future for the Palestinians, Sadat could not convince his Arab colleagues. His pretension was regarded mostly as window dressing, but, if we can trust modern Egyptian observers,[210] it was not. We have

---

210 I was told in Cairo, in March 2002, that seen in retrospect, Sadat´s move was rational because he did include the Palestinian question in the agreement, all the more so since Egypt always regards itself as the protector of the other Arab states´ interests, something Syria has in common with Egypt. This feeling is, in my view, partly rhetoric, partly true.

therefore to conclude that the division in the Arab world was a fact of life from then on, and it was going to have severe consequences for Egypt over the coming years. Those in Israel who were constantly looking for splits in the Arab World could now take some comfort from this development.

Under these circumstances, Sadat hoped that the US government would compensate the lost aid and increase its assistance to the Egyptian government and people, which did also occur, to a great extent. Likewise, the EU countries and others provided large amounts of aid, so much, in fact, that in the early nineties, Egypt received more than all other African countries combined, according to what the World Bank representative in Cairo at the time told me. As soon as the other Arab nations realised that Sadat would not accept their conditions for a continuation and increase in the aid to Cairo, they reassembled in Baghdad and decided to impose the following severe measures:

Diplomatic relations with Cairo were to be severed, Egypt was expelled from the *Arab League*, banned from other common Arab institutions and excluded from trade. The worst for Egypt was that money promised for the purchase of arms would no longer be forthcoming. In order to prove that he at least had his own people behind him, Sadat again arranged a referendum in April 1979, which gave him more than (the usual) 99 % backing, but hardly more than 10 % of all registered voters participated.

In order to fulfil his promises to the Palestinians, the Egyptian President did at a later stage enter into negotiations with the Israelis on their behalf, but against the wishes of their long-standing leader, Arafat; thus, almost no one took these talks seriously. Even as an exercise in public relations it was eventually futile, convincing no one, probably not even the President himself.

In July 1980, the *Knesset* passed a bill as part of the Fundamental Law, confirming the final inclusion of Jerusalem (both Eastern and Western parts and a large surrounding area) into Israel, and this provoked an outcry in the Arab world. But it did not dissuade Sadat from continuing negotiations with the Israelis on the status of Palestine and other questions.

Begin and Sadat met many times, the eleventh and last one in August 1981, to discuss the final stage withdrawals of Israeli forces from the Sinai. But even to moderate Egyptians, the President had now gone too far in humiliating himself and his nation, at a time when most Arabs and their leaders were disgusted by the hard-line Israeli policy, especially in and around Jerusalem. Did Sadat provoke the signing of his death warrant on this occasion? We do not know, but it may have been the last straw in Sadat's long line of what was regarded by traditional Arabs as insulting procedures and policies.

In Washington there was a new President from early 1981, Ronald Reagan, and Sadat saw Carter's disappearance from the political scene as a great loss. The former President had envisaged a new Camp David meeting pending his re-election. Reagan, on the other hand, showed no particular interest in the region when he took over in Washington.

Sadat seemed convinced that only an even closer collaboration with the Americans and Israelis would compensate for the loss of his former Arab friends. At the end of 1979, the Egyptian President said in a casual way that he was ready to grant the Americans military facilities in Egypt, something new in this region, where the Soviets had been very active until only a few years before. He even talked of joining NATO.[211] The new American President Reagan's Secretary of State, General Haig, found Sadat most accommodating when he visited Cairo in April 1981. "We agreed on everything", stressed Sadat, only a few months before his assassination, which occurred in October 1981. Sadat certainly became a victim of his own brave policies, viewed with contempt by more narrow-minded fundamentalists and Pan-Arabists, but these circles were already a factor of decreasing importance in Arab politics. Sadat probably counted on a return to the Arab fold within a short period.

The Sadat biographers mentioned above characterise Western policies and the Egyptian President Sadat in very sarcastic terms at the end of their controversial, but interesting, book, in this way: "The infatuation for Sadat therefore represented the crossing of yet another threshold of irrationality — an irrationality which, because it is the outgrowth of its love-affair with Israel, has forever caused the West to pursue Middle East policies which run counter to its own interests".

Although this statement is in accordance with the views expressed by other sarcastic observers such as the above-mentioned Georges Corm,[212] I prefer to disagree with its one-sided pro-Arab and somewhat narrow-minded angle, despite its reference to the irrationality of Sadat and the West. And although one can perhaps understand the feelings behind such views, they do not seem correct in the long-term historical perspective, as I see it.

A more balanced view of Sadat emerges from Fouad Ajami's *The Arab Predicament*,[213] in which it is stated that "Sadat had never excited a Pan-Arab audience; he had never been a hero, and if he lacked the hero's status, he also lacked the hero's reputation and was free from the chains that tie heroes to their great deeds [...]. There was perhaps in Sadat's Egyptianness a desire to move from Nasser's shadow into a smaller area". The book emphasises at the same time that "Egypt's

---

211 Similar Israeli thoughts have been referred to above.
212 See his op.cit. p. 490, in which he states about Sadat: "L'Occident garde du president Sadate l'image d'un homme de la paix exceptionnel, mais isolé au milieu de ses pairs Arabes. Il n'a évidemment pas pris la peine de regarder ce qu'il y a d'explosif dans cette "paix" qui n'est pas celle des braves".
213 Cambridge, 1981.

centrality in the Arab world was natural and inevitable".[214] Elsewhere the same writer states that "Sadat was able to move all the way from the first disengagement agreement in early 1974 [...] to the journey to Jerusalem [...] then to the exchange of ambassadors with Israel (in what can be seen) as an instrument of Egyptian history [...]. Other Arabs may not agree, but there are grounds for arguing that Sadat may have been [...] an instrument of Arab history as well".[215]

---

214 Ibid., p. 94 and p. 80. Somewhat illogically the same author, who has just mentioned Sadat´s freedom from the chains that bind heroes to their great deeds, later emphasises that "the October War took on an almost mythical dimension. Sadat was called upon to make good on his promise of October - his new order of peace and prosperity. *This dictated his policies. He had become a captive of his own promises*" [my emphasis]. Ibid., p. 100.
215 Ibid., p. 107.

XI. Slow Arab recognition of Israel

1. Arab League Summits

We have focused on the important events in Egypt, Jordan and Lebanon in the 1970s that had a great impact on the regional pattern of conflict but which did not bring about much change in the situation within the occupied territories. Although the above-mentioned Arab summit in November 1978 had rejected the understanding reached by Egypt and Israel leading to the peace treaty in 1979, this did not mean that all the Arab countries continued to oppose an arrangement with the enemy; if not yet a final agreement, at least some accommodation of Israel could be reached.

Many surely began to realise that for a long time to come, the Israelis had no intention of obliging the Arabs in general or of granting the PLO, in particular, autonomy, not to mention independence. In the late seventies and eighties, with the exception of one brief period, Israel had right-wing governments, and for these (under Begin and Shamir) no compromise on an autonomous Palestinian unit was likely. By Israeli law, it remained forbidden for a long time to have official contact with the PLO or other Palestinian organisations. The Arab governments had to take this into account.

Sadat had certainly calculated that eventually most of the Arab states, even some of the more radical regimes, would understand, little by little, that the wheel of history was turning and that the *fait accompli* of the peace treaty could not be removed from the political pattern of the Middle East. Saudi Arabia was an influential partner with close links with the West, just like the Hashemite Kingdom of Jordan; the regime of Hafez Assad in Syria was busy with internal difficulties in the early eighties and with the problem of Lebanon. Iraq was engaged from 1980 to 1988 in a violent war with Iran that had split the Arab world, with Syria supporting Iran against the general trend, which made it natural for the Arab states to support Iraq rather than Iran, since only the former is an Arab country. Lebanon was in the middle of its dramatic civil war and suffered, as we remember, Israeli onslaughts in 1978 and 1982 – 83.

The Crown Prince of Saudi Arabia, later King Fahd, proposed a peace plan at the Arab League Summit in Fez in November 1981, which surprisingly involved a *de facto recognition* of Israel, but the meeting did not last more than a few hours before it was suspended. The following year (1982), however, a new summit took place — also in Fez — that recognised a similar plan presented by Fahd, who was now the Saudi King. It involved a peace plan on the same lines as the previous one and based itself on the UN resolution 242, granting *land for peace*. It also spoke of Palestinian self-determination under the PLO, which would result in a Palestinian state in the occupied territories (West Bank and Gaza), and of the necessity of dismantling the Jewish settlements in these areas.

This decision by the Arab League, which, however, was not backed by all member states,[216] constituted a very important step forward in the history of the conflict, because it involved an indirect recognition of the fact that Israel had been established in the area as a *fait accompli* and could therefore not be revoked. This was exactly the same understanding that had moved Sadat to make his peace arrangement with Israel.

Some years passed before the Arab League went even further in November 1987 and took the important decision to accept the restoration of diplomatic relations with Egypt by individual member states. The League was finally bowing to the *fait accompli* of the peace treaty between Israel and Egypt signed almost a decade earlier, but the decision was still frustrating to those Arabs who would not accept the unjust situation implied by the continuous occupation of the West Bank and Gaza. Despite this disagreement, the League also indirectly approved the idea that Egypt should no longer remain isolated in the Arab world.

2. Abortive American Peace Proposals

On several occasions the USA took peace initiatives that were never carried out. One of them, prepared under Ronald Reagan, was presented by the President on 1 September 1982. The American government was angered by the confusing situation and the losses in Lebanon during the Israeli occupation, and its plan involved self-government for the Palestinians in the West Bank and Gaza, in association with Jordan. Despite this link with the pro-Western kingdom, the Israeli government rejected the Reagan Plan, which also involved a prohibition of expanded Israeli settlements in the occupied territories.

A good deal later, in March 1988, Secretary of State George Schultz presented another plan that tried to link the Middle East conflict with the Reagan-Gorbachev summit, which was to take place at the end of the year. But King Hussein would

---

216 The most radical states, Iraq and Libya, were not participating.

not accept this plan because he suspected that Prime Minister Shamir, whom he disliked, and who — after some hesitation — had accepted the plan, would implement only some of its initial parts and never relinquish an inch of territory. Shamir wrote in his memoirs that he was weary of all the peace plans presented,[217] but that was of course due to the fact that he — like Begin before him — would not give up the *status quo* after the 1967 conquest, and would certainly not recognise the PLO, let alone grant it any influence at all. The Israeli governments also continued to expand settlements in the occupied areas, regardless of Washington's admonishments.

When George Bush became President of the USA in early 1989, a more difficult relationship developed between Jerusalem and Washington. The new Secretary of State, James Baker, criticised indirectly, but clearly, Shamir's policy in the occupied territories. He said, among other things that "[i]t is time for Israel to lay aside, once and for all, the unrealistic vision of a Greater Israel. Its interests in the West Bank and Gaza — security and otherwise — can (only) be accommodated in a settlement based on resolution 242".[218] These unusually blunt words certainly did not please the Israeli leadership, but as so often before, they were not backed by pressure from Washington that was strong enough to change the Israeli way of thinking. This has been an almost permanent aspect of the relationship between Washington and Israel since the 1970s.

Yitzhak Rabin was Minister of Defence in the Shamir/Peres government in the late 1980s, and finally realised that a new approach was required in the treatment of the Palestinians. He therefore presented a plan which he eventually managed get approved by the Prime Minister. It involved the calling of elections in the occupied territories, thereby setting aside the PLO, in order to find new leaders whom Israel could trust. All terrorist acts should cease before the elections, but autonomy would be granted in exchange for the stopping of the *intifada*, (see below) that had begun in late 1987. This plan was presented to Secretary of State James Baker in Washington in May 1989. Baker was cautiously sympathetic, but insisted on the *land for peace* formula and even angered the government in Jerusalem with his continued blunt talk, as mentioned above. Generally speaking, both George Bush and his Secretary of State were not as easily convinced of the need always to support Israel as their predecessors, especially Reagan, had been. Bush felt that Reagan's almost unconditional support of Israel's provocative or aggressive policies, for instance in Lebanon, had not helped the new President to get much political support from the American Jews.

The Palestinians had no wish to give up their general support for the PLO, which was one of the main elements of the Rabin Plan, and the organisation could take comfort in the fact that it was again backed more decisively by the other Arab

---

217 Here quoted from Shlaim, op.cit., p. 450.
218 Quandt, op.cit., p. 296.

states after the breakout of the *intifada*. When energetic opposition from the Shamir government's own hard-liners, such as Sharon, emerged, the Prime Minister gave up Rabin's plan, which he had previously endorsed, and which thus died an inglorious death like so many other plans before.

3. The First *Intifada*

In December 1987 the first *intifada* (revolt, or *shaking off*, in Arabic) broke out, and Shlaim calls this *the Palestinian War of Independence*.[219] It came as a surprise to almost everyone because it was a spontaneous revolt, but it was nurtured by the many humiliations and practical difficulties that the Palestinians had long experienced. The general feeling of hopelessness had increased in Palestinian political circles after the failure of the secret *London Agreement*. This understanding had been reached during secret meetings in London between Simon Peres and King Hussein in early 1987, but never materialised.[220] "The *intifada* was not an armed rebellion but a massive, persistent campaign of civil resistance, with strikes and commercial shutdowns, accompanied by violent (though unarmed) demonstrations against the occupying forces", writes Benny Morris.[221] The first spark was a traffic incident, in which an Israeli truck driver accidentally killed four Gaza (Arab) residents. Morris also tells us that "Israelis liked to believe, and tell the world, that they were running an *enlightened* or *benign* occupation, qualitatively different from other military occupations the world has seen. The truth was radically different. Like all occupations, Israel's was founded on brute force, repression and fear, collaboration and treachery, beatings and torture […]".[222] The PLO had lost substantial support after two decades of struggle against the occupation, which had not, it was felt, led to any results in the occupied territories. During the latest Arab summit in November 1987, the weakness of the PLO had been exposed, since the meeting focused mostly on the Iran-Iraq war and almost totally ignored the Palestinian problem.

The PLO leadership was now quick to exploit this strong and unusually popular movement, one of whose offspring was the establishment of the radical Palestinian Liberation movement, *Hamas*.

---

219 Op.cit., p. 450.
220 Birgitte Rahbek, in her already mentioned book *En Stat for enhver Pris* recalls many of the reasons that motivated the Palestinians´ feeling of frustration, see pp. 249 - 252. She notes that Rabin, as Defence Minister, ordered the beating of prisoners that amounted to obvious torture and shocked the world.
221 Op.cit., p. 561.
222 Ibid., p. 341.

As Defence Minister responsible for the occupied territories, Rabin took surprisingly harsh measures against the uprising, and this only made the frustrations and anger worse among the downtrodden population. He was probably closer to the Prime Minister (Shamir) in this matter than Peres, who understood the need for further negotiations, despite the failure of the above-mentioned London Agreement, which Shamir had not wanted to accept. Israel again became the target of severe international criticism, from the UN, too, because of brutal and unnecessary killings of (often) unarmed insurgents, and it was the worst exposure of Israel since the invasion in Lebanon. The David-Goliath syndrome that Israel originally tried to exploit could now be reversed, because it was evident to all international observers, including those of the press, that most of those suffering were the Palestinians, often armed with nothing but stones, and living in dreadful surroundings with little hope for a better future. The death rate was several times higher for Palestinians than for Israelis, and has remained so over the years, including during the second *intifada*.

Impressed by the *intifada*, the Arab League called a special meeting in Algiers in June 1988, which confirmed the special role of the PLO and pledged support for the *intifada*.

Not only Israel suffered a loss of prestige because of the uprising; King Hussein's Jordan also felt it necessary to revise the status of the occupied territories that had up to that time formally been under Jordanian administration. Hussein severed those administrative and legal ties in July 1988, and admitted that it was due to the *intifada*. It was the end of the popular idea in Israel (and in the USA) that one could negotiate the future of the West Bank with the moderate King, and many Israelis, not least Peres, had invested much work in that scheme.

4. PLO's Recognition of Israel

The PLO wanted to exploit the success of the *intifada* and therefore called a meeting in Algiers in mid-November 1988, where the Palestinian National Council took a decisive step: It was agreed that the *State of Palestine* should be established as an independent country. But the hope of acquiring the whole of old Palestine was now abandoned, because the decision mentioned Palestinian self-determination *in co-existence with Israel*. It was therefore implied that the PLO now recognised the legitimacy of Israel. Arafat repeated these new signals in his speech to the UN in December 1988, which in the light of history must be seen as a major step forward for Israel. One would have thought that this very important new step in the Israeli-Palestinian conflict would have been received with open arms by the Jews, but the right-wing Israeli government responded negatively. Prime Minister Shamir called the Palestinian decision "a propaganda exercise", because he wanted to remain sceptical towards the Arabs. Even the Labour ministers retained their sceptical attitude towards the PLO at this stage, despite the change in the Organisation's way of thinking.[223]

While Foreign Minister Peres was always eager to find a political solution, Shamir was strongly convinced of the necessity of maintaining the *status quo* in the occupied territories. Eventually also Rabin, who had often disagreed with Peres, found out that a new tack was necessary, and the two competing Labour leaders now agreed more and more on the necessity of new political ideas. Rabin was finally beginning to realise that the Jordanian side could no longer be helpful in finding a solution with the Palestinians. We have already mentioned Rabin's idea of calling for elections in the occupied territories, which never materialised because of political opposition from many sides.

The final peace effort in this period with regard to Israel and the PLO was a proposal put forward by the Egyptian President in September 1989; the plan never materialised, however, because of Shamir's resistance to sitting at the same table as the PLO, which was also involved in this plan.

In 1990 the Labour members left the Cabinet after Peres' serious disagreement with Shamir, who therefore became more powerful, leading a government of right-wing parties alone. He had already been in power for a long time when the *intifada* broke out in December 1987, which eventually led to the above-mentioned indirect recognition of Israel by the Palestinians in 1988, probably due to their newly won self confidence.

---

223 Recently, a liberal mind like Shlomo Ben-Ami, Foreign Minister under Barak, has expressed doubts as to whether the PLO leader, Arafat, had really recognised the existence of Israel; see his above mentioned book, *What is the Future of Israel (Cual es el futuro de Israel)*, p. 84.

XII. THE MADRID PEACE CONFERENCE

As will be recalled, this study does not intend to go into historical detail regarding countries other than Israel and its direct Arab neighbours. Thus the Iraq-Iran conflict lies outside the scope of this book, as does the Gulf Conflict in 1990 – 91 during and after the invasion of Kuwait, as well as the very recent war in Iraq. But the (first) Gulf War had of course immense repercussions in Israel and on the conflict we are studying, especially because Israel became the direct target of Iraqi attacks in early 1991 during the American-led joint Arab-Western war, which aimed at expelling the Iraqi forces from Kuwait. This conflict between the West and Iraq under Saddam Hussein is still unsolved and even after the American occupation or "liberation of Iraq", as President Bush terms it, which led to the capture of Saddam in late 2003, Saddam's evil spirit seems to influence Iraq. But in addition to mentioning the fact that dangerous Scud missiles were directed against Israel by Iraq (fortunately without causing too much damage) in early 1991 and the fact that Israel did not retaliate and intervene in the war due to heavy American pressure (in order to avoid an unnecessary escalation of it), we have to stress here the importance of the new political pattern that was the result of the Gulf War.

Before the first war ended, Saddam Hussein had suggested that the Kuwait and Middle East conflicts be solved in accordance with the relevant UN resolutions, thereby implying the necessity of a withdrawal from occupied territories, not only by the Baghdad forces from Kuwait, but also by the IDF from all occupied Arab territories. Saddam Hussein was not able to *sell* this idea —a logical formula, by appearances — because he had managed to make almost all of the Arab states turn away from him. Several, such as Egypt, Saudi Arabia and Syria, to mention only the largest countries, had taken part in the war against Baghdad. They were all angered by Saddam's brutal invasion of Kuwait, which could not be compared to the Israeli occupation of Arab land that was due to wars more or less imposed on Israel.

The new pattern of world politics was due to the fact that the USSR had almost surrendered as a superpower and was soon going to be replaced by a much weaker Russia and the other, former Soviet states. The USA was now the world leader without rival and its success in the brief Gulf War underscored this fact. President George Bush talked of a *new world order*, which we — in retrospect — may regard as too pretentious, especially seen from our angle in this new millennium, more than ten years later. Because of the Gulf War, the Arab world had been in turmoil and split not only for or against Saddam Hussein, but also over some other problems. One contributing factor was the pro-Iraqi position of the kingdom of Jordan, or at least its different policies, opposed to the Arab-Western alliance against Baghdad, which we have mentioned above. While Amman could normally be counted among the more moderate regimes as seen from our Western perspective, its population was, generally speaking, pro-Iraqi for various reasons, and the King did not dare go against the mood of his people. The same could be said of the PLO, whose members were generally pro-Iraqi, because the Baghdad regime, in its strong anti-Israel sentiment, often supported Palestinian organisations, including terrorist ones. During the war, Arafat even declared himself openly against the allied military effort to throw the Iraqi forces out of occupied Kuwait; this was a position that soon reduced the influence of the PLO inside the Arab world and among its other sympathisers and also cost the Organisation financial support from the richer Arab nations such as Kuwait and Saudi Arabia. The same can be said, though to a lesser degree, of the Jordanian kingdom.

President Bush and James Baker, his Secretary of State, thought that the time was ripe for improvements in the Middle East and that the meeting of the former enemies, in the Spanish capital would signal to the world that time had come for a solution, however difficult it might appear. Bush wanted a solution to the Middle East problem because it had taken up too much of Washington's time, creating problems with the US-Arab relationship and with the Jewish lobby in the United States. He therefore suggested a peace conference, together with the USSR and other concerned states, such as those of the area and the EU. Arab countries that had participated in the anti-Iraq alliance — especially Syria, which was about to lose the support from its long time protector, the USSR — realised that they had better follow the proposals of the sole superpower. Jordan was also eager to help the Americans forget its lack of co-operation, which had angered Washington during the Gulf War.

An agreement was reached on Madrid as the meeting place, and although this conference gave some impetus to progress in the Middle East, it was not much to speak of, again considered in hindsight. This time it was the Jerusalem government led by Shamir, rather than the Arab states, which created a problem. Bush employed a great deal of persuasion and even some arm-twisting to get Shamir to the conference table. We know that the intentions of the Israeli Prime Minister, an angry hawk, were those of obstructing, not of collaborating with Washington or showing any goodwill with regard to a peace settlement.[224] Shamir would not accept a separate Palestinian delegation, but only a common Jordanian-Palestinian one. Eventually the two delegations acted on an individual basis and this must be seen as a limited, but important, diplomatic victory for the PLO.

The conference was held in late October 1991 in the Spanish capital, under the joint chairmanship of George Bush and, in his eleventh hour, Mikhail Gorbachev, who would soon disappear from the scene of world politics. There was participation from the following Arab countries: Lebanon, Syria and a combined Jordanian-Palestinian delegation. Israel was there, of course, on the other side of the table, and there were the two co-sponsors, the superpower(s), the EU and several other countries.

An agreement was reached fairly soon to begin peace negotiations, and at the same time it was also decided that these should follow both bilateral and multilateral paths. With regard to the latter, the plan was that questions of common interest should be negotiated, but the Syrians and the Lebanese objected to starting such negotiations until there was progress in the bilateral paths.

Notwithstanding Shamir's indirect boycott of the talks, and in spite of the reservations we may have today, the Madrid result was the most important first step towards a genuine, comprehensive and just peace arrangement for the area that had ever seen the light of day.

It took time for positive negotiations to begin; they had to wait until a new and more understanding leadership was in place in Israel under Rabin's second government, from June 1992. It was certainly not easy for the parties to initiate negotiations after so many years of bitterness and fighting, punctuated by some attempts at rapprochement. One would have expected that the most difficult country to convince would be Syria, but President Hafez Assad spoke of the need for a "peace of the brave" (a phrase borrowed from President de Gaulle-after the Algeria War), and his Foreign Minister talked of "total peace for total withdrawal". With its fairly large-scale participation in the allied war effort against Iraq, Syria could feel that it had come in from the cold. The Lebanese were surely sceptical for various reasons, especially because of their complicated situation haunted by memories of the brutal Israeli occupation in 1982 – 83, which was still felt in large areas of their country. But having just concluded their long civil war, they were weak and had to follow the in the path of the Syrians, their new masters with regard to foreign politics. The long-time former (and later) Prime Minister, Selim Hoss, directly advised against Lebanese participation. The Palestinians, who had to work within

---

224 It makes sad reading to see to what extent Shamir, by his own admission in his memoirs, did not invest any trust in the negotiations with the Arab side. His instructions to his aides were also devoid of anything that could help the peace process. See Shlaim, op.cit., pp. 492 – 501.

the Jordanian delegation, were happy because it was the first time they could act on the international scene almost on a par with the Israelis. No one knew yet that they were not far from the direct negotiations with the Israelis leading to the *Oslo Accord*, and the same was the case for the Jordanians. Eventually each of these countries or entities negotiated individually. The improving atmosphere in the area resulting from the Madrid meeting certainly had its positive effects.

Shlaim writes that "the Madrid peace conference was carefully stage-managed by the Americans, with James Baker acting as the chief puppeteer. It was he and his aides, who came to be known as the peace processors […] and stipulated that the basis for the negotiations would be SC resolutions 242 and 338 and the principle of exchanging territory for peace".[225] Shlaim also stresses the degree to which the Israeli Prime Minister was an obstacle to progress in Madrid, and that this fact explains the intervention of Farouk Shaara (the Foreign Minister of Syria); in his address to the conference, Shaara alluded to the fact that Prime Minister Shamir had assassinated the UN representative, Bernadotte, in 1948: "**Here stands the man who killed a peace mediator**", said Shaara. When describing the negative attitudes of Shamir, Shlaim compares him to the former Bourbon Kings of France who "had neither learnt nor forgotten anything".[226]

The Madrid meeting was soon followed by five rounds of bilateral talks in Washington under American supervision. Not unexpectedly did they almost become abortive because of the Shamir government's obstructive policy, and soon the US election campaign was taking up most of the attention of the Washington administration.

Only two negotiation rounds, which were carried out in secret to begin with, led to positive results. They will be dealt with separately because of their importance in the overall conflict pattern: first, the Oslo Process, begun in late 1992 and early 1993, and secondly, the bilateral talks between Israel and Jordan in 1994 leading to a peace treaty.

---

225 Op.cit., p. 487.
226 Ibid., p. 488 and p. 490.

XIII. Oslo talks and agreements

Only a few years after the Israeli governments under Begin and Shamir had denounced any thought of negotiations with the PLO or other representatives of the Palestinians in the West Bank, unofficial and secret talks began near Oslo in early 1993, in order to find a solution. There had already been an earlier contact in London to prepare the ground for these secret negotiations, and they were of course influenced by the generally improved atmosphere in the region after the Gulf War and the Madrid Conference. The Israeli government was not directly involved initially but eventually joined the talks under the Norwegian umbrella. Two respected Israeli academics, Dr. Yair Hirschfeld and Dr. Ron Pundak, encouraged by Peres' assistant, Yossi Beilin, took the initiative to begin these contacts with the PLO, and Arafat had already expressed his eagerness to meet secretly with Israeli officials. At first, preliminary contact with the Danish government had been attempted through the Danish Ambassador in Tel Aviv, but the Danish Foreign Minister at the time, Uffe Ellemann-Jensen, did not want to be involved in this, because he was going to take over the presidency of the EU as of early January 1993.[227]

The two academics mentioned above were forming the first Israeli delegation, but neither the Israeli Foreign Minister, Simon Peres, nor Prime Minister Rabin, was duly informed from the beginning. Beilin, however, informed Peres of the attempt at contact in the first week of February, and the Foreign Minister then informed Rabin; neither of them seemed very enthusiastic at the beginning, remaining sceptical of Arafat and his organisation. The role of the Nordic country was to guard the negotiators from any curious international press, in its remote

---

227 I have this comment from this former Danish Ambassador to Israel, through whom the first contacts were established in November 1992. The later Louisiana process, in which Dr. Ron Pundak´s father, Herbert Pundik, was (and is) very active, may be said to derive from this first effort in the direction of Danish involvement in the peace process. It may confuse some of my readers that father and son have different spelling of their names. But Pundik is the old Russian/Danish version; Pundak the Hebrew one.

mountains.[228] The Norwegian Foreign Minister, Johan J. Holst, had approved the contacts taking place in a secret place in the mountains, and the social scientist, Roed Larsen, and others were facilitators during the meetings, in which Abu Ala was one of the leading PLO negotiators, reporting directly to Arafat. For the PLO leader it was not easy to convince his colleagues in the fight for independence that these talks were necessary at all; according to Morris, he had to use all his political skills fully to overcome his internal opposition. Many Palestinians regarded the agreement as a sell-out.[229]

The Norwegians succeeded in providing enough protection and also allowing a degree of confidence to be established between the parties, who of course were quite sceptical about each other to start with.[230]

As already stated, the Israeli Prime Minister was noncommittal at the beginning, but later saw his interest in proceeding with these useful contacts. He also prepared the Jewish public when he stated in August 1993 that in the long run, recognition of the PLO would be unavoidable.

In the same month, August 1993, Peres, who had been following the latest rounds of talks in detail, *initialled* the Accord at a secret session in Oslo, on 20 August. He then flew on to the USA together with the Norwegian Foreign Minister, J.J. Holst, and they both informed the US Secretary of State, Warren Christopher, of the positive results. The latter was surprised of the scope of the accord, but agreed to support it publicly in order to assist the Israeli government when it had to obtain the approval from the Knesset. At the end of the month, Rabin introduced the Accord to his Cabinet, where the atmosphere was generally positive.

These secret talks led to what was called a "Declaration of Principles on Interim Self Government" that was signed in Washington soon afterwards, on 13 September 1993. The role of the superpower had not been instrumental, either in creating the Oslo venue or in promoting the promising result, but the US government wanted to be associated with this positive progress. The two main parties concerned were of course eager to have the endorsement of the superpower, especially from President Bill Clinton personally, all the more because the positive result was very much in line with what had been aimed at during the Madrid Meeting. Clinton was eager to show his youthful energy (especially compared with that of his predecessors) in foreign affairs.

The Norwegians had to accept that their role as a small nation would not allow them to implement the results, and that it would be useful if a larger power — especially *the* superpower – could give it its blessing. For Israel it was of course essential

---

228 Morris writes that "the Norwegians played an important role in mediating, bridging, and smoothing ruffled feathers". Op.cit., p. 620.
229 Ibid., p. 621.
230 Confirmed to me by Ron Pundak in a conversation in Tel Aviv in late March 2002.

to have the backing of its *big brother* in the future, but nobody could guarantee a final, positive result; the same may be said for the Palestinians. With the arrival in power of Bill Clinton, the Israelis would soon feel that there was more understanding for their views than under the Bush administration. This does not mean that the new US administration was biased in favour of the Jewish side, because Clinton surely wanted to be as objective in the matter as an American president can. That was probably also the feeling Arafat had during the difficult talks.

The picture of the President shaking hands with the two old opponents, Yassir Arafat and Yitzhak Rabin, in front of the White House became the focus of attention for quite some time, just as the photo of Sadat speaking to the Knesset in Jerusalem 16 years earlier and of the Egyptian President signing the peace treaty with Prime Minister Begin in the year 1979; all will remain as the best symbols of the peace process.[231]

What was achieved in Oslo? Briefly, we may emphasise that the arrangements entailed the recognition of one party by the other, that is, that Israel recognised the role of the PLO as representing the Palestinians and that the Organisation as such recognised the State of Israel. This of course was a very essential step forward, giving hope of a much better future for both of these entities, who had fought against each other right from the establishment of Israel, and even long before that.

It was further agreed that Israel would accept progressive expansion of the autonomous areas of the PLO in the West Bank. There was still no question of an official Israeli recognition of a sovereign state, Palestine, but the idea was in the air. It was also agreed that the transition period would last a maximum of five years, and that the area of Gaza should be included under the coming Palestinian Authority (PA) administration. The UN resolutions 242 and 338 were mentioned and as such recognised by Israel. Jerusalem, surely the most difficult problem to solve, should be left to the final stage negotiations.

The new autonomous Palestinian Authority (or government) could establish its control over the Gaza and Jericho areas and would be responsible for schools, culture, health, tourism and welfare, plus taxes, among other issues (40 in all). The PA administration was granted permission to establish its own police force and the right to hold free elections. It was not stated but implied that the PLO leader, Arafat, would also be in command of the autonomous body. The original Declaration of Principles stipulated that the final agreement should be implemented within five years of the withdrawal of Israeli forces, i.e. in 1998.

As mentioned, it was indeed a historic event that the two national forces competing for sovereignty over the Holy Land, the Jewish/Zionist and the Palestinian/Arab ones, now agreed on a compromise, granting both a share in the old British

---

231 We have already mentioned above (footnote 212) the negative comment by the always critical Georges Corm.

Israeli Prime Minister Yitzhak Rabin, President of the United States Bill Clinton and PLO chairman Yassir Arafat in Washington 1993.

mandate of Palestine. But the Palestinian side now got a much smaller part than what it could have obtained through the UN decision on partition in 1948, if it had not rejected the plan at the outset. In the meantime, Israel had gained a powerful position as the strongest military nation in the region and was still keeping — and intended to go on keeping — a good deal of influence or power over the West Bank and Gaza, which the later developments have so sadly confirmed. It was therefore not an agreement between two equal partners — far from it — but a compromise that granted some form of autonomy to the weaker part, the Palestinian leader and his PLO.

Probably because of this, the new agreement was not met with much sympathy by other Arab states, especially not by neighbouring Syria. The Damascus government found that the Accord went against the agreed lines of solidarity among the Arab states, dictating that no one should ever try to go alone in the direction of peace. This common aim implied that the various states should co-ordinate possible negotiations in order to obtain a comprehensive peace arrangement. It was in keeping with the previous condemnation of the Egyptian leader, Anwar Sadat, when he had decided to enter into a peace agreement with Israel. Syria was now one of the lone defenders of the old Pan-Arab principles.

The agreed Declaration of Principles meant that the Palestianians' situation was now separate from the Jordanians. The latter soon had their own plans ready and these were to materialise the following year.

In the following section we shall look into what subsequently happened between Jordan and Israel. It seems relevant to recall here that King Hussein had in 1988 already given up his responsibility for the administration of the West Bank, a step that allowed the PLO to negotiate the agreement with the Israelis.

The *intifada* that had begun in December 1987 was of course a sign of the Palestinians' deep distrust of the Israelis, but also gave them more self-confidence than ever. One may here recall the old saying, "you have to earn your own freedom and independence". The King's relinquishing of his share of responsibility — even if it had carried little weight after the 1967 Israeli conquest of the West Bank — probably prompted the feelings of frustration among the population of the occupied territories, Gaza and the West Bank. But the *intifada*, which the PLO leadership endorsed soon after it began, also strengthened the latter in its continuous fight for approval by the Israeli governments. We have already mentioned that Shlaim calls this fight the *Palestinian War of Independence*; and on that fair basis we may say that the seeds of recognition by Israel of a Palestinian national feeling had been planted in late December 1987 by this genuine fight for independence by the Palestinian youth. The PLO, on its part, had implicitly recognised Israel, as mentioned above, in November 1988, fairly soon after the outbreak of the *intifada*, but this was arrogantly ignored by the right-wing government then in power in Jerusalem.[232]

The Declaration of Principles was to be followed by more precise agreements, as we know. The next step in this direction was the *Cairo Agreement* of 4 May 1994 on Gaza and Jericho, which laid down guidelines for the security of these areas and for the withdrawal of Israeli forces.

The Gaza and the West Bank were to be divided into three zones: A, B and C. The new authority or government, the PA, would have almost full control over the heavily populated A zones, including the larger urban areas such as Hebron, Jericho, Nablus and Ramallah and nearly the whole of Gaza, but little or no control over B and C. The withdrawal of Israeli forces was to take place in accordance with a special agreement to be found later, but this agreement has been difficult to reach or implement over the last many years.

After a three-day debate, the Knesset approved the Oslo Agreement in a close confrontation between the liberal Labour side and the negative Likud, and the result was 61 in favour and 50 against, with nine abstentions. It is strange to record

---

232 Friedman, in his op.cit., p. 381, writes that "only through the Intifada, did the West Bankers and the Gazans really emerge as a nation in the fullest sense".

that the later Labour Prime Minister, Ehud Barak, warned against the acceptance of the Accord in his capacity of Chief of Staff.

Finally, the Oslo II Agreement, which stipulated the conditions pertaining to the continuation of the Israeli occupation and the withdrawal of forces, and the limited autonomy for the Palestinians, was signed in Washington in September 1995.

The five-year period that was set for the transition did not suffice, and at the time of writing an agreement seems further away than ever.

The second Oslo Agreement was passed by the Israeli Parliament with a majority of only one vote, which shows the serious opposition that many right-wing members and others demonstrated against any form of Palestinian autonomy and/or recognition of the PLO.

XIV. THE PEACE TREATY BETWEEN ISRAEL AND JORDAN OF 1994

We have already mentioned that King Hussein was often eager to deal with his Jewish neighbours and had held many secret meetings with especially Labour leaders over the years. He had been out in the cold during the Gulf War because he did not join the alliance against Saddam Hussein and even tried to be a mediator between the Iraqi leader and the West; not only was the attempt in vain, but it also angered his Western, especially his American, friends. After the Madrid Conference, which gave Jordan new access to Washington, and after the PLO-Israel Accord negotiated in Oslo, where Arafat had shown his willingness to go it alone, the King found it easy to forget all previous engagements committing him to respect Arab solidarity. Arafat and the King had had similar feelings of frustration during and immediately after the Gulf War because of their common position, which was seen as pro-Iraqi by the West and most of the Arab countries.

In matters of foreign politics, the King was, and increasingly so, the unchallenged master of his country, and he never allowed much discussion about the final aim of policy. In this case, it was a peace treaty with Israel which aimed to settle, once and for all, the question of whether the *intruding nation* had a right to remain in the region. With his understanding of history and tradition, he could surely not forget that his own royal ancestors were not masters of the same desert Kingdom along and east of the river Jordan (which never existed as a separate, political entity, at least not before King Abdullah), but had ruled for centuries in smaller or larger areas of (Saudi) Arabia, now lost territories for the Hashemites. They could thus also be considered *intruders* under imperialist British protection. But even without that reflection, the mature King Hussein had become a realist and saw clearly that the Israelis had come to the area to stay. In that respect his thinking was in keeping with that of his grandfather, King Abdullah, and that of the late, pragmatic President of Egypt, Anwar Sadat. Hussein only dared to admit this later than the President, both because of the often delicate internal situation in the Kingdom, where Hussein surely wielded less absolute power than was the case with his colleague as head of state in Egypt, and because the King had to take his difficult neighbour, Iraq, into account.

What the King must especially have taken into consideration before going to the negotiating table was that the Israelis had impressed the world with their military successes against evident Arab weaknesses, but what was more, any Jerusalem government was now supported by the most important nation on earth. Since its support of Sadat in his opening towards Israel, the USA had never shown any tendency to abandon the Jewish *client state*. Even during the worst excesses of a new brand of nationalism under Begin, the Reagan administration never openly condemned Israeli actions in Lebanon or towards the settlers, let alone tried to stop them. Nor did the Bush administration, despite its frustrations with the Shamir government, which were clearly expressed to the leaders in Jerusalem though with no noticeable result.

As his chief negotiator, the King nominated a trusted man, Dr. Majali, who later became Prime Minister. The problems between the two countries, Israel and Jordan, were not too difficult to settle, and the negotiations lasted only around a year. Majali has recently told me that there was generally a good atmosphere between the parties during the negotiations and that these never threatened to run into a definite failure.

The King and the Israeli Prime Minister, Yitzhak Rabin, signed the peace treaty in October 1994, in a ceremony that took place at the border between the two countries, a little north of Aqaba and was witnessed by President Clinton. It opened up diplomatic and other relations between the two nations in a way very similar to that paved by the treaty between Egypt and Israel. But in the case of Jordan there were no great difficulties with regard to land, and the King, as we remember, had already abdicated sovereignty over his lost territories on the West Bank. Still, the monarch retained a special role, a custodianship, over the holy, Islamic places in Jerusalem with the tacit acceptance of the PLO leader, who had eventually come to speaking terms with the Jordanian King some years earlier. There was a small correction of some border lines, in both directions, and Jordan agreed to grant permanent residence to those many Palestinian refugees already in the country who wanted it.

The King felt relieved when the treaty was signed, but only few Jordanians joined him in the celebrations. Probably most of the educated elite and the middle class accepted it as a *fait accompli* and trusted the King when he affirmed that there would be economic benefits from this treaty. But surely not all Jordanians agreed with this new policy and many sceptics raised their voices against any policy of accommodating the luring tones from Jerusalem. Until today, and especially under the rule of right-wing governments in Jerusalem, the general sympathy in Israel for the Kingdom and its royal leader has been evident, but there has been little support for the reverse direction from the majority of Jordanians, in favour of opening up to the Jewish state. Most people accepted, or had to accept, the decisions of His Majesty, but in their hearts they surely felt more sympathy for the Syrian attitude, not to speak of the Iraqi one; the former indicated that it was premature to deal with Jerusalem before all Arab nations could accept a comprehensive peace agreement. In that respect the Jordanians did not differ very much from those Egyptians who did not easily follow the ideas of Sadat when he opened up towards Israel in 1977.

Adnan Abu-Odeh, a long-time adviser to the King and former minister and ambassador, was originally a Palestinian citizen (or refugee) from Nablus. In his already mentioned recent book on the relationship between Palestinians and (Trans)Jordanians,[233] he emphasises how difficult this relationship became in the aftermath of the Peace Accord with Israel. He writes: "The two accords [The Oslo Agreement and the Jordanian-Israeli Peace Treaty] dispelled the ambiguity in which the status and destiny of Palestinian-Jordanians had been shrouded by the Rabat Resolution of October 1974, which recognised the *PLO as the legitimate and sole representative of the Palestinian people*... Taken together, the two accords implied that Jordan is Jordan and Palestine is Palestine [...;] these [Transjordanian] nationalists could now treat the Palestinian-Jordanians as an alien community whose legal status had to be reconsidered so that the Jordanian identity would not be compromised".

Abu-Odeh further stresses that a heated debate exploded in the local press in November 1995 and that this was quite normal, considering the importance of this sensitive subject, whether a citizen of Jordan felt primarily like a Palestinian if born in that area, or like those (Trans)Jordanians who had no link to the Palestine territories. I find it is sufficient to add here that while Palestinians in Jordan normally feel that they are not discriminated against, except perhaps in the army and some high-level government functions, the locally born Jordanians sometimes feel left out of business life, often controlled by Palestinian-born citizens. The interesting book gives more details on this difficult subject, which is often treated in a low-key way in Jordan. Eventually the debate surrounding this honest book made Odeh's own position as adviser to the new King Abdullah (after 1999) unsustainable, since many (Trans)Jordanians remained sceptical with regard to Palestinians in high positions. It must surely have been a great disappointment to him, but, having reached a normal age for retirement, he could continue to live a peaceful life in his adopted country.

The peace treaty of 1994 was of course — and almost as a matter of routine — condemned by some of the more radical Arab states, such as Iraq, Syria and Lebanon. That an anti-Israel organisation like *Hamas* condemned the treaty came as no surprise, but it was strange that the PLO, which had already signed its own agreement with the former enemy a year earlier, in September 1993, joined in the criticism of the new treaty.

Many Jordanians objected to the very term *normalisation*, rightly pointing out

---

233 Op.cit., pp. 193 - 194.

that it was not *normal* for Jordan to make peace with its former enemy and neighbour. They saw the new situation as one of a trial period in which both sides had obligations to show that they wanted to live in peace. Acts such as the one in which the *Mossad*, the Israeli secret service, tried to assassinate a citizen of Jordan in the heart of Amman, were fiercely condemned and made the King furious. The attack mentioned took place in early 1998, and the life of the victim, a *Hamas* leader, was saved only through an immediate personal intervention by the King, who informed the Netanyahu government how angry and frustrated he was over Israeli interference. Not only the victim, (who, as it turned out, did survive), but also the entire atmosphere between the two governments was poisoned by that very abnormal occurrence involving two neighbouring states.

After King Hussein's death in early 1999, the relationship between the two countries has become more difficult, exacerbated by the more brutal policies of the Israeli governments after the right-wing take-over in 1996 (partly excepting the Barak interlude in 1999-2001), and also because the young King Abdullah has had other priorities than those of preserving a special relationship with Jerusalem, as his father tried to do till his death, in spite of many difficulties.

XV. DETERIORATION OF THE CONFLICT UNDER NETANYAHU 1996-99

1. Right-Wing Victory at May 1996 Elections

The two preceding chapters on the Oslo Agreements and the Jordanian-Israel Peace Treaty, respectively, dealt with the promising time when Yitzhak Rabin was at the head of the Israeli government with Simon Peres as his Foreign Minister. This is one of the few periods in recent years when those believing in the peace process — promoted again with the 1991 Madrid Conference — could indeed believe in progress.

The Rabin period of government came to a sad end when the Prime Minister was assassinated in November 1995 by a radical Jewish extremist during a pro-peace rally in Tel Aviv. He was succeeded for a short while by his Foreign Minister, Simon Peres, who had long been his competitor for the leadership of the Labour party. Both had received the Nobel Peace Prize in Oslo in 1994 together with Arafat, but the euphoria after the Oslo Accord did not last long. The *intifada* had come to a halt, but when Peres took over in November 1995, there was a period of insecurity which some hard-line Palestinians misused to sow discord in the political setting of Israel through acts of violence. The Lebanon-based *Hisbollah* also attacked Northern Israel with rockets, and eventually Peres reacted in the same violent way, in order not to be accused of being too soft, and allowed the IDF to carry out heavy air and artillery bombings in South Lebanon in April 1996 — an operation called *Grapes of Wrath*. These attacks aimed primarily at destroying Lebanese infrastructure in the south of the country, and they resulted in great civilian losses, even of peasants who had sought refuge in a UN camp, *Kafi Quana*. This was a sad chain of events demonstrating once again that a vicious circle of violence will automatically worsen the political situation. The Israeli show of force caused an outcry internationally.

The elections took place on 29 May 1996, at a difficult time when the repercussions of the *Grapes of Wrath* bombings were still felt internationally and within Israel. Through French and US mediation, a monitoring group was set up to control attacks and retaliations in the South Lebanon area, in accordance with what was referred to as the *April 1996 Memorandum of Understanding*.[234] The consequences of the violence from both sides seemed to confirm the failure of the outgoing Peres government to ensure national security, let alone promote the peace process that had been so dear to his own and to Rabin's heart. The incumbent Labour government almost gave up in its difficult choice between security or peace, and that factor must be seen as the background of the May 1996 elections, called earlier than necessary according to standard rules. Because of the apparent upsurge in radical national feeling, as represented by the Likud block and by parties even more radical, Peres perhaps did not have much choice left in the national political pattern than to ask for these elections. But what may surprise was his apparent reluctance to continue the fight for a peaceful settlement, because this could be seen as the abandonment of the Rabin course, which Peres had so openly endorsed in the latter's last government. As a new Prime Minister, he had tried to show *robust* (to use a modern, but not quite strong enough, word) ways towards little Lebanon, but it is evident that the majority felt that this long term number two in the Labour Party only showed lack of leadership. His fairly high age, 73, was not in his favour, either, and Peres apparently conducted an uninspiring election campaign, what Shlaim termed "lackluster".[235] He had long earned a reputation for being arrogant and too self-confident, which may explain his many failures at elections and nominations in recent years. If Shlaim at one point stresses that Rabin in his second government "enjoyed a towering dominance of the making of his government's foreign and domestic policies [… whereas] Peres was the Statesman", apparently Peres had now lost this qualification.[236]

It did not help him that just after the assassination of Rabin, the Labour Party had achieved fine results in the opinion polls. It only proves that in Israel (as in other democratic countries), the fate of political parties can easily change at elections. At least Peres lost this time, not only due to his own errors, we may think, but because he faced a much younger politician, Benjamin Netanyahu, from the Likud Party, who was not yet 50 years old and was running a modern American-

---

234 A *Memorandum of Understanding* is a less formal agreement than a treaty, but has binding effects on the signing parties, here Israel, Syria, Lebanon and the two foreign powers, France and the USA. Each side was represented by a diplomat and a military officer, and for a long time, Syria has been sitting around the same table as Israel, its old enemy. This Memorandum of April stipulated that no attack on *civilian* targets was allowed.
235 Op.cit., p. 562.
236 Ibid., p. 505.

style election campaign. It did not help Peres, either, that many of the Arab voters inside Israel (there are quite a few) might have found that Peres was never a man to be fully trusted. He often said *yes* or *no*, while these terms could just as well be understood as *maybe*. Rabin was renowned for being honest, and I have heard many Arabs say that the late Prime Minister — though he could sometimes be harsh — could always be fully trusted. If Peres's influence did not completely end with this lost election, at least he never again returned as Prime Minister. Today (at the beginning of 2005), he has recently been appointed Foreign Minister in the Sharon cabinet, at the age of 82.

The May 1996 elections brought forth a new element in Israeli politics, since it was the first time that a Prime Minister was elected directly by the electorate and not chosen by the most successful party after the elections. Benjamin Netanyahu's victory was marginal (50.4%), and in the Knesset, Labour had still more representatives than Likud, but Netanyahu obtained support initially from a coalition supported by 66 members of Parliament in the 120-seat Knesset. What was most satisfying for him was the above-mentioned fact that he had got the personal backing of a majority, however slight it was. The Constitution now made it rather difficult to set aside an elected Prime Minister. He therefore began to rule the land like an American President.

Netanyahu's main theme during the election campaign was the security issue, much more than the peace process, to which he only paid lip service.

2. Worsened Conditions with Regard to the Arabs

The new Prime Minister, who had been ambassador and minister in former Likud governments, had published a book in 1993: *Place among the Nations: Israel and the World*. It showed him as an ultra-nationalist and indeed as a very anti-Arab politician, in an almost absurd way. The book's central theme was the same as the one his predecessors in the Likud, Begin and Shamir, propagated: That the Jewish people had a right to the whole country of Israel. He stressed that the relationship with the Arab world was one of permanent conflict and "he reserved special vehemence and venom for the Palestinians", according to Shlaim.[237]

On this background, it was no wonder that hardly any progress could be made in the direction of peace during Netanyahu's three years of government. We may even say that this period showed serious lack of good government in Israel right

---

237 Op.cit., p. 566, where many examples are given of the absurdities contained in this Israeli *Mein Kampf*. (My expression, but I am of course not suggesting that there was an identity of views with Hitler's in this book, but only talking of similar ultra-nationalist ways of thinking and about the style of the book.)

from the start. It was no wonder, therefore, that the Arabs felt frustrated, especially those who had cared to read his above-mentioned book.

Despite some of the Prime Minister's lukewarm promises of goodwill, almost all the Arab states soon grew concerned over the new right-wing government. Netanyahu's inaugural speech did not promise much, because he talked down, like a schoolmaster, to most of his Arab neighbours. He also spoke of the necessity of continued Israeli strength and told the Syrians that they could not ask for preconditions for resuming the negotiations (i.e. he indirectly declared that the Golan would not be returned to Syria), and finally he reminded the Palestinians that he expected strict adherence to what had been agreed. But they were surely aware of his well-publicised animosity to the Oslo Accords, which could not be easily forgotten. The day before Rabin signed the Oslo II Accord, Netanyahu had even declared, "[t]he Prime Minister will soon be able to announce the establishment of a Palestinian terrorist state".[238] In addition, it was soon a fact that Netanyahu decided to close his eyes to the expansion of Jewish settlements in the West Bank, especially in the Greater Jerusalem area. In this, he merely followed the line of his predecessors, only more wholeheartedly.

3. The Palestinian Problem

The most burning issue was evidently the Palestinians/the PLO, on which so much effort had been invested by Netanyahu's predecessors, Peres and not least Rabin. If the new Prime Minister's opening statements in the Knesset had not been promising, Netanyahu soon created shock waves when he permitted the digging of a tunnel below or near the Aqsa Mosque in the old City of Jerusalem in September 1996. It provoked an outcry by the Arab world and made any dialogue with the Palestinians most difficult from the beginning.

Despite American efforts to heal the wounds during a hastily organised summit meeting hosted by Clinton in Washington in October 1996— at which Netanyahu met King Hussein and Arafat, while President Mubarak of Egypt declined the invitation — the atmosphere hardly improved. Seen from an Arab perspective, Netanyahu had already become a person not to be trusted. His attitudes soon placed the peace process in jeopardy. Shlaim writes, in his clear-cut sarcastic way, about "Netanyahu's declaration of war against the Peace Process".[239]

Only in January 1997 was some progress made with regard to the city of Hebron. An agreement was reached which allowed for some Israeli forces to remain in order to protect the limited but very nationalistic Jewish settlement there, as compensa-

---

238 Morris, op.cit., p. 635.
239 Op.cit., p. 568.

tion for withdrawal from most of the city, inhabited mainly by Palestinians. King Hussein of Jordan helped to bring about this agreement, signed in Egypt.

The positive reaction to this overdue agreement soon evaporated, however, when the Israeli government permitted new Jewish settlements in the (Arab) area between Jerusalem and Bethlehem. They were named the *Har Homa*, or in Arabic, *Jabal Abu Ghaneim*, and were closing the ring of Jewish settlements around the holy city and making Arab movements almost impossible there. This new comprehensive settlement policy in the Greater Jerusalem area was made public in February 1997 and created a new uproar in many places. It was based on a fairly old plan that had been proposed in Rabin's days, but was postponed at the time, when the Palestinians protested. In Israel the government owns most of the land and thus no settlement can occur without government interference or control.

The American government vetoed a resolution of the UN Security Council that criticised this new building and settlement plan, but the rest of the UN members, with the exception of Israel, the USA and Micronesia, voted in favour of a similar resolution at the UN General Assembly.[240]

After about a year in power, Netanyahu presented his Cabinet with a plan that deviated strongly from the Oslo Agreements and involved the return to the Palestinians of only 40 % of the occupied territories. It was therefore abortive since the PLO rejected it outright, saying, "[t]his is not acceptable. Netanyahu is negotiating with himself [...]. He has forgotten that he has a partner".[241]

At the Labour Party's convention in May 1997, Ehud Barak, who had replaced Peres as the Party leader after the latter's election defeat, managed to have deleted from the Party's election manifesto its long-time declared opposition to the establishment of a Palestinian state. This change was immediately denounced by the Netanyahu government as appeasement of the Palestinians. In his above-mentioned book, Netanyahu had spoken against any giving-in to the Arabs by the Israelis and compared any concession to them, to Chamberlain's naive giving-in to dangerous Hitler in 1938. The Arab states were, in Netanyahus's view, similar to Nazi Germany, Israel to defenceless Czechoslovakia and the Palestinians to the Sudeten Germans – a very strange comparison, indeed, considering the obvious dissimilarities with military and national facts and the historical background.

Despite these unhappy events, the peace process was not completely dead. Because of pressure from Washington, which Netanyahu could not ignore, an

---

240 It has been seen quite often that resolutions unable to pass the Security Council because of a veto from one of the big powers (or permanent members) will be presented at the UN General Assembly (GA) and passed there. The GA resolutions only have a moral, as opposed to a legally binding value, however. But even the Security Council resolutions have often *not* been accepted as binding, not least by Israel.

241 Shlaim, op.cit., p. 584.

Israeli Prime Minister Benjamin Netanyahu and Palestinian leader Yassir Arafat during news conference at the White House in October 1996.

agreement was reached 20 months after the new government had come to power, on the more general problem of Israeli withdrawals. After a long session in the USA, the *Wye River Memorandum* was signed on 23 October 1998 by the Palestinian leader, Yassir Arafat, and Benjamin Netanyahu. President Clinton had again made a great personal effort in order to achieve this step forward, and he was of course present at the ceremony, together with the King of Jordan, now marked by fatal illness. The agreement primarily confirmed previous arrangements with regard to the control of almost 40% of the West Bank by the Palestinians, but also fixed dates for the various withdrawals. Many hoped that it was a signal of new willingness by the Israeli government to further the peace process, but the agreement was never fully respected by the Jerusalem government, under various pretexts. Since then other efforts have been equally abortive. The new agreement was passed by the Knesset on 15 November 1998 by a great majority in support of it, with 75 voting for, 19 against and 9 abstaining.

This vote showed that there was a national consensus behind the continuation of the Oslo process, even if the government party itself was split on the matter.

On this background it was absurd that only six weeks later, on 20 December 1998, the Israeli government decided to impose a standstill on the Wye Agreement. The Knesset approved this decision a few days later, but — on the initiative of the Labour Party — at the same time called for new general elections in May 1999, thus cutting Netanyahu's period of government short. The first decision was an affront not only to the Palestinians but also to Washington, which had invested so much in resuming the peace process. The Netanyahu government's motive was that the PA had not lived up to its obligations as set forth by the arrangement, concerning the combatting of terrorists. But Shlaim tells us that "the PLO had scrupulously adhered to what was agreed at Wye Plantation".[242] This was also the general feeling of most diplomats and other observers in the region.

The Palestinian Authority was now confronted with a serious challenge, the expiration of the originally determined transition period of five years (according to the signed agreement) on 4 May 1999, just before the Israeli elections of 17 May. Many countries tried to persuade Arafat to refrain from a unilateral declaration of independence immediately before the elections. In a declaration from the European Council in Berlin (24 and 25 March 1999) the heads of governments confirmed the right of the Palestinians to form a sovereign state, and this important and clear statement of course made it easier for Arafat to postpone his declaration of independence. He had already learnt pragmatism the hard way over many years.

4. The Syrian/Lebanese Relationship

The Syrian attitude towards Netanyahu was one of disgust, most of the time. Shlaim quotes from a Damascus newspaper that describes the new Israeli government in the following harsh terms: "It is dominated by rabbis, generals, racists, mass murderers and advocates of transfer, all wanting to destroy the foundations of peace".[243] The Damascus government felt that the rapidly changing attitudes of Netanyahu towards the settlement of the Golan problem confirmed that Syria and the other Arabs were faced with a politician whom it was impossible to trust. Even if Netanyahu had originally emphasised that the Syrians ought to enter into

---

242 Ibid., p. 605.
243 Op.cit., p. 572. Shlaim does not say that the press in Syria, mostly written by the government's own propaganda people, normally carries a harsh tone in relation to Israel. This does not mean, however, that the characteristics of the quoted article did not hold water. It expressed, to a large extent, the feelings among the radical Arabs in Syria and elsewhere, even in those moderate countries like Jordan and Egypt where the governments had made peace with Israel. Netanyahu was definitely seen as a politician representing a big step backward.

negotiations without pre-conditions — meaning that they should not expect Israel to give up all of the Golan — on other occasions, he would declare his willingness to negotiate all aspects of the Golan. Then again, he also maintained on and off that this matter was not negotiable, which frustrated and confused observers. In keeping with his lack of respect for the Arabs, he generally ignored the feelings of this important neighbouring state, Syria.

Netanyahu's obsession with security made him pay more attention to the relationship with Lebanon than his predecessors had done. The government in Beirut under President Hrawi and Prime Minister Hariri could not enter into separate negotiations with Israel, because of Lebanon's special relationship with Syria. As already stated above, Syria was, actually, if not legally speaking, responsible for Lebanon's overall foreign policy. Neither the President nor Hariri had the power to oppose the *Hisbollah* "liberation movement", as it is regarded in the Arab world. Netanyahu tried a "Lebanon first" solution that was not workable, due to Lebanon's protectorate status, which Netanyahu or his advisers should have known beforehand. On various occasions, Israel did send bombers into the Lebanese mountains, creating havoc. Sometimes Jerusalem openly ignored the April 1996 *Memorandum of Understanding* and the results of the Monitoring Group's findings, which often placed the blame on the Israeli government for the IDF's "acts of punishment" inside Lebanon, when they were killing innocent victims. On other occasions, of course, the Monitoring Group accused the *Hisbollah* of unreasonable attacks on civilians.

Without going into detail here, it is significant that one of the last acts of the Netanyahu government before resigning in the Spring of 1999 was to bomb Lebanese bridges and electric power stations, killing several civilians and causing meaningless havoc in this already badly hit land. The Israeli philosophy of striking hard in order to subdue the *Hisbollah* movement showed Jerusalem's ignorance of Arab feelings in this matter. But again, we have to realise that all Israeli governments, supported by general opinion in the nation, often believed, and still do, that only through very hard retaliations is it possible to make the Arabs understand that force and violence from their side will *always* be met with an even stronger reaction from Israel. Ben-Gurion, the founding father, established this philosophy, Golda Meir followed it right away and even Rabin and Peres did the same — Rabin, in his violent reaction to the *intifada* and Peres with his fatal *Grapes of Wrath*— so there was basically nothing new in Netanyahu's militant move. In the eyes of Israeli leaders, these acts of retaliation constitute a necessary policy, but seen from the outside, including the often quoted Israeli historian, Shlaim, it is one that creates a vicious circle very painful to those civilians who suffer anywhere, whether in Israel, inside Lebanon or in the West Bank and Gaza areas. It is also killing the hopes for a final, comprehensive peace arrangement based on mutual understanding, as established by the few peace accords, such as the initial one with Egypt at Camp David, the Oslo Accord, and more recently the agreement with Jordan.

Netanyahu eventually admitted that the growing number of victims in the Israeli armed forces (with up to as many as 50 young soldiers dying every year) due to the *Hisbollah* attacks inside Lebanon made it necessary to rethink the policy of occupation. Therefore a withdrawal from the *Security Zone* in Southern Lebanon had already become a subject of open debate in Israel in the last period of the Netanyahu government, but a decisive change had to wait for the arrival of his successor. Netanyahu admitted, however, that Israel could now accept the UN resolution 425 with regard to a withdrawal, a resolution which had been passed after the first invasion of 1978, but which the various Israeli governments had ignored until then.

The direct negotiations between Israel and Syria, which were broken off in early 1996, were never resumed in Netanyahu's days, and the Syrians simply ignored provocations from Israel, such as the legal decision taken by the Knesset *not* to hand back the Golan — formally long integrated into Israel — without a majority vote in favour in a referendum among the Jewish population. Damascus of course denounced it and spoke of a new aggressive attitude but these vague protests were not followed up.[244]

In the autumn of 1997, a false Mossad report on Syrian war preparations against Israel created a great deal of fuss in Israel, but not in Syria, where the governmment and its press played down any rumours. In this case they definitely knew that the story was based entirely on false information. Shlaim is therefore not correct in telling us that the two countries were pushed almost "to the brink of war",[245] since it was obvious then to the observers on the Syrian side that no such war preparations were being carried out by the Arab side. I was a personal witness to what was happening in Syria in those days and based my own reports on the various Western defence attachés who were examining the situation along the Syrian borders with Israel. I happened to live near a big military cantonment and saw absolutely no signs of war preparations in those days. Eventually the Israelis also found out that this was the whole truth, and that their problem was only a Mossad liar.

At the funeral of King Hussein in Amman in February 1999, the two leaders, Assad and Netanyahu, were both present, but no dialogue was accepted on this

---

244 If one asked them — as I did — Syrian officials would say that it was not worthwhile to take any serious action against the Israeli policy in this regard. First of all, nobody trusted Netanyahu; second, in a serious negotiation with Israel at a later stage, the two governments would have to ignore all such meaningless declarations. A very sensible attitude, I find. If a war had broken out then, it would have been Israel`s sole responsibility.

245 Op.cit., p. 592.

occasion by the Syrian side, since the President found no reason to be optimistic regarding the usefulness of beginning a new start with unpredictable Netanyahu. At any rate it was felt that the Israeli Prime Minister would not stay in power for long, which soon proved to be true.

5. The Jordanian and Egyptian Relationship

With regard to the relationship with Jordan, Netanyahu almost took it for granted that the little Kingdom could be trusted as a special friend of Israel, so that he need not pay extraordinary attention to it. But, as mentioned above, King Hussein had great difficulties in getting solid backing in his own country for the peace treaty signed in 1994, only one year before Rabin's death. And two episodes marred the relations between the governments of Amman and Jerusalem, only less than two hours' drive from each other. The first was the above-mentioned episode of late 1997 when the secret service of Israel attempted to assassinate, by poisoning, one of the *Hamas* leaders during his stay in Jordan's capital. Netanyahu had directly ordered it, and it occurred only a few weeks after the first visit to Israel in September 1997 by the new US Secretary of State, Madeleine Albright, who had only mild criticism for Netanyahu, and might therefore have given a green light, Netanyahu believed, for more harsh measures against the Arabs. She had visited the area after some *Hamas* bomb attacks, in order to try and promote more peaceful surroundings in the area.

As mentioned above, the *Hamas* leader did not die in Amman, thanks mostly to a resolute reaction by the Jordanian authorities, and especially to the intervention of the King himself, who demanded from the Israeli authorities the secret formula utilised in the poison. The Jordanians were furious that Netanyahu allowed such an attack on their territory. The King, who declared that it was "like being spit in the face" also demanded that the top *Hamas* leader, Sheikh Ahmad Yassin, who was imprisoned in Israel, should be set free if Jordan was to send the (would-be) assassins back to Israel. The government in Jerusalem gave in to these demands, since it hardly had any other choice. Otherwise the Jordanians would have pursued in Amman the responsible Mossad people, who were caught red-handed. No Israeli government could easily accept that.

The foul atmosphere may have influenced a Jordanian soldier in a new ugly episode sometime afterwards. He killed several Israeli school children when they were playing near the border.[246] The King immediately expressed his dismay, but

---

246 Prince Hassan has told me that the episode took place in 1996 and not in 1998. I feel confident that it was in 1998, but this is not important, because only the reaction of the King is to be noted as remarkable.

despite his friendly gesture (very unpopular in his own country and among Arabs in general[247]) in paying a condolence visit in Israel to the parents of the dead children, there soon arose new episodes. Some highly placed Israelis expressed themselves in a way that showed lack of respect for the King or his government. This should again underscore the great difference between Israeli bluntness (some would say tactlessness) and Arab pride, which we so often find in this conflict.

With regard to the Egyptians, the relationship was correct but cool, all the more so because no one in the Arab world looked at the Israeli government in Netanyahu's time with friendly eyes, especially because of the expanded Jewish settlements policy and the general feeling that one could not trust the Prime Minister as a person. The Egyptians, who maintained friendly relationships with both the US government and the Syrian one, had to steer a careful course, not offending either of them. But President Mubarak was normally capable of avoiding any offence. We saw that the Egyptian leader — unlike King Hussein — had not wanted to join in Clinton's efforts to improve the atmosphere after the tunnel problem in Jerusalem.

6. Internal Disagreements

The Netanyahu government was often split between the radical religious elements and the more liberal forces, and a man such as Foreign Minister Levy eventually gave up and left the government, because he found the policies of Netanyahu too dangerous with regard to *the other side* (i.e. the Arabs). Defence Minister Sharon (now Prime Minister), the general who brutalised Lebanon in 1982 and many other places, could not agree with Netanyahu, because he saw him as too lenient, which shows how difficult it was and is to steer a middle course in Israeli politics. But in this respect we may also understand that these two very strong and ambitious politicians, one — Sharon — of the older, and the other of the younger generation, were engaged in a serious struggle for power. There were also some scandals involving Prime Minister Netanyahu and his wife that weakened his position in the country; these episodes, however, had little to do with the relationship to other countries, always the main topic of this study. Elections were organised on 17 May 1999 and were won by Ehud Barak.

---

247 Many Arabs have asked the pertinent question of whether one could imagine an Israeli Prime Minister doing the same with regard to condolence visits to parents of innocent children killed by the IDF in retaliation attacks. I think not.

XVI. Barak's abortive peace efforts

Whereas in most countries foreign policy is not an important subject during election time, in Israel it is often the other way round, reflecting the isolated and often seriously exposed situation of the Jewish nation.

Ehud Barak was fortunate in evoking the memories of Y. Rabin, another famous general turned statesman, and in that respect Netanyahu was more of a civilian than the two Labour leaders. They (Barak and Rabin) could both be described as military hard-liners turned softer in the course of time, Rabin to the point of receiving the Nobel Peace Prize together with Peres and Arafat. Before the election of May 1999, the Labour party under Barak insisted in moving forward in the direction of a peaceful settlement with all Arab states, or at least with those involved in the peace process, which had been made utterly difficult by Netanyahu, to the point of reducing it to meaningless. The Israeli public, longing for real peace if combined with respect for their security needs, voted for Barak in order to give him a more comfortable victory than the Likud block had enjoyed before. He received 56% of the votes and Netanyahu only 44, but in the Knesset, both the Labour Party and the Likud-Block saw the number of their respective seats reduced, Labour from 34 to 26; Likud from 32 to 19. Thereby the already existing split into smaller parties in the 120-seat parliament was further deepened.

Only in July 1999 did Barak manage to form a coalition government. He chose as his first Foreign Minister David Levy, who had held that position before, under Netanyahu, but who resigned as early as August 2000. He had not participated in Camp David and was now replaced by Shlomo Ben-Ami as new Foreign Minister, a man who knew the Arab world better than most, since he was born in Tangier, Morocco, and spoke Arabic and Spanish. He had come to Israel as a young man and became a historian turned politician after having served as Israel's ambassador to Madrid. He was fairly liberal-minded and got along well with Barak, it seems, but their time was short, and they did not manage to move things as they had wished.[248]

---

[248] We have already above referred to a recent book containing interviews with Ben-Ami. It explains his personal views on the immediate past and its title is *The Future of Israel*, which I have read in its Spanish version, published in Madrid, 2002. There is also a French edition.

Israeli Prime Minister Ehud Barak during speech on the development regarding the West Bank.

After its formation, the government repeated what the Prime Minister and party had declared before the elections, that it was its aim to enter into serious negotiations with the Palestinians' new government, the PA, in order to complete the talks already begun in the previous government's time or attempted more seriously under Rabin and Peres. It was clear that Barak wanted to profit from the fine image of Rabin in the more tolerant sectors of the electorate while at the same time promising the other sectors of the public not to forget their security needs. But despite his demonstration of good intentions, Barak (or his government) permitted a fairly large amount of new settlements in the occupied territories in his first three months, claiming that he was only approving earlier permits granted under Netanyahu.[249] But, as already mentioned, even Labour governments have generally not withheld such permits; they have sometimes even widened what

---

249 Rahbek, op.cit., p. 318.

only Jewish eyes would see as a *liberal* policy of allowing settlements, condemned by all other governments, including that of the US as illegal.

1. Resumption of the Peace Process

There have been many public discussions in Israel and elsewhere as to whether it would be easier for an Israeli government to begin with a resumption of the Palestinian track or with the Syrian one. Barak initially declared that he aimed at both, and he soon promised to withdraw the IDF troops from the occupied parts of Lebanon. He also stressed that he regarded the Syrian President as a man one could trust, since previous agreements, for instance on the cease-fire line in the Golan, had been fully respected by the Damascus government. Hafez Assad, on his part, reciprocated in order to have meaningful negotiations with the Jerusalem government, and declared that Syria viewed with great expectations the new leadership taking over in Israel. The British journalist/writer, Patrick Seale, Hafez Assad's main biographer, was instrumental in bringing about this happy, positive opening between the parties.

This was a promising start, but difficulties soon arose again.

2. Negotiations with the PA

As early as 4 September 1999, Arafat and Barak signed a new agreement at Sharm-el-Sheikh after several preparatory meetings between themselves and officials from both sides. The agreement involved a carefully listed timetable for the further withdrawals of Israeli troops from the West Bank, and other outstanding issues, such as special corridors between Gaza and the West Bank cut off by Israeli territory, the building of a harbour in Gaza and liberation of prisoners by Israel. A new date for the final agreement was set for 13 September 2000, seven years after the first agreement (Oslo I) was signed at the White House in Washington. But the Barak government soon disappointed the other side, and also the friends of peace in Israel, when it declared that Israel "was not going to carry out the terms of the original Wye Memorandum", signed in 1998 by Netanyahu. Arafat appealed in vain to Barak to live up to those terms that had already been pushed aside by the then right-wing government. At a Cabinet meeting in November 1999[250] Barak further declared that UN resolution 242 — mentioned as the basis of the final agreement in the Oslo Accord — was relevant for sovereign nations only and not for occupied territories; this was a rather meaningless statement, which clearly

---

250 Rahbek, op.cit., p. 320.

contradicted the opinions held by other nations, not only the Arab states, but also the EU and even the USA.[251] So if Barak showed goodwill verbally, he was at the same time humiliating Arafat once again, because in reality the PLO did not obtain much, and no final agreement was reached before the envisaged date.[252] The Barak government's instructions before the negotiations at Camp David, which followed in the summer of 2000, also set forth rather harsh conditions, seen from the Palestinian side: "No concession on Jerusalem, which must remain the Capital of Israel in its undivided shape, nor a return of refugees to Israel, no acceptance of a foreign army west of the Jordan river and necessary PLO acknowledgement of the existing settlements to be annexed by Israel".

These conditions were surely no good omen for the coming round of negotiations in the USA, and it was therefore not fully unexpected that these did not succeed. We must also not forget that with the extended system of settlements in many areas of the occupied territories, Israel had made the establishment of an autonomous Palestinian state very difficult, if not impossible. No wonder that many — including American policymakers such as Brzezinski many years ago — have talked of a Jewish tendency to create Palestinian *Bantustan's* that could easily be controlled by Israel and have no real autonomy, let alone independence.

3. Negotiations with Syria

It took somewhat longer for the new Israeli government to resume the negotiations with Syria that had been dormant since early 1996, when the Israeli government (of Simon Peres before the elections), not the Syrians, pulled out of them. During the Netanyahu period there was hardly any contact, nor much hope, as we know. Now a new beginning was envisaged. After the initial words of goodwill, expressed publicly by both sides, and already referred to, Foreign Minister Sharaa of Syria — one of President Hafez Assad's trusted men, and long-time minister — met with Prime Minister Barak in the USA in December 1999. It was the first time ever that such a bilateral meeting had taken place at this high level. Many Israelis had — according to their press — wanted Hafez Assad to come to Jerusalem in person as Sadat had in 1977, but this shows a lack of understanding of the personality of the (then) Syrian President. He was a very proud and logical man and not inclined

---

251 The supposedly liberal minister, M. Melchior, told me the same thing when I saw him in April 2002, and also expressed the strange opinion that the occupation of the West Bank and Gaza was *not illegal*. Most observers and governments, however, do not question this illegality.

252 Rahbek expresses it in her blunt was as follows: "Once again Arafat had his back broken by Barak", (my translation) op.cit., p. 318.

to gamble or show off in the same way as his former Egyptian colleague. If he had already invested great efforts in respect of bilateral negotiations, he insisted that they would have to be resumed from the point where they had stopped in 1996. "The Israelis must admit", he said, "as a prerequisite for further talks, that the Golan should be returned to Syria, regardless of anything else". Hafez Assad also reminded the Barak government that *land for peace* was the principle upon which the peace process had been initiated. For the Syrian government, therefore, this principle was (and remains) a *sine qua non*, as it was for Sadat before he got back the whole of Sinai. That Rabin did concede this to the Syrians in the first round, soon after the Madrid Conference, is a contested fact, maintained by the Syrian side but denied by most Israelis.

The Israeli government had its own way of approaching these negotiations, as we have seen already: They accepted that the Jewish nation had no historical rights in the Golan (unlike old Jewish land inside Palestine), even if the government and Parliament had taken all the legal steps necessary to integrate the area. This expression, "legal steps", pertains only to Israel, of course, since no other nation has accepted that the conquest of land can grant any right of possession to the occupiers, *vide* also UN resolution 242. Probably this Israeli decision was taken in order to grant the many settlers there more security, to highlight the sheer economic value of the area — a great provider of water resources — and of course to ensure military protection in threatening situations.

Enough here to confirm that the meetings at high level in late 1999 eventually ran out of steam because the parties could not agree. This may appear odd since the disparity between them only involved a few square kilometres, however much we talk of land of high strategic value. Ben-Ami says that for him, the negotiations with the Palestinians must have the highest priority, whereas Barak — like his predecessor Rabin — hoped that agreements with the Arab neighbours would ease the situation, also vis-à-vis the Palestinians. Ben-Ami admits that it was the question of Syrian access to Lake Tiberias that was the pivotal point on which Barak would not give in,[253] which shows the failure of Barak as a statesman, according to his second Foreign Minister. I tend to agree.

With regard to Lebanon, Barak had, as we know, already declared that he intended to withdraw the IDF from the south of Lebanon. He had hoped to obtain an agreement with Lebanon and Syria on this *redeployment* in order to avoid too much bloodshed,[254] but Syria was not willing to oblige as long as there was no definite opening from the Israeli government with regard to the much more important

---

253 Ibid., p. 126.
254 The word *redeployment* is the Israeli euphemism for the more blunt *withdrawal*, just as *Security Zone* was used instead of *occupation zone*. The UN, of course, uses the latter word, *withdrawal*.

matter of IDF pulling out of the Golan. The withdrawal of the IDF therefore took place in May 2000, without any pre-arrangement with Syria or Lebanon, and the *Hisbollah* followed the retiring troops to the border, harassing them to the end, but not causing much havoc; this was partly out of fear of retaliation, but also because of Syrian pressure not to destroy completely any hope of a bilateral opening with Israel. In May 2000 Prime Minister Barak declared that with the accomplishment of the withdrawal, Israel had now ended 18 years of tragedy in Lebanon.[255] At the same time he wrote a letter to the UN Secretary-General accusing Syria of trying to hinder the withdrawal of IDF from Lebanon, speculating, he stressed, in the presence of Palestinian refugees in Lebanese camps, on organising new terrorist attacks on Israel. He also pointed out that Damascus left the door open for Iranian interference in Lebanon through the *Hisbollah*. This was nothing new and did not show much constructive thought, as I see it. But surely Barak's motive was to avoid further accusations from the right wing, which saw the withdrawal as a sign of weakness. I tend to agree with Thomas Friedman who, in an article in *International Herald Tribune* of 3 – 4 June 2000, stressed that, on the contrary, the withdrawal showed Israeli strength and was a courageous decision restoring for the first time in 22 years a clear-cut border between Israel and Lebanon.

Barak did not find it necessary to confirm publicly that the IDF had finally fulfilled the requirements of UN resolution 425, passed 22 years earlier in 1978 and demanding its withdrawal, which Israel had ignored over those many years. Even Netanyahu had belatedly recognised that it would be necessary to withdraw, because of the continuous losses for the IDF; he had, however, left it to his successor to act in this field. The withdrawal neither satisfied the expectations of Israeli pessimists, who had dreaded that it would lead to new acts of terrorism by the *Hisbollah*, including attacks on Northern Israel, nor those of the optimists who had thought that it might bring a new opening in the relationship with Lebanon. Syria could not of course oppose this withdrawal officially, even if Damascus thereby lost some means to place pressure on Israel through the *Hisbollah* — which was under Syrian control — albeit only in a limited way. Many observers, including some of my diplomatic colleagues in Damascus in the late nineties, argued that Syria would do whatever it could to oppose an IDF withdrawal. But the always careful Hafez Assad, who was almost dying at the time of the redeployment, would never be so blunt, either in words or in action, as to oppose an Israeli withdrawal from Lebanon, if he had been able to do so. He realistically knew that he had to accept this event as a *fait accompli,* whether he liked it or not.

I also belong to those who believe that in recent years, under Hafez Assad, the Syrian influence has been of a somewhat moderating nature with regard to *Hisbol-*

---

255 He ought to have said 22 years, because the drama of Israeli intrusions began in 1978 and not only later, in 1982, even if the latter was by far the worst.

lah. Although this seems to continue under the successor regime of Bashar Assad, we still know little about his real power in Syria. But we may conclude at this stage that hardly any large-scale attacks by the *Hisbollah* have occurred in Israel lately, after the withdrawal of the IDF from Lebanon. The Lebanese were surely happy to see the disappearance of the last occupying force in the South as a sad vestige, or one of them, of their long civil war and its foreign interference. But as long as the *Hisbollah* survives (which it has —both as an armed militia and as a political party — at the time of this writing), this movement remains one of the built-in weaknesses of the Lebanese nation, which the people and the fragile governments in Beirut have to live with. Because of the ambivalent attitude of the regime in Damascus, which continued to keep Syrian troops in Lebanon until very recently, Lebanese citizens did not really feel independent in their own nation.

4. Doldrums in 2000 – 2001

The Clinton government had already invested a great deal of energy in promoting solutions to the Middle East conflict, but now it made another effort. At a meeting in Geneva on 25 March 2000, President Clinton tried hard to persuade his colleague, Hafez Assad, of the necessity of resuming talks with the Jerusalem government. According to the Syrian side, however, the American President brought no promise from the Israelis to accommodate the Syrians with regard to acceptance of the *land for peace* formula, only expecting Assad to yield, it seems. The two presidents had already met before in 1994, in the same city of Geneva, and with the same meagre result.

The death of the long-time Syrian ruler came soon after, in the summer of 2000, but has not yet changed much in Syria's foreign relationship. Assad's son has now survived more than four years and seems to have managed to consolidate his power. But it remains an open question whether he is the real ruler in his own right, like his father, or is only dependent on the late President's strong adherents, ruling as they think Hafez Assad would have done. Therefore Bashar has had little choice in his own government and has had to keep the foreign minister, Farouk Sharaa, and most of the other strong political personalities in their place. The foreign political situation remains more or less the same as under his father's long-time regime, but after the advent of Sharon no hope of a settlement is in sight.

The long negotiation between Arafat and Barak, assisted by President Clinton in Camp David in July 2000, as mentioned above, ended without any final agreement. The last effort under Barak and Clinton was made at Taba (Egypt) in early 2001, when the parties seemed to have come close to a final conclusion. But the holy city of Jerusalem was once again one of the stumbling blocks, together with the unsolved refugee question and the problem of the border crossings. Therefore no final agreement was reached at this last stage of serious negotiations, and there is still no agreement today. The second *intifada*, which broke out on 28 September 2000, continued throughout the year 2001, and has been on the increase since then. Ben-Ami, who took part in the negotiations with the Palestinians until the end, emphasises in his book that Arafat was a very difficult personality, who was never able to take the final responsibility for an agreement. But Ben-Ami also admits that Barak should perhaps have taken a more personal interest in these final, but abortive talks.[256] Here, one might recall Ben-Ami's comment that Barak was a failure as a statesman.

Barak already had many difficulties at home because of the very insecure political situation threatening him, and had to endure severe criticism even from within the Party, where some called him "the little Bonaparte", thinking him a very arrogant politician, not keen on consulting even his own party leaders. In that respect he could be compared to his predecessor, Netanyahu. Strange to note the fact that the right-wing forces in Israel openly welcomed the failure in Camp David in July 2000! We have quoted above that it was very difficult for Arafat to get approval from his colleagues after the Oslo Accord, which confirms that he was not the only power centre in the PLO. He had to persuade his colleagues, and it apparently proved too difficult this time. It was probably not only Barak (who had tried seven years earlier to persuade Rabin against accepting the Oslo I Agreement, when he was the Chief of Staff) who showed a lack of statesmanship in his last round of negotiations with the PLO leader, but also his opponent Yassir Arafat, never an easy politician for outsiders to grasp, who failed in leadership.

Discussions between the parties continued on and off, but no real agreement was in sight, even at the end when President Clinton was about to be replaced by George W. Bush and Barak by Ariel Sharon, in late January 2001. Whereas Birgitte Rahbek gives expression to the many who doubt that any concrete offer was ever presented by the Israeli side,[257] official Israeli sources point out just the opposite, saying that the Prime Minister in his last effort urged Arafat to accept his *generous offer*, as it was termed.[258] It all came to nothing, however, but we do not know

---

256 Ibid., p. 104 and p. 105. Ben-Ami, in his interesting account of the talks, shows respect for the Palestinian leader, but also underscores that Arafat lives in another world, so to say.

257 See her article in *Politiken* of 27 December 2000.

258 All the historical facts are not yet known, but the Arabs pretend that the offer was not very concrete or as generous as the Israeli side has stipulated. Even if Israel offered 96 or 97% of the occupied territory to the Palestinians, not only Jerusalem, but also the question of refugees, still created stumbling blocks. One of the Egyptian delegates to the talks at Taba, in Egypt, near Eilat in Israel, told me in March 2002 that "Barak himself was hesitating" because he knew the hostile atmosphere in many circles in

exactly why, and the two versions are not compatible, as will be seen. The atmosphere between the parties had definitely worsened in the preceding months and especially since the new *intifada* started after a provocation by the soon-to-be Prime Minister, Ariel Sharon. He visited the place of the holy Mosques on 28 September 2000, accompanied by several hundred heavily armed bodyguards — a totally unnecessary demonstration of power, for which Barak was also partly to blame (because he had accepted the massive protection of Sharon, or at least it was authorised by his government). The well-known American commentator William Pfaff wrote in the *International Herald Tribune* on 10 October 2000, that "Sharon's visit to the contested area, meant to undercut any concessions that Mr. Barak might have offered, proved a terminal provocation. It was meant to be that". I entirely agree.

Ben-Ami, who had been Minister for the Police before becoming Foreign Minister, thinks that this provocation was not the reason for the outbreak of a new violent wave; he forgets, however, or rather omits, I think, to mention the fact that Sharon came to the holy Muslim area with numerous armed guards. From an Arab point of view this was a special provocation, and we may here recall the fatal visit of King Abdullah to the same place in 1951, ending in his assassination. But unlike Sharon, he had come almost without any special protection, despite the fact that he was also a very controversial leader. We have to take into account here the fact that the failure in July 2000 of the important negotiation round in Camp David had added to the frustrations of the Palestinians, who could not easily forget the difficulties and humiliations under the three-year government of Netanyahu, ending only little more than a year ago.

At a conference in Tel Aviv in June 2003, political scientists and policymakers from Israel and the USA met in order to try to throw more light on the failure of the peace efforts in the Barak period. Only one representative from *the other side* (the Arabs), Dr. Samith el–Abed, Vice Minister in the PA Ministry of Planning, took part. *A comedy of errors* was probably the most significant comment heard from among the many participants who were critical, not only of the Israeli Prime Minister, but equally of the American delegates and also of Arafat, of course. Ron

---

> Israel to these concessions. Therefore his lack of flexibility on the hard-core questions meant that Arafat could not accept the terms offered, even if many of them seemed generous. Ben-Ami states that it was rather the uncertainties of the Oslo Accord that brought about the lack of agreement between Barak and Arafat. He also underlines that even within the Labour-led government there was disagreement with regard to the concessions to be granted to the PLO. Op.cit. p., 118. The increase in Jewish settlements since Oslo (from 50,000 to 220,000 settlers) is another reason for the lack of agreement, he adds. Now there are 400,000 settlers, according to Rahbek; see her above-mentioned article in *Politiken*, dated 27 December 2001. Pundik operates with almost the same figure.

Pundak, one of the advisers behind the Oslo Agreement, emphasised that the whole Israeli strategy failed, and he was also very critical of Barak's role, just as we have mentioned was the case with the then Foreign Minister, Ben – Ami.[259]

When we evaluate what was behind the failure of the 2000 – 2001 talks between Israel and the Palestinians, assisted by the outgoing Clinton administration, it is surely not enough to take note of the official Israeli version, according to which Arafat was so stupid as not to accept the *generous offer* granting a coming Palestinian State almost 96% of the occupied territory and other positive solutions, for instance, on Jerusalem. I feel it very appropriate also to listen to Clinton's Secretary of State, Madeleine Albright, who has recently published her *Madame Secretary, A Memoir* (2003).[260] She writes that she spent 15 days in Camp David, locked in with Israeli and Palestinian leaders, and that "after three days we had drafted one paper rejected by Barak and a second rejected by the Palestinians".[261] Her description of the two main leaders is significant in helping to understand the atmosphere, when she writes, "Barak was clearly drained by the hours he spent on the telephone tending political forces at home" and Arafat just "seemed a tired and isolated old man".[262] After the final negative result she simply concludes "Camp David was over", but later adds that it was the most disappointing event in her long period as Secretary.[263] She also gives an account of how Clinton eventually put forward a final paper, which was not presented as an American proposal, but which — on the basis of the negotiations so far — the President thought would be needed on core issues, in order to reach an agreement. The Palestinians never gave a definite answer, and at one point Madeleine Albright writes about "Arafat's intransigence", whereas "the Israeli's had given all they could".[264] Basically, her account as an important witness corresponds to the Israeli version. But we also have other American representatives, who gave their account at a seminar in Tel Aviv (see footnote 259). Let us first quote Dr. Rob Malley, who took part as a Middle East adviser to the President, and later confirmed that "in Camp David there was never any complete proposal presented which the Palestinians could really have accepted". He added that some of Arafat's advisors were even more intransigent than the PLO leader himself. Another American participant, however, Martin Indyk, did accuse Arafat

---

259 Hanne Foighel has recently written an interesting article about this conference in Tel Aviv; see *Udenrigs* (the regular publication from the Danish *Udenrigspolitiske Selskab*, no.3, 2003), p. 58 in *Camp David in retrospect*, which gives a full picture of the Conference.
260 Madeleine Albright, *Madame Secretary, A Memoir* NY, Miramax Books, 2003.
261 Ibid., p. 619.
262 Ibid., p. 622 - 623.
263 Ibid., p. 629 and p. 634.
264 Ibid., p. 629.

of being unreasonably adamant, "which his own people ought to blame him for".[265] We may recall again that the then Foreign Minister of Israel, Ben-Ami, admitted failure on the Israeli side during the talks, in agreement with some other Israeli witnesses who spoke out at the seminar in Tel Aviv.

If Arafat, therefore, all in all, may have miscalculated and *missed the boat* at this important juncture in history, the other side had apparently not presented its offer in a generous way. The PLO leader was, at any rate, generally speaking not very forthcoming during diplomatic negotiations, which were never his strong side, to put it mildly. But we must also take into account that for a long time, the PLO had felt from their opponents a great lack of respect for agreements, as we have mentioned above. This had been the case, not only under such a negative opponent as Netanyahu with regard to the Oslo agreement, but also, and very recently, under Barak, with regard to the Wye or other minor agreements.

These were either ignored by the Jerusalem governments (under Netanyahu as well as under Barak) or purposely pushed aside, mostly with reference to Palestinian terrorism. Combined with the steady increase in Jewish illegal settlements in the occupied territories, even under Labour Party governments, this explains a lot. Even if we concede, as I surely do, that terrorism was and remains a serious problem, we may also ask "Why?" With this question mark, I certainly do not intend to exonerate Arafat of any guilt he might have had. He definitely played his cards badly, and ignored the fact that he should have tried as far as possible to suppress any terrorist acts, especially when he had a fairly liberal opponent, as in the Barak period. On the contrary, he made an agreement with *Hamas* and *Jihad* in September 2000 in order to co-ordinate their fight, and he also freed several *Hamas* prisoners, making the Israeli government angry and frustrated. By not co-operating with the Barak government, Arafat therefore antagonised even those peace-loving Israelis who wanted to grant concessions, also real ones, to the PLO side.

We may here repeat that even this last Labour government had allowed new settlements in the occupied territories during Barak's short term — almost as many as Netanyahu did. In this respect there has been little difference between Labour and Likud governments.[266]

The still active *intifada* has cost more than two thousand Palestinians their lives and thousands wounded, plus a great number of Israeli losses, though they were well below the one- hundred mark in 2001. This number has steadily increased since then. It must be worrisome to the Israelis that whereas the death rate at an earlier stage was one to ten in favour of the Jews, it has recently (in 2002) changed to one out of three killed being Israeli. The Israeli Secret Service[267] has at the same

---

265 *Udenrigs* op.cit., p. 63 - 64.
266 See Birgitte Rahbek, op.cit., p. 318.
267 For those interested in knowing more about the Mossad, the most well-known secret

time carried out a brutal series of killings of those supposedly responsible for the *intifada*, and we were confronted with almost the worst scenario, when the two new leaders took over in early 2001 in the USA and Israel.

The lack of progress in the final peace talks resulted not only in the poor result for Prime Minister Barak in the February 2001 elections, but also in his soon losing the chairmanship of the party, which was given back to Simon Peres, albeit only for a short while. People had lost confidence not only in the Labour Party, but sadly enough also in the peace process. It had looked promising when Barak took over after the negative years of Netanyahu, but also he ended his leadership in failure, after hardly two years in power. The political situation was now dominated by confusion, influenced by an almost desperate lack of security in Israel, because of the violence of the second *intifada*.

The ill-famed General Ariel Sharon won the elections, this time with a more secure result (over 62%) than his Likud predecessor and rival in the party, Benjamin Netanyahu, who left politics for a while, bitter that he had not been elected as chairman of the Likud. He could have joined hands with the coming Prime Minister, perhaps, if they had been on speaking terms. But Netanyahu — unlike Barak, who lost the elections and his chairmanship of the Party — was to have a comeback in Israeli politics as Foreign Minister for a while.

---

agency of Israel, I can refer to Victor Ostrovsky and Claire Hoy´s *By Way of Deception. A Devastating Insider´s Portrait of the Mossad*, Canada, 1990. Many countries have such secret services, but the Israeli one has probably got more power than most and — even if we accept that Israel is a democracy — operates more independently of government control than is normally the case in Western nations. Israelis will point out that this is due to the violent environment in which the country has had to survive. But others, including myself, will maintain that good government cannot be reconciled with such actions as indiscriminate killings of terrorist opponents, except if there is proof of guilt in a legal process. More than 300 people have been killed in such state- authorized killings, unfortunately also often involving the death of completely innocent persons. The nomination of an Israeli ambassador to Denmark in 2001, who as a former leader of the Mossad admitted the necessity of using *mild* torture in the fight against terrorists — albeit in a limited way — created quite a debate in Denmark about him as a person. He had been granted *agrément* before his attitudes were disclosed publicly in an interview with a Danish newspaper, and the government would not deny him his post. The (then) Foreign Minister of Denmark, Mogens Lykketoft, said that he did not want to criticise the Ambassador, who was nothing but the representative of his government. But he took the opportunity to heavily criticise the Israeli policies with regard to *Human Rights*.

XVII. THE BRUTALISATION OF CONFLICT UNDER SHARON

1. Man of War

During the election campaign, Barak had accused Sharon of being "a man of war and not of peace". He referred to Sharon's aggressive role in the invasion of Lebanon in 1982, which is a fact no one can deny. That Sharon also had a personal responsibility for the sad massacres there may be seen from the findings of the Commission set up afterwards in Israel to investigate the matter. It concluded that Sharon could not escape serious criticism in this regard, and he was thus degraded by the Begin government at the time. But as we know, he soon staged a political comeback and became minister in several governments. Now he won more than 62% of the votes in the February 2001 general elections, in the special vote for the Prime Ministership, used for the third time only, and later abolished again in Israel. This blunt and brutal general, who was known in the Arab world as a strongman who never hesitated to give orders to kill rather than to negotiate, was now the leader of a right-wing coalition government in Israel, even if his political basis in the Knesset was not convincing at all. He could not persuade the Labour Party as such to enter into the government, but the always ready Simon Peres, now an old man of 78, entered willingly once again as Foreign Minister, a post he did not enjoy under Barak, as we remember.

Sharon, after taking over, criticised his predecessor for having negotiated with Arafat before the *intifada* had stopped. For his part, he stressed in a TV interview in March 2001 that he "would not proceed with the peace process until violence had stopped". He repeated his slogan from before the elections: "Security for the people comes first". Sharon was more lenient with the PLO leader initially than later on, and only said that he was disappointed because Arafat had not called for a halt to hostilities when the Palestinian leader had addressed his lawmakers, only a few days back. Sharon stressed the fact that, as he saw it, Arafat *could* stop the violence, if only he had the intention and will to do it.

This point is exactly where observers disagree. Some of course find, as Sharon does, that basically all the Palestinian resistance groups were controlled by Arafat, whose leadership remained dominant and unchallenged within the PLO. Others, however, tend to think that Arafat had no such absolute power or influence, because extremists — like the *Hamas* or the *Jihad* movements — normally act independently. I tend to believe in the second theory,[268] but, with the lack of openness, nobody knows exactly who decides what in this undercover world of the Palestinian resistance movements. We may conclude here that Arafat was often blamed by both sides and increasingly pushed around by the Israelis in Sharon's period — blamed by the right-wing government in Israel for not suppressing the violence; by his own extremists for giving in to Israeli demands without getting the only thing in return that the PLO wants: Full independence within a reasonable state of its own, generally speaking, in all the occupied territories.

Initially, Sharon also added, in a subdued, diplomatic way that he was soon to abandon: "It is not up to us to decide who leads the Palestinians. Arafat is their leader and a man with whom we have to negotiate […] but not under fire. This government will not negotiate under fire".

Sharon was soon going to have more fire than anybody could want. The escalation of violence that the Prime Minister had indirectly started with his visit, under heavy guard, to the Muslim Holy places soon became a fact of life in the course of 2001 and even more so in 2002, and still continued until recently. To give an example of the extent of the violence, I may quote from a letter sent by the Permanent Representative of the PLO to the UN Secretary General only one month after the takeover of Sharon. In his letter from March 2001, he stresses that more than 400 Palestinians have died since the beginning of the second *intifada* in September 2000, and 60 Israelis, whereas over 14,000, many of them children, have been wounded; of the victims, almost a thousand were seriously wounded. He also pointed out that the IDF was using special munitions, illegal according to relevant UN conventions and far more damaging than necessary. (This is a fact that has been confirmed by several conferences and reported in the international press.) Not only the arms utilised by the IDF, but also the occupation methods — already extremely severe — were made even harsher in Sharon's time, thereby increasing, not abating, the violence. Almost as a matter of routine, some of the more damaging bomb attacks from the Palestinian side that killed many innocent Israelis were met immediately with brutal measures and also resulted in acts of government-ordered killings of *terrorists* by the Israelis.

---

268 When I said so, in an interview with the Danish-origin member of the (first) Sharon government, Michael Melchior, then Vice-Minister of Foreign Affairs, he arrogantly told me: "You know nothing of the Conflict". I hope I do, otherwise this book would not have been written. In an interview with a Danish newspaper, *Politiken,* 15 December 2001, under the headline "The Arabs hate us" he stresses the fact that it was "Arafat who was responsible for the election of Sharon because he declined the peace-offer he got from Barak". A typical, simplistic Israeli view, which is not correct, as explained above.

Israeli Prime Minister Ariel Sharon flanked by bodyguards as a response to extremist threats against the Minister.

But measures such as the closing of whole cities, as was the case with Bethlehem as early as March 2000 and later on again at Christmas time, and isolating other areas for security reasons, was hitting not only the freedom fighters/terrorists, but the whole civilian population and creating havoc in the Palestinian economy. Of course no tourist would dare enter the besieged city where Christ was born; until then the city's economy was based mainly on the income from visitors. Similar damaging effects of the violence and brutal occupation measures were of course to be seen in Israel, but its economy had better possibilities for recovery because of US aid and a much more resilient infrastructure. That Israel certainly also suffers great losses of all kinds is equally evident. The Palestinian economy is in most regards directly dependent on the Israeli authorities, who often withhold customs duties, despite protests from the EU and others.

Arafat was repeatedly asked to stop the violence, also by the new US President, George Bush, when the latter willingly received the Israeli Prime Minister in Washington in March 2001, very shortly after Sharon's takeover. Bush never received Arafat, however,[269] and when feeling left out in the cold, the PLO leader

---

[269] A marked difference from the Clinton period just finished, when the American President had seen the leaders of both sides frequently.

replied in a defiant mood, in the same month of March 2001: "The *intifada* is going to continue until the Palestinians obtain their independence". Bush had initially been very careful not to become involved in the Middle East conflict, where his predecessor, Bill Clinton, had acted with such energy until the end, albeit without any positive result in his last phase, as we remember, due to the lack of will on both sides necessary for compromise. But the new Secretary of State, Colin Powell, soon stressed publicly that the USA had not pulled out of the conflict and would try to assist in finding a solution. Washington had no monopoly in this respect, though, he emphasised. He did not accuse the PLO leader in any direct way, as Sharon soon began to do and surely wanted Washington to imitate. After some specially destructive and brutal Palestinian attacks on civilians in Israel, Sharon began to publicly accuse Arafat of being responsible for the terrorist acts. As punishment, he ordered an IDF attack on Arafat's Guards' barracks in Ramallah at the end of March, wounding more than 60 civilians and others, including two killed in the act. At the same time the UN Human Rights Commission in Geneva condemned the excess of violence used by the IDF. We may therefore conclude that a new vicious circle had begun already in the first month of the Sharon government.

The new Prime Minister himself soon began to speak of an *open war* with the Palestinians, and if we accept Shlaim's description of the first *intifada* as the Palestinian War of Independence, the second, more violent one must surely be seen in the same way. As I have indicated in the title of this book, we may call it a war, albeit between very unequal participants. In April 2001 the IDF was ordered to bomb some refugee camps (after an attack from them) in the Gaza strip with heavy artillery, destroying several houses and wounding and killing more than 30 people.

Two American politicians visited Arafat in the second half of April 2001, and were happy to be asked to transmit a message from the PLO leader to Sharon. In it Arafat proposed a joint declaration by the Israeli Prime Minister and himself to the effect that both ordered their respective armed forces to stop hostilities and begin a series of talks. The two senators later informed the press that Sharon was at first taken aback by this offer, but soon declared that it was not satisfactory. Arafat had to show in practice that he ordered the stopping of hostilities.[270]

The proud (many would say stubborn) PLO leader would not oblige, and peace lovers regretted Sharon's refusal to accept Arafat's opening; the Prime Minister thereby confirmed his distrust of Arafat and his wish to eradicate by force the terrorism so damaging to both peoples. The American professor James Petras wrote an article in April 2001 that the final aim of Sharon was the total evacuation of the Arab population from the occupied territories.[271]

---

270 Here quoted from *El Mundo*, 21 April 2001.
271 *El Mundo*, 3 April 2001.

In early April of the same year, the French government issued a statement condemning the strategy of the Sharon government, stressing that the vicious circle must be broken by the Israeli administration, which had entered a dead-end street. In addition, the new Danish Foreign Minister at the time, Mogens Lykketoft, publicly regretted — and thereby indirectly condemned — the Israeli policy. It was probably the first time that an official person in Denmark called a spade a spade, thereby satisfying parts of the Danish public while offending the rather outspoken, but smaller than before, pro-Israeli circles. Some other observers openly declared that Sharon would lead the whole area into catastrophe. This was also the view of the Danish Minister of Foreign Affairs, who, at the end of 2001, again condemned the Israeli policy of retaliation, which in his view was damaging the situation not only for the Palestinians but also for the Israelis themselves.[272]

Inside the EU it has been difficult up to now to condemn Israeli actions, because at least one member state, Germany, for obvious historical reasons normally does not want to antagonise the Israelis. The five Nordic Ministers of Foreign Affairs[273] had no such problem and openly criticised the Israeli government in this period. Furthermore, the *Mitchell Commission*, established by President Clinton in the autumn of 2000, urged both parties in May 2001 to restore mutual confidence through the stopping of new settlements by the Israeli side and through the imprisonment of terrorists by the Palestinian administration.

Neither of the fighting parties seemed to pay much attention to this well-intentioned advice from the Mitchell Commission. Especially the many attacks by suicide bombers were seen by most observers as a dramatic turn for the worse.

In the same way, several warnings to the government in Jerusalem from the American Vice-President, the EU Commission and by the UN Secretary General against the exaggerated use of force during Israeli acts of retaliation, in particular the use of the modern Israeli Air Force against civilian areas, also went almost unnoticed, it seems. On 9 April 2001, the *International Herald Tribune* carried the headline "Sharon, defying US, vows to press ahead. Bush repeats demand". It seems as if these US demands had not been made in terms strong enough to be respected, which was an experience Reagan and other US presidents had previously had with stubborn Israeli leaders, despite their dependence on the USA. Of course this negative attitude in Jerusalem is due to the knowledge that at the end of the day, Washington will never cut off assistance to Israel, because of the important Jewish lobby in the United States and for American geo-political reasons.

The same negative fate met an appeal from the official representatives of the group of the eight most industrialised countries in the world, when they held a

---

272 *Politiken*, 27 December 2001.
273 Denmark, Iceland, Finland, Norway and Sweden, with a close collaboration in a Nordic Union.

meeting in Rome in July 2001 and expressed their concern about the increasing conflict. They suggested a mission of "international observers" to be sent to the area of conflict. They also demanded that both sides respect and comply with the Mitchell Report.[274] The Israeli government bluntly told these powerful nations that it was hostile to the sending out of new foreign observers because such a mission would only amount to a fulfilment of the Palestinians' request.[275] In July, President Mubarak warned Israel of dangerous consequences, if the Israeli offensive against the Palestinians continued inside the occupied territories as if the IDF were at home there (as in Israel). The IDF now played a decisive role in combatting terrorism with its heavy armament in all occupied territories. The warning to Sharon stressed that Egypt might break off those diplomatic relations that Sadat had granted Israel as the first Arab nation long ago.

In an attack with missiles on 27 August 2001, the IAF killed the leader of the Popular Front for the Liberation of Palestine (PFLP) Mustapha Ali Zahri, who literally lost his head in this brutal operation.

In early September 2001, the EU Foreign Ministers *demanded* that Arafat eliminate the terrorist nets and that Israel withdraw its forces from the occupied territories. Neither of the warring parties seemed to listen to these requests from a EU that still had its difficulties in finding an appropriate role, because — as mentioned above — the individual countries among the fifteen-member Union had different opinions with regard to the Middle East. Germany was generally more positive towards the Israelis, while the French and most Southern European nations were also trying to accommodate the Palestinian side as much as possible. The other member states — the UK, the Benelux and the Scandinavian members[276] — were in the middle. Soon after this balanced EU-appeal, the world experienced the worst terrorist attack ever recorded in history.

---

274 The Report demanded *a cease-fire* as the first step, followed after some time by direct talks between the parties aiming at a final status peace agreement. George Tennet, the director of the US CIA was chosen to supervise the withdrawal of Israeli forces and monitor the new arrangement.

275 Strange reasoning behind this rejection, because it refers only to the fact that the other part had requested this same solution. During a visit to Washington, Vice-Minister for Foreign Affairs Michael Melchior told the American authorities, that the suggestion would not work in practice. Only a more diplomatic rejection, it seems, than the first mentioned one.

276 Only Denmark, Finland and Sweden, whereas Norway and Iceland remain outside the EU.

2. After 11 September 2001

Terrorism took on a new dimension in the world after the shocking attack on the World Trade Towers and the Pentagon on 11 September 2001, which not only confronted the American government with a challenge of huge proportions, but also had serious repercussions in the Arab world. The Danish journalist Herbert Pundik, quoted here several times, wrote about the "Roots of Hatred", emphasising that the continuous and unsolved conflict in the Middle East, and the pro-Israeli US policies, must be seen as one of the reasons behind this tremendous terrorist attack.[277] Others, of course, found different reasons behind the attack, but I tend to agree with the first finding, i.e. that the *main* cause behind 11 September was the unsolved and humiliating conflict we are analysing here. Many Arabs or Muslims had come to hate the USA because of the dominant world power's all-permeating international influence; this hatred mirrored in particular the serious frustrations felt by the Arabs and Palestinians because of their continuous humiliations under the harsh measures imposed by Sharon, combined with the US support of Israel, despite some warnings on and off, to which I have already referred. The Arab world saw only the humiliations, the extreme use of force in the occupied territories, and forgot the terrorist acts, which they could only recognise as a *result* of the humiliations, not as *the cause* of the basic conflict.

Just to give an example from the Arab world, it is worthwhile quoting a well-known Jordanian journalist, Alia Toukan, who on 27 November 2001 wrote, in the normally fairly objective *Jordan Times*: "US administrations' unwavering support for the Jewish state is providing fodder for extremists".

Sharon, on his part, again reacted wrongly after 11 September. He arrogantly pretended that the new fight against terrorism which Bush was soon going to launch united Israelis and Americans and the whole free world in the same *crusade*. He had, however, to endure some corrections from Washington, which wanted Arab understanding for the US elimination of the Taliban regime in Afghanistan, that had supported Bin Laden and his horribly destructive movement. But after the success of the American intervention in Afghanistan, at the end of 2001, Washington and Sharon seemed again to speak the same language, with Sharon enjoying even more support and understanding — up to a point.

The internal co-operation inside the Israeli coalition government was very fragile and lacked harmony, and Simon Peres had patiently to swallow many of his former ideals, living with a leader who surely not only neglected the other side in the conflict, but did not seem to want any real peace arrangement at all. Peres endeavoured to continue an open dialogue with Arafat, but Sharon generally ig-

---

277 *Politiken*, 23 September 2001.

nored or even opposed such meetings. The Prime Minister's policies soon forced the Palestinians into a more desperate fight, which is still going on.

In one instance (at the end of September 2001), according to an Israeli newspaper, *Yediot Aharonot*, Foreign Minister Peres accused the army, in particular general Moshe Yaalon, a very high-ranking officer, of wanting to kill Arafat.[278] It would not last long before his own political master, Sharon, openly declared that he regretted not having killed the PLO leader when it had been in his power to do so during the occupation of Lebanon in 1982 – 83;[279] this was a rare and absurd declaration from a would-be statesman, but it proves beyond much doubt that Sharon only thinks and acts as a military person of the hardest school. When Peres was in Spain in November 2001, he gave an interview to *el Mundo*, in which he was asked whether he would agree that Arafat was unable to control all the Palestinian armed movements. He answered, "[i]f one desires to have a state, one has to be able to control the armed forces. Whereas Israel has many (different) visions, it has only one army. In the Palestinian camp, on the contrary, there are many armies but only one vision".[280] Peres seemed to forget that exactly the same could be said about Israel when it was fighting for the consolidation of a Jewish state before and immediately after Independence. The various armed fractions acted as the worst terrorists one can imagine, some of them under later prime ministers such as Begin and Shamir (e.g. the bomb attack on Hotel David, the assassination of Bernadotte), and Ben-Gurion could hardly control them until he got his state. And if we compare the two situations, a Palestinian state seems much further away from real acceptance today than Israel was in 1947 – 48, when the new Jewish nation was surely not humiliated in any way comparable with what is the case for the PA/PLO now.

As a symbolic gesture to the Arab world, President Bush stated in October 2001 that a solution to the Middle East Conflict suggested the establishment of a Palestinian State. At the UN General Assembly in November 2001, Peres declared that there was support in Israel for a Palestinian state, but this was not yet fully in keeping with the official policy of the Ariel Sharon government. If Sharon had perhaps in some instances accepted the idea vaguely, it was clear that the Palestinian state he envisaged would not be a viable one. The Foreign Minister of Israel received a good deal of criticism from right-wing circles at home with regard to his statement in New York.

Some limited cease-fire arrangements between the parties were reached in the second half of 2001 but never lasted very long. In one instance, when the *Hamas*

---

278 Quoted from *el Mundo*, 1 October 2001.
279 In an article in *el Mundo*, on 1 February 2002, it is pointed out that Sharon *did try to kill Arafat* with the repeated bombings of his headquarters in 1982. This makes the bombastic declaration by Sharon even more absurd.
280 El Mundo, 4 November 2001.

had declared that it had stopped its armed activities and actually respected this declaration in practice, Israel did not resist the temptation to murder one of the *Hamas* leaders, with the result, of course, that violence resurged immediately.

The assassination on 17 October 2001 of the Tourist Minister of Israel, R. Zeevi — an extremist who had declared that he wanted all Palestinians to be sent out of the occupied territories — and the murder of several Israeli settlers in December led to the sad result not only that the IDF destroyed many PA buildings in Ramallah, but also that the Sharon government officially declared that the PLO and its leader represented the terrorists and that Israel would therefore cease all contact with them. Sharon thus viewed Arafat as simply *irrelevant to the conflict*, despite the fact that the PLO leader still represented some millions of adherents who accepted no other leader. Sharon had apparently completely forgotten his own initial statement as Prime Minister that it was up to the Palestinians to choose their leader.

In November 2001 the US sent a peace mission to the area, headed by General Zinni, in order to press for a settlement of the conflict; but at the same time, the IDF carried out a heavy retaliation-attack on Gaza, wounding several, including a pregnant woman, and killing a young boy of 13. The spiralling violence soon killed many innocent Israelis in a shooting attack organised by the extremist Palestinian organisation, *Jihad*.

When the EU and the USA, following new attacks, including those by dramatic suicide bombers (a total of 30 in 2001), urged Arafat to arrange a cease-fire, the PLO leader eventually agreed, declaring on 17 December 2001 that he would order a stop to all armed attacks and disarm radical groups. But this did not impress Sharon enough to let the PLO leader visit the town of Bethlehem at Christmas-time, where he had often before participated in a mass, together with his Christian wife.

We cannot of course give a detailed list here of all the serious incidents in the area of conflict, but it will easily be understood that we have to conclude as follows: The year 2001, when Sharon had taken over, saw a steady escalation of violence and brutal retaliations that in late December was resulting in more bloodshed than ever. Hardly anyone could now realistically hope for a peaceful settlement between the parties.[281] Arafat was weakened physically, but gained in stature in his own world, it seems. The EU and the USA continued to declare that they still regarded Arafat as the legitimate Palestinian leader. But this President of a humiliated small entity, not recognised as a state and not even as a negotiation partner by Israel, could not enter 2002 with much hope. Arafat feared not only the continuous onslaught from the Israeli side, but also the competition from the radical movements such as *Hamas* and *Jihad*, which were strengthened by the public uproar over the brutal

---

281 In a humoristic way, the already mentioned Israeli deputy minister, Melchior, said in an interview in a Danish newspaper that the faint light he saw at the end of the tunnel might come from tanks driving in the opposite direction.

repressive methods of the occupying forces.

Sharon had surely not obtained security for his population, as he had promised, and was further away from peace than most of his predecessors had ever been, except in open wartime. The Prime Minister himself liked to use the phrase *war with the PLO*, whereas others still hesitated to call it war as such.[282] But surely there is now a warlike situation between two very unequal opponents, the Prime Minister of a strong military power, Israel, and the leader of a weak, humiliated and insecure entity, the occupied territories of the PA.

3. Dangerous Years, 2002-2004

During his visit to the area of conflict, the American Vice President Cheney agreed to see the PA leader, Yassir Arafat, whom the Bush government had so far tried to ignore or put under the obligation to stop entirely any form of violence — a demand that seemed difficult for two reasons: 1) Arafat did not wield absolute power over the organisations that were not directly under his command, such as *Jihad* or *Hamas*; and 2) Only if there were an Israeli withdrawal from all significant areas of the occupied lands these organisations might comply with a direct demand to stop violence.

The year 2002 had hardly begun when Sharon accused Arafat of being *an enemy of Israel*, as if much else could be expected. Was the Prime Minister himself a friend of the PLO and its long-time leader, whom he only shortly before had wished assassinated twenty years ago? In January the IDF intercepted a shipment full of arms, which was — according to the Sharon government — supposed to be delivered to the PNA, Arafat's armed forces. This was denied by the PLO leader, but of course any army or police force will be looking for weapons from any possible source. If this is so, the timing of this consignment was badly chosen, and the arms of a rather *offensive* nature.[283]

With the takeover of the EU Presidency by Spain[284] in early January 2002, it was even less easy for the Israeli government to convince the EU leadership of

---

282 Pundik, in early 2002, told me that I should not use the word *War*, because that would play into Sharon´s hands. Later on, however, he used the same word himself, and so do most observers now. What else can one do?

283 See also Pundik in *Politiken*, January 2001, where he writes that "the Israeli occupation of Palestine is illegal" and that it is only natural that the PA must fight against it as long as the Sharon government does not grant the PA any concessions.

284 Normally opinions held in Spain are supposed to be rather close to Arabs opinions and therefore Madrid from time to time has a difficult relationship with the Jerusalem government.

its just cause with regard to the policy of intrusions into, and brutal retaliation attacks against, the occupied territories. The Chairman of the EU Foreign Ministers, Spain's Josep Piqué, openly declared that the recent retaliation attacks by the IDF in the Gaza were unjustified and could never be said to be of a *defensive* nature. Not unexpectedly, Sharon did not accept this criticism and now accused the PNA of collusion with Iran and Syria to form a terrorist coalition.

When Piqué was in Cairo in January 2002, he stated that it would be a good idea to work out an estimate of all the damage to buildings and infrastructure in the occupied areas that had been established or supported through the substantial EU financial aid to the PA. In the years 1994 to 1998, the PA received European aid of more than $600 million, and individual EU countries also contributed to the Palestinian entity.[285] The purpose of the suggested review of financial support might be to demand compensation from Israel for some of the damage. This more or less direct criticism of Israel does not mean that the EU as such, or any of its member states, condoned the worst excesses of terrorism, which was of course the background of the Israeli retaliations.

On 18 January 2002, the IDF encircled the Arafat residence in Ramallah with tanks, in retaliation for a violent terrorist attack in Hadera, killing six persons at a Jewish celebration of a *bar mitzvah*. The terrorist action was immediately condemned by Piqué, as spokesman for the EU, during his visit to Damascus, while he also regretted the retaliation attack. This attack was to be understood as a warning to the PA of even worse things to come. Despite Piqué's expressed fear that the peace process had now collapsed, the EU could see no other alternative than to continue to re-establish contact between the warring parties, he stressed.

On 24 January, Elie Hobeika was assassinated in Beirut, shortly before he was due to be a witness in Brussels during a process of investigation of the war crimes of Ariel Sharon. Hobeika was a man with several enemies, but many observers saw in this murderous act the hand of the secret service of Israel, which would eliminate a person who had a great deal of blood on his hands and could give dangerous testimony. Hobeika had been the leader of one of the right-wing militias that had perpetrated the terrible massacre of Palestinians in refugee camps near Beirut, which had taken place twenty years earlier under the eyes of the IDF. We have already mentioned that Sharon was indirectly condemned at the time by a Commission of Inquiry in Israel, for serious negligence or worse, and it is therefore not unlikely that the Prime Minister would now have found it tempting to see to it that an awkward witness was eliminated. A local politician, who had just seen Hobeika beforehand in Belgium, had got the impression that the latter was going to accuse Sharon of being responsible for the orders given with regard to the mas-

---

285 Denmark alone more than $100 million over a five-year period in the nineties.

sacre,[286] but that he (Hobeika) had not wanted to come forward with his accusation until he could give an open testimony before the investigating commission. Fortunately for Sharon, Hobeika's death was timely, so an open accusation against the Israeli Prime Minister was averted. Sharon's government naturally denied any complicity in the assassination.

In early 2002, the EU had planned to recognise a Palestinian state, in accordance with a French proposal, but this was avoided in the last minute, at the EU's meeting of Foreign Ministers, in Caceres, Spain, on 9 February. If this decision (negative for Israel) had been taken, it would have amounted to an open confrontation with Israel, and therefore, pressure from Washington stopped it. The US government argued that the conditions were not appropriate in this early part of 2002, because of recent terrorist attacks. The EU also seemed to acknowledge at this meeting that the Oslo Process and the Mitchell Report were no longer of any relevance at this difficult moment.

But even President Bush declined once again to follow the advice given by Sharon during the latter's fourth visit to Washington in less than a year, to withdraw the US recognition of the RAIS, as Arafat was named by his own adherents.

The US Secretary of State, Colin Powell, wrote an article in February 2002, in which he defined the US policy in the Middle East as follows: "We still want to adopt all the elements of the Mitchell Plan and eventually see a Jewish state that is sure within its borders, and a Palestinian land also free and sure within its borders, and a prosperous trade between the parties, combined with friendship and good neighbourliness, not hatred".[287]

In February, the still hopeful (or opportunistic) Simon Peres told a Spanish newspaper that after having negotiated for a long time with one of the Palestinian leaders, Abu Ala, he could now mention that the discussed plan aimed at granting the PLO autonomy/independence in some 40% of the occupied territories. This was the same idea that Netanyahu had had in mind, but surely a far cry from [the generous offer] of Barak, presented — or was it? — only little more than one year earlier.[288] But the day after this interview, the IDF reduced Arafat's headquarters to ruins. How can official politicians or diplomats of a state negotiate with representatives of another entity — not yet recognised as a state — when the government of the former is at the same time using violent methods against what we could term the *underdog entity*?

---

286 An article in *el Mundo,* 25 January 2002 states that all fingers point to the South and more specifically to Ariel Sharon as responsible for this heinous murder.
287 Here quoted from *el Mundo,* 16 February 2002. I have therefore translated from Spanish, not fully sure of the original version in English. One notices the difference between the word *state* for Israel and *land* for Palestine, literally translated from *tierra*.
288 *El Mundo,* 20 February.

In the brutal IDF attack on Ramallah and Gaza on 20 February, 18 innocent victims lost their lives and a huge amount of property was destroyed. The almost simultaneous presentation of the above-mentioned plan during Peres's visit to Madrid therefore seemed rather absurd, all the more so because Sharon ignored it, being engaged in his war on the terrorists and PNA, actually on Arafat and the whole PA. The Prime Minister could therefore not be interested in such niceties as a peace plan which no one could visualise at the moment.

One of the more positive signs in the conflict at this otherwise sad moment was a peace plan presented by the Saudi Arabian government, to which we shall soon return. It was received with some positive remarks by lone voices in a sea of hatred, by the always ready Simon Peres and by the Israeli President, Moshe Katsav. The latter offered to travel personally to Riyadh to further the process. This gesture from a personality without political power, but with the prestige of his high office, shows us to what absurd and opposing extremes the negative and positive tendencies run in this conflict.

All the Israeli acts of punishment against Arafat, who now lived isolated in semi-destroyed headquarters surrounded by many ruins, did not stop the violence, if Sharon had ever really believed in his own policy of retaliation. In the first days of March seven Israeli soldiers and three settlers were shot dead by an (apparently) lone terrorist; altogether, 21 Israelis lost their lives in 24 hours on 3 March. The day before, six Palestinians, including a small boy who was killed by a tank, had lost their lives, when the IDF attacked refugee camps, which gives some explanation — if no justification, of course — for the above-mentioned attack on Israeli soldiers and settlers. After more violence of the same kind from both sides, the IAF attacked Gaza on 6 March, killing several Palestinians, and this led to open US criticism, presented by Colin Powell in the American Congress, of Sharon's retaliation policies.

In the middle of this desperate situation, Sharon had to give Arafat permission to leave Ramallah in order to participate in the Arab summit at the end of the month, and this concession was surely due to pressure from Washington, in the hope that the coming discussion of the Saudi Arabian peace plan could at least bring some new opening to a desperate situation. But soon orders were again given, prohibiting Arafat from leaving, and the situation became absurd when, on 12 March 2002, the IDF launched the biggest military operation in the occupied territories, with 20,000 soldiers and 150 tanks. On the same date, the UN Security Council passed a resolution, 1397, which for the first time mentioned "a vision of two states, Israel and Palestine, (that) live side by side within secure and recognised borders". The resolution also welcomed the contribution of the Saudi Crown Prince, Abdullah (in reality the leader of his country) and the diplomatic efforts by other powers, while expressing concern at the continuation of the tragic and violent events that have taken place since September 2000.

On 1 April, the *International Herald Tribune* carried a leading article entitled "The

Limits of Force", in which the *New York Times*, from where the article originated, emphasised that "if anything has been learned in 18 blood-soaked months, it is that military responses have caused only minimal interruption to the Palestinian terrorist infrastructure, while fanning the flames of anger and resolve. Israelis need security, Palestinians need a state". With these few words, the description of the conflict at this sad stage could not be more accurate.

This same month of April began with the publication of most of the content of the plan put forward by Anthony Zinni, the US general, who — as already mentioned — had been sent by President Bush in order to promote some form of progress between the parties. But a suicide bomber killed 14 Israelis at almost the same time,[289] inaugurating a month that was going to be one of the bloodiest in Israel's history, and therefore one of the saddest within our framework.

The Palestinians complained that the Zinni report did not mention the final status talks, but only referred to the first step in the Mitchell Report, the cease-fire. They wanted a clear link between the two elements. The UN and many individual countries at the same time urged Israel to stop the siege of Arafat, encircled and not able to get out of his bunker, as it were. The opinion in the USA with regard to Sharon's brutality was also turning negative, and the *Washington Post* wrote that "Sharon's offensive must stop" (from the *International Herald Tribune*, 2 April 2002). The article criticised Bush for being too lenient with Sharon, saying, "he cannot focus the pressure on a Palestinian leader effectively under Israeli arrest". Very just and significant words that I can easily endorse.

Despite the fact that world public opinion, as illustrated by the above quotations, now went against the Jerusalem government more than ever before (or at least for many years) even in the USA, Sharon pressed his armed forces forward in early April. They occupied large areas of the West Bank, including the holy Christian city of Bethlehem, and ignored the fact that, according to the Oslo Agreements, these areas were no longer under direct Israeli control.

The EU tried to mediate through its Chairman of the Council, the Spanish Prime Minister, J.M. Aznar, but in this instance, the crisis had passed the mediation level. The former Prime Minister of Lebanon, Selim Hoss, sent an open letter to President Bush, in which he tried to urge the latter to see the damage done because of the Israeli policies. "Is this what your glorification of freedom, democracy and human rights implies?" he asked sarcastically about the American policy, and pointed out that Washington was now seen by the Arab world "as an ally of the slaughterer of the epoch, Sharon".[290] At the same time, huge demonstrations took place in Beirut, in favour of the Palestinian cause that had created such havoc in Lebanon up to only a decade earlier.

---

289 It took place in Haifa, at the time when I happened to be in the country.
290 Quoted from *Daily Star*, Beirut, 2 April 2002.

A respected American commentator, William Pfaff was right, I find, when he emphasised that "Sharon was exploiting America's war on terrorism", adding, "[i]t offers Israel an expedient ride on the US government's post-Sept. 11 obsession".[291] Even more critical was the well-known (Jewish) American commentator, Thomas Friedman, who in the same newspaper of 4 April wrote: "Only because of the collaboration of feckless American Jewish leaders, fundamentalist Christians and neoconservatives, has it been impossible for anyone in the American administration to talk seriously about halting the Israeli settlement building, thereby *prolonging a colonial Israeli occupation that threatens the entire Zionist enterprise*" (my emphasis).

Finally President George Bush spoke on the Middle East, on 4 April 2002, pointing out the following elements: "The situation has deteriorated dramatically in the last week, just when we were almost reaching a cease-fire, according to my special envoy, Anthony Zinni. [That may seem over-optimistic (my remark).] That hope fell away when a terrorist attacked a group of innocent people at a Netanya hotel, killing many men and women in what is a mounting toll of terror […].[292] Across the world, people are grieving for Israelis and Palestinians […,] the future is dying, the future of the Palestinian people and the future the Israeli people. Terror must be stopped […] the United States is supporting the legitimate aspirations of the Palestinian people for a Palestinian state and Israel has recognised the goal of a Palestinian state. This could be a hopeful moment for the Middle East. The proposal of the Crown Prince Abdullah of Saudi Arabia, supported by the Arab League, has put a number of Arab countries closer than ever to recognising Israel's right to exist […]. Israeli settlements must stop. Israel should also show a respect for and concern about the dignity of the Palestinian people who are and will be their neighbours. I ask Israel to halt incursions into Palestinian-controlled areas and begin the withdrawal".

If I have emphasised the President's positive remarks about Palestine (and omitted those about Israel), it is because we have here a clear American recognition of the rights of the Palestinians to have their own state, which the US had already endorsed with the above-mentioned UN Security Council resolution of 12 March. President Bush also mentioned that Israel recognises a Palestinian state. Does the President here include Sharon?[293] As far as our experience goes with the government now in Jerusalem, this would be the case only if we talk of a small *Bantustan* state of Palestine, completely controlled by the Israeli government. I have also

---

291 *International Herald Tribune*, 4 April.
292 I was in a hotel in Tel Aviv at that time, and experienced the fear among most Jews around the country in this very dangerous period. The suicide attack took place among people celebrating the Jewish festival of Passover.
293 George Bush may think, as the saying goes: "Free me from my friends, I can cope with my enemies".

referred to the US President's positive remark with regard to the Saudi Arabian plan — again endorsed by the UN resolution — to which we shall return later. If only the American government would carry out in the real world, what amounts to a balanced policy on paper, the conflict might have stopped long ago.

During Zinni's visit in Arafat's headquarters, the PLO leader accepted the American President's suggestions for resumed peace negotiations with the Israeli government. But despite the appeal by the US President, Sharon, on his part, vowed to continue his brutal military operation in the occupied areas, aiming at eradicating terrorism, as he saw it. Bush was not amused and declared on 8 April that he had meant what he said when he asked the IDF to withdraw, but Sharon seemed deaf, even to friendly calls. Bush seems to be good at blowing hot and cold at the same time, because in one instance shortly after his complaint, he called Sharon *a man of peace*.

In the real world, the IDF not only continued its occupation and encirclement of the PLO headquarters in Ramallah, but it also waged a war of nerves against the encircled Arafat. IDF tanks used their noisy engines at night outside the PLO headquarters, or what was left of the buildings. Electricity and water supplies were cut off and life became intolerable in Arafat's residence. But the PLO leader seemed to thrive in these challenging times. Extreme situations arose frequently, however, for instance when the IDF soldiers shot at Palestinian ambulances, which enraged doctors and others in the civilised world. The Israeli excuse was that these ambulances often carried weapons. Taking into consideration the differences in the number of armed forces and their strength on the respective sides, the Israeli excuse carries little weight.

On 9 April 2002, the Chairman of the EU Foreign Ministers, Piqué, suggested the introduction of sanctions against Israel if the IDF were not pulled out of the occupied territories; at a meeting in Madrid the following day with representatives from the UN, the EU, the USA and Russia, he also announced a new peace plan, of fairly modest ambitions, to be launched by the EU, Russia, the USA and the UN together. It was based on the recent UN SC resolution 1402, which imposed an immediate cease-fire that also applied to terrorism, and urged talks on a new peace arrangement. Despite this plan of goodwill, terrorism and retaliation attacks continued unabated. At almost the same time as the plan was revealed, 13 Israeli soldiers were killed in a bomb attack in the refugee camp of Jenin (in the West Bank), when they were conducting a search for terrorists in what the Israeli government called the largest factory of illicit weapons, especially bombs for the suicide attacks. Sharon therefore declined to stop his militant actions against the terrorists, as he regarded them, and his IDF arrested 4,000 Palestinians in the first two weeks of April 2002.

On 18 April, UN Secretary General Kofi Annan suggested to the UN Security Council that an international mission should be sent to Israel and Palestine with a mandate that would also allow the use of arms. Just like the Mitchell Plan, or the one put forward more recently by *the Quartet* (see below), this UN plan never materialised. Because of the noise from the heavy guns, nobody could hear these pacifist voices. Many accused Israel of carrying out a massacre in the Jenin refugee camp, but later investigations did not confirm this angry accusation. Several Palestinians and Israeli soldiers were killed in the course of the occupation of the camp in the search for terrorists, which eventually developed into a real battle; most of the buildings were destroyed, and afterwards the camp reminded one of a real war scene. The US Secretary of State arrived in Israel in the middle of this critical situation on 12 April, when several suicide bombs were again killing innocent victims.

Later in April, many Palestinian so-called terrorists had sought refuge in the Nativity Church in Bethlehem, and difficult negotiations now took place in order to give them a free passage out of the IDF siege. The Israeli government pretended that some of the murderers of minister Zeeni were among them, but eventually most were allowed free passage and granted asylum in some European countries.[294] In the second half of the month of April, Israel undertook a degree of withdrawal of the IDF from the occupied areas, but not enough to give a convincing sign of more tolerance or a new political opening. At the end of April, Bush received the Saudi Crown Prince and used this occasion to declare again that it was time for the IDF to pull out.

In early May, Colin Powell proposed an international peace conference, which Arafat agreed to attend, whereas Sharon, on his part, had another plan that he termed the most serious up to now. All these abortive proposals, however, did not change the picture in the occupied territories at all, and the humiliation of Arafat and the PLO continued, together with that of the Palestinian population. And the Israeli population continued to live in fear because of the unrelenting terrorism. In an interview with *el Mundo* (14 May), Arafat thanked the Prime Minister of Spain, because he was one of the few outsiders to have kept in contact with him by telephone during his 34 days of almost complete isolation.

We have mentioned above that some of the fairly rational observers in the USA were becoming more sceptical with regard to the American pro-Israel attitude in Sharon's time. But there were others who went in the opposite direction. The right-wing Christian circles or fundamentalists in the USA (Protestant) have generally been pro-Israeli over the years, and they now intensified their support for Sharon and urged Bush to give the Prime Minister (even) more support than before. A personal friend of Bush, the Republican Dick Armey, declared in May 2002 that

---

294 Some of those affected have declared how brutal the Israeli intrusion into the Church of Nativity was; see for instance the Spanish magazine, *Interviú*, of March 17, 2003. Those who came to Spain deplore their sad fate because they feel isolated.

Israel ought to claim all the occupied land as part of Israel. A huge demonstration in favour of continued American support for Israel took place in New York on 5 May, giving the White House an indication of the popularity of the American tilt in favour of Jerusalem, just before a new visit by Sharon to Washington (his fifth as Prime Minister). Generally speaking, the Jews have tended to vote for the Democratic rather than for the Republican Party in the USA, but this competition for the support from a marginal, but important electorate normally assures the Israeli government of continuous American understanding, whatever government is in place in Washington.

In Europe, the former pro-Israeli sentiments, for instance in Scandinavia, have turned almost in the opposite direction in recent years. This is also the case with regard to the public feeling in Spain. An opinion poll from May 2002 shows that only 8,8% think that Arafat is to blame for the worsening of the conflict, whereas 35,4% find that Sharon's government is to blame. Another 38% think that both parties are responsible for the negative development.[295]

Sharon cut off his May visit to the USA and, when back in his own country, talked about the necessity of expelling the *terrorist* leader Arafat, because of new bomb attacks in Israel. The Sharon government had worked out a paper which confirmed that Arafat was behind the financing of the suicide bombers and other terrorists. We do not know if this paper, which was presented in Washington, did convince the American administration, but a majority of observers — outside the right-wing circles in Israel and the USA — certainly were not impressed. Even Peres, still Foreign Minister, but paralysed inside the government, strongly warned against a deportation of the PLO leader. Not until the middle of May could Arafat leave his bombed headquarters with a view to visiting some of the Palestinian towns such as Bethlehem, Nablus and Jenin. In Nablus he defiantly declared that "with thousands of martyrs with us we shall arrive in Jerusalem", a statement which certainly did nothing to improve his standing in Israel.

Without explaining his peace plan, Sharon told the Knesset on 14 May 2002 that he would only discuss peace with the Palestinians after a reformation of the PA regime. In this connection he accused Arafat and his PLO of being "terrorist, rotten and tyrannic". Whereas many Palestinians might have negative opinions about their leader, whose regime was certainly no democratic model — far from it — the Palestinian people needed no foreign oppressor to tell them that. And many would excuse Arafat for remaining the peculiar *Byzantine* personality that he was: A clever, but enigmatic and corrupt politician who was certainly no statesman, but an expert in manoeuvring the various fractions in the PLO against each other in order to maintain his own dominant influence. He remained the only real leader, therefore, whether we liked him or not, and he might perhaps have carried out re-

---

295 *El Mundo*, 4 May 2002.

forms, if the siege of his headquarters and the Israeli oppression had not made such reforms almost impossible. Or a rebellion might have begun against his dominant authority, had he not been sitting as a lame duck in his bunker. Surely his popularity was beginning to decline in early 2002, while Sharon — unwittingly — did his best to support him morally in the course of the year. Again a vicious circle.

According to a poll in Israel, most Israelis were against the establishment of new settlements in the occupied territories, but the Sharon government continued to promote them. According to some opinion polls, the majority of Israelis also wanted a new round of negotiations with the PLO on a peace settlement. Sharon still did nothing in this regard, except to decide on the building of a controversial cement wall with sections of barbed wire fence (reminiscent of the *Iron Wall* mentioned by Jabotinsky) in June 2002, in order to protect the Israeli side against intrusions from the occupied territories; this was a double-edged sword, because it emphasised the differences between the two sides and also made the Israeli weakness quite clear to most observers. Many Israelis had asked for this protective wall, whereas the settlers feared that they would be left alone on *the other side*. The Foreign Minister, Simon Peres, did not agree with the new plan, fearing that it would make a peace settlement more difficult, and the wall was altogether very controversial within the Israeli government and even more so with the Israeli public. But the building continued, albeit not very quickly, not least because of the heavy costs involved. What makes it particularly offensive to the Palestinian side is the fact that it expands Israeli territory beyond the 1967 border line in many places, at the expense of the Palestinians. Sometimes Arab villages are cut in two. That was the basis of the action taken at the *International Court* at the Haag.

The terrorist acts also continued, however, and on 18 June 2002, 19 innocent victims were killed in a bus by a suicide terrorist attack, and later on the same day seven more Israelis were murdered. This led soon afterwards to a Palestinian advertisement in an important newspaper, *Al Quds* (meaning *Jerusalem*), protesting and openly condemning suicide attacks against civilian targets. Fifty personalities, some of whom were well-known and collaborated with the PLO leader, signed this public appeal in the Palestinian newspaper. Because of the latest wave of bomb attacks, the IDF again occupied many cities in the West Bank and Gaza, and the PLO headquarters were also surrounded anew in the second half of June. An IDF missile attack killed six Palestinians in Gaza, one (or more) of whom was a *Hamas* member according to the Israeli side.

On 24 June 2002, President Bush openly supported the idea of the establishment of a Palestinian state, and suggested that a transition period of three years be set for Palestine's independence. On the other side, the President also obliged Sharon when at the same time he urged the Palestinians to find a new leader. This shocked many of them, and probably further weakened the already feeble respect for the US President, who had never been able to control the Israeli Prime Minister and now tried to push aside the already humiliated Arafat. The effect was therefore counterproductive and led to a new political backing of the PLO leader. He, on his part, reacted in a clever way, calling for elections in January 2003.

In mid-August 2002, Arafat also tried to persuade all the Palestinian resistance or terrorist groups to agree on a common approach to keeping terrorist attacks down and to an opening towards Israel, but — not unexpectedly — *Hamas* and other radical organisations would not oblige. This happened at the same time as Israel began a process against Marwan Barghouti, one of the imprisoned PA leaders and a candidate to take over the PLO leadership after Arafat's death. He was accused of being behind many murderous acts (37 in all), killing 26 and wounding more.

Later in the same month, there was another case, now before a Commission of Inquiry in Israel, where the former Prime Minister, Ehud Barak, stood accused of using too much violence against *Israeli* Arabs (not Palestinians) when the second *intifada* broke out in late 2000 and 13 were killed by the police force. The accusation showed two things: First, a positive aspect regarding the state of law obtaining in Israel, since in most nations it is unusual to see a former politician having to defend his acts before such a Commission. Not unexpectedly, however, Barak denied having given orders to use any force. The official documents showing the wording of the orders given to the police had disappeared, and thus the more negative side of the same Israeli society was revealed.

In September the Supreme Court of Israel accepted the government's deportation of two young people from the West Bank to Gaza, only because their brother had been shot by the Israeli police while he was producing bombs to be used in suicide attacks; the police had a certain suspicion that these two were also involved in terrorism, but could not prove it. Human Rights organisations protested against this measure, which is of course against all rules of law. The Danish newspaper *Politiken* wrote a leading article (6 September 2002) pointing out that this decision showed a further descent down the ladder of democratic behaviour and that Israel was now approaching the low level of anti-human behaviour of countries such as China and Saudi Arabia, where these methods have been used in many cases.

In his speech to the UN General Assembly on 12 September 2002, President Bush said as follows regarding the Middle East: "There can be no peace for either side without freedom for both sides. America stands committed to an independent and democratic Palestine living side by side with Israel in peace and security. Like all other peoples, Palestinians deserve a government that serves their interests and listens to their voices. My nation will continue to encourage all parties to step up their responsibilities as we seek a just and comprehensive settlement to the conflict".

Nice words without any specification as to how the superpower envisaged the peaceful solution that everybody wanted, but which had been drowning in bloodshed since the takeover by the Sharon government that was supported — and still is — almost unconditionally by Washington.

The horrible suicide bomb attacks in Israel continued through September, which again gave rise to retaliation by the IDF, which surrounded Arafat's headquarters and shot at some of the few standing PLO buildings. Sharon's verbal reaction repeated his former declarations along the lines that "Arafat must be removed from here once and for all". The popular anger among the Palestinians was again increasing, and the situation in the occupied territories became even worse when an Israeli attack against a *Hamas* leader in Gaza killed at least two militants and wounded 40, including many children. Sharon said the attack was a success, completely forgetting the heavy toll of civilian losses in this bomb action, which indiscriminately struck far beyond any reasonable measure. Maybe because of American pressure, the siege around the Arafat headquarters was lifted to some extent in late September.

To commemorate the second year after the start of the latest *intifada*, a group of Danish Jews arranged a small, but significant demonstration in front of the Israeli Embassy in Copenhagen,[296] *demanding* the retreat of the IDF from the occupied territories and the stop to meaningless bomb actions from the other side. They had also publicised an appeal beforehand on 24 September, for peace and the stopping of further bloodshed. In this appeal, they declared that the American-Israeli alliance was an unlucky one, and accused Sharon of showing an aggressive and senseless continuation of the vicious circle of violence, in the same way as *Hamas*. They also declared that the Sharon government's blindness and lack of compassion for the Palestinian suffering was unworthy of the Jewish people.[297] The statement ends by expressing the belief that a sovereign Palestinian state in worthy co-existence with Israel, and with secure borders for both, is the only way to assure peace.[298]

In October one of Arafat's collaborators, Mohammed Dahlan, left the PA, and sent the PLO leader an open letter, in which he criticised the slow progress with regard to reforms of the Palestinian society. This was an unusual step, since none of Arafat's nearest collaborators had been able to leave the administration after 1994.

On 21 October a new violent attack (by the *Jihad*) killed 14 innocent bus passengers in the north of Israel, thus confirming, as if that were needed, that no serious change had occurred in Israel with regard to the security situation. A few days later a smaller attack took place, killing three Israeli soldiers and the suicide bomber.

On 30 October the few Labour party members of the Sharon coalition-government, such as the Foreign Minister, Simon Peres and the Minister of Defence, Ben

---

296 There are only about 7,000 very integrated Jews in all of Denmark and normally they would not demonstrate against an Israeli government.
297 King Hussein, in one of his speeches, said something similar: That he could not understand why the Jews, who had suffered so much themselves, hardly ever showed any compassion for other peoples' sufferings.
298 Here quoted from *Politiken*, 24 September 2002.

Eliezer, leader of the Party, finally pulled out of the Cabinet. The formal protest was against a new budget granting more financial support to the (*illegal*[299]) Jewish settlements in the occupied territories, but the real reason seemed to be the coming election of a new Labour party leader, in which Ben Eliaser hoped to be re-elected. He could not present himself as a candidate, if still a minister in a coalition government headed by a Likud Prime Minister.

On his last day in office, Peres met some of the Palestinian leaders on the Spanish island of Mallorca and stressed the fact that it was necessary to continue the mediation efforts of the *Quartet* (see below). The above-mentioned PA leader, Mohammed Dahlan, who was leaving the PA, also took part in the meeting and emphasised that no elections could take place in Palestine as long as the Israeli forces occupied it. He mentioned to a Spanish paper — which asked him about rumours pointing to him as the preferred candidate, from an Israeli perspective, to follow Arafat — that the Sharon government had twice tried to kill him. In Israel, the Sharon rival in the Likud block, Netanyahu, was now taking over as the new Foreign Minister, but he imposed the condition that Parliamentary elections should be held ahead of schedule in Israel. Even if Peres had held little influence inside the Sharon Cabinet, the taking over of Netanyahu as his successor in the Foreign Ministry surely did not augur well for any peace settlement.

In the middle of November 2002 a new serious event added more casualties to the already long list. Twelve Israeli settlers were killed in Hebron, where the Jews live surrounded by Palestinians but protected by the IDF. It soon became public knowledge that the first information which told of a *massacre* was not correct; it was in reality a fight between the often very aggressive settlers, heavily armed, and a small group of Palestinian activists.[300]

It was a shocking piece of news to most peace-loving observers that Netanyahu, in his capacity as new Foreign Affairs Minister, soon declared the Oslo Agreements null and void, with a reference to the *massacre* in Hebron that was — as just mentioned — an armed fight between the illegal settlers and a Palestinian group. He also warned Arafat that his expulsion from the West Bank was soon to come. On 21 November a new attack, killing twelve persons, took place on a bus in Jerusalem, thereby confirming the saying of a newspaper with regard to the daily life in Israel that it was dominated by a sad *death routine*.

---

299 All settlements in the occupied territories are *illegal*, according to international law and to most observers, including those governments that are otherwise on friendly terms with Israel. Only the right-wing circles in Israel consider them as a right, whereas the Labour politicians have mostly held an ambiguous position. They even established new settlements themselves as we have seen, generally speaking because of political expediency.

300 *El Mundo* of 18 November 2002, which quotes the *Haaretz*.

Just before the Christmas period, the IDF re-occupied all of Bethlehem after some serious new attacks, in anticipation of the elections to the Knesset fixed for 28 January 2003. A very serious attack on an Israeli-run hotel in Kenya on 28 November, combined with an abortive missile attack on an aircraft, pointed to a shocking link between *al Qaeda* (responsible for the attack in New York on 11 September 2001) and terrorism in Israel. Almost at the same time, Netanyahu lost the election for chairmanship of the Likud party, which was not unexpected.

After some American pressure, the EU had to postpone the promotion of the *Quartet Plan* till after the elections in Israel, but Washington also persuaded Sharon to vaguely accept the so-called *Road Map* to a general settlement of the conflict. All in all no success could be noted in our Conflict picture during 2002; only a development going down the drain, involving a dramatic turn in the direction of further distance and tragedy between the parties.

At the end of the year 2002, the world was more and more taken up by the increasing threat against Iraq, which the Washington administration — with bellicose Bush at its head — wanted to occupy in order to avoid further risks to humanity. The Western world was — and is — split, with France and Germany against any attack, at least without a new UN resolution to this effect. The fighting between so-called terrorists in Israel and the IDF continued without any hope of an improvement of the situation in the near future.

It may be worth mentioning here, as we are nearing the end of our historic account of the recent conflict, what Thomas Friedman wrote on 12 December 2002 in *The New York Times*: He recalled his suggestion a year earlier that a joint NATO force should take control of the West Bank in order to secure the establishment of a Palestinian state. He now repeated it, saying that even the Israeli newspaper, *Jerusalem Post* had recently recommended a Kosovo-style international trusteeship of the occupied Palestinian territories. He also quoted the former US Ambassador to Israel, Indyk, who had written: "President Bush has laid out a great vision of a democratic Palestinian state, living peacefully alongside Israel […] but he has failed to articulate an effective mechanism for achieving it". According to Friedman, some form of trusteeship is the only workable alternative to permanent conflict, and he points out that Europe has a role in demonstrating its goodwill here. I entirely agree, but it is frustrating to see that the EU has apparently abdicated its role, playing instead that of a rather unimportant second fiddle in this matter.

Just before the elections on 28 January 2003, the IDF launched one of its many violent attacks on Gaza, killing several civilian Palestinians, as if Israel wanted to give a final serious warning to the electorate, which probably needed no lesson about the war-like situation.

One of the PA members, Minister Saeb Erekat, said in an interview with *el Mundo* (on the day of elections, 28 January 2003) that Sharon wanted to kill Arafat — if he could not expel him — and completely destroy the PA, profiting from the attention given to the coming war with Iraq. Arafat would never surrender, he continues, but rather become a martyr than be expelled by the IDF, which Sharon was also planning. Erekat deplores the continuous destruction by the IDF of the Palestinian infrastructure and the fact that the USA seems to condone the prolonged Israeli occupation, which is today the only one in the world. Finally he stresses as his only hope (in which he does not seem to believe) that the *Quartet proposals* be carried out and that international observers may come to the PA area. But he ends the pessimistic interview by underscoring the fact that no elections can take place in the Palestinian territories as long as Sharon is in power in Israel.

Even some Jewish commentators pretend that, generally speaking, people in Israel have lost hope of a peaceful settlement and only want to strike back against the terrorists, along the lines of what Sharon offers. That is why they continue to support Sharon and probably also because of the weakness of the Labour Party, which remains a factor after the many changes at the top level, and was responsible for the Party's bad results at the last two elections.

The same day as the above-mentioned interview, 28 January 2003, Erekat's pessimism proved justified, because as predicted, Sharon won a significant victory for his Likud Party, obtaining 36 seats in the 120-member Parliament. While this was a fine result for him he still needed a coalition government to ensure a viable administration. This is a normal factor in Israeli politics, however, and it did not take much time before a new coalition (without Labour members this time) was in place.

The Israeli writer David Grossman's comment with regard to the election was that it was characterised by *fear and hatred*.[301]

4. The 2003 War in Iraq

Even if Iraq is outside the scope of this study, we cannot avoid mentioning this momentous event of 2003. The war in Iraq, which began in March, was launched by the US President against the recalcitrant and brutal regime of Saddam Hussein. Some Western allies joined in the military onslaught or in the later occupation of the country (primarily the UK, but also Italy, Japan, Poland and Spain, in addition to several smaller countries, like Denmark) that was approved neither by the UN nor by most countries in the world organisation. It was surely looked upon very negatively or with scepticism by almost all Arab countries, and opposed by such important European countries as France and Germany. What initially gave some sort of comfort to observers of the conflict between Israel and most of her neighbours was the tactical move by President Bush when at an early stage he

---

301 Quoted from an article in *el País*, 3 February 2003.

Palestinian women in Hebron demonstrating with Saddam Hussein banners against the US-lead war against Iraq.

declared his renewed interest in a solution of the Middle East conflict. In this he was certainly encouraged by the British Prime Minister, Tony Blair, and the Spanish leader, J.-M. Aznar, both of whom had more internal problems than the US President because of their participation in the military coalition. Sharon, on his part, could not help demonstrate his satisfaction with a war that would certainly eliminate an unpredictable and dangerous enemy; as time went by after the quick victory in Iraq (April 2003), Sharon demonstrated some of his usual arrogance towards his opposite number in Palestine, Arafat, whom he disregarded more and more.

The joint effort of the *Quartet* to which we have dedicated a special chapter (XIX), had hardly had any effect before the war started, and the aftermath was soon characterised by other problems. As early as 15 May 2003, Herbert Pundik wrote in *Politiken* that the *Road Map* process had "ended in a ditch because of a collision with the Israeli Prime Minister". He stressed at the same time, however, that Arafat was no less a manipulator than Sharon, and that the EU should avoid contact with him and leave the conflict to Mahmoud Abbas, better known as Abu Mazen, the new Prime Minister of Palestine.

This new government was approved by the Palestinian Council on 29 April 2003, shortly after Abu Mazen's nomination by President Arafat, but only 41 members voted in favour and 18 against him in the Parliament of 85 members. Arafat, who must have been under continuous strain because of his isolation, both physical and political, had finally understood that only through relinquishing some of his overwhelming power could he hope for a settlement. The appointment of the first Palestinian Prime Minister, however, was controversial, as will be seen from the voting, and therefore did not have the positive effects hoped for — all the more so because *Hamas* and other radical groups were against Abu Mazen, whom they considered to be too lenient towards the enemy.

A massacre of Jews in Jerusalem took place soon afterwards, in May 2003, and was followed by an Israeli retaliation attack, proving that the Sharon government did not trust that Abu Mazen could stop terrorism. As we know, this was still the *sine qua non* for any collaboration between the parties, and Abu Mazen must have felt the negative impact of the violence.

Under pressure from Washington, Sharon agreed to meet the new Prime Minister, Abu Mazen, and the meeting took place in July 2003. But a general improvement between Israel and the PLO was still far away; Abu Mazen therefore almost gave up immediately since he felt that he had to fight against the influence of the above-mentioned radical groups and at the same time appeal for any liberal concession from President Arafat, still very much in power. Therefore the influence of Abu Mazen in this first period could hardly be registered in any positive way for the conflict.

He finally decided to resign in early September 2003 and was replaced by Ahmed Qurei, also known as Abu Ala, one of the main negotiators in Oslo. That the open war between the parties, which took so many lives, continued, did not help people abroad understand Israel, because its brutal retaliation attacks were often considered too harsh. This increasingly negative attitude towards Israel may be confirmed by the fact that a poll carried out in the EU countries showed less understanding than ever for the Jewish nation. 58% of the Europeans asked even found that Israel posed *a threat against humanity*. At the same time, the organisation *Amnesty International* published a strongly critical report on the Israeli measures in the occupied territories.[302] In Israel and in some Jewish circles this development was taken as a sign of a new wave of anti-Semitism in Europe. They seemed to ignore the fact that in the USA, too, public opinion was beginning to be much more critical of Israel, as many quotations above have amply demonstrated. As a recent example we may here refer to the *International Herald Tribune*, which on 14 August 2003 stressed that "Israel is turning the Road Map into a Road Block".

---

302 *Berlingske Tidende*, 9 September, 2003.

XVIII. New opening from the Arab League Summit

The Arab Summit took place in the Lebanese capital on 27 and 28 March 2002, in the beautifully restored Phoenicia Hotel, destroyed during the civil war, and it was chaotic in many ways. First of all, moderate Arab leaders such as the King of Jordan and the Egyptian President did not attend, for various reasons. But it is not worthwhile speculating here on the reasons, not always given in an honest way, because all the member countries were represented — if not by their top leaders, at least by important substitutes, such as Prime Ministers or other responsible government members. What was more significant was that Arafat did not come, which was due to the fact that he would not accept the strict Israeli conditions imposed on him before the government would grant him permission to leave his bunker. A planned speech by the PLO leader on a screen did not materialise initially but only later, after intervention by the Syrian President to the host-country's President, E. Lahoud. Altogether, the Lebanese government left the impression on the outside observers present that it had organised the meeting in a rather inefficient and negligent way. This may seem surprising, since it would have been an ideal occasion for the Beirut leadership to present reborn Lebanon as a well functioning nation after so many confusing and dramatic years of civil war.

The main topic of the summit was the acceptance of the Saudi Arabian Crown Prince's proposal with regard to the conflict with Israel. Therefore the important factor in our study of the conflict is that a faint hope arose from this summit of the Arab League, in the middle of the sea of violence that plagued its neighbours, Israel and Palestine. The final declaration from the Arab League was remarkable in many ways:

1. First it united *all* the member states, even those generally negative when it comes to negotiations with Israel: Iraq and Libya, and to a lesser degree, Syria. (Damascus had already been negotiating with Israel after Madrid.)

2. It did not insist, as earlier proposals from the Arab League had, on the unconditional right to return for all refugees, but only on aiming for the reaching of a "just settlement" of the problem of the Palestinian refugees, along the lines of the UN General Assembly resolution 194 (from 11 December 1948). The latter stipulated that "the refugees wishing to return to their homes and live at peace with their

neighbours should be permitted to do so at the earliest practicable date, and that compensation should be paid for the property of those choosing not to return".

On that basis, of course, there is not much room for a compromise, if the refugees insist on their right of return, which the Israeli side has consistently rejected as not realistic or possible.[303] But the change in the formulation of the final Arab League text, as compared to the first Saudi Arabian version, leaves a hope that there is now a will on the Arab side to find some sort of compromise. One has to remember in this connection that the UN resolution dates from 1948 and that so many changes have taken place in the area since then. Most of the original refugees have died, anyhow, or are now very old, unless they were small children then.

3. The Arab League resolution otherwise takes as a point of departure the UN resolution 242, granting *land for peace* and demands IDF's withdrawal from all occupied territories and the establishment of a Palestinian state in the territories occupied in 1967. When this happens, the Arab states will establish "normal relations with Israel"[304].

The last paragraph was the one that caused Sharon and his right-wing forces to dismiss the new Arab decision almost instantaneously. They would accept no withdrawal, or only a very partial one, as we have seen above, and they still concentrate their thoughts on a guarantee of security that nobody wants to give them unless they show more understanding and flexibility.

We may here quote extracts from one of the moderate Arab speakers, King Abdullah of Jordan, during the Summit in Beirut, whose speech was read out by his Prime Minister. He said among other things, "the Palestinian cause is the Arab nation's main cause [...]. The problem is principally one of politics and not of security [...; the] eruption of violence is due to Israel's stalling in implementing what it had agreed with the Palestinians, as well as Israel's evasiveness to realise these commitments [...]. [T]he Israeli occupation of Palestinian territories is the fundamental base of conflict[...]. [T]he peace process is a whole. [...] The PLO under Arafat is the legitimate Palestinian leadership".

At their meeting the League also emphasised that the Arab world condemned and rejected all forms of terrorism and added that terrorism is contrary to the Islamic way of thinking. The Syrian Head of State, the young President Bashar Assad, while also condemning terrorism, especially the *state terrorism* of Israel, said that it was still desirable to reach a definition of what terrorism is, as Syria had already

---

303 The Syrian Foreign Minister once asked me why, if Israel in recent years could absorb so many Russian Jews, some of which were even not Jews at all, could it not absorb those refugees who might want to return? Probably not many, he added.

304 It is said by some Arabs that "normal relations" is less than "normalization", but it is not worthwhile discussing this semantic detail, when we are still so far from a real negotiation phase.

suggested in vain in 1985, with a proposal that it should be worked out by an international conference. It is necessary, he continued, to distinguish between terrorism as such and a legitimate, popular resistance against an occupying force.

The EU was represented not only by its Council President, the Spanish Prime Minister, but also by the relevant EU Commission representative, Solana, and the special envoy for the Middle East, Moratinos, all three of them Spanish citizens. The latter worked steadily for peace in the area over the last six to seven years, until he was replaced by another EU official recently. (Today he is the Foreign Minister of Spain in the Zapatero government.) The UN Secretary General, Kofi Annan, was also present during the summit.

XIX. Joint Mediation Efforts by the EU, Russia, the UN and the USA

We have already mentioned the joint efforts begun in the *Quartet*, a collaborative effort among the most powerful nations and organisations in the world. It was originally based upon a Danish proposal within the EU to further the peace process and to avoid unclear elements, such as some aspects of the Oslo accords. The Danish proposal was fairly easily adopted by the EU — for once in complete agreement — and taken up with the US government and also with Russia and the UN Secretary General. During the Spanish Presidency of the EU (in the first half of 2002) it became formalised on 10 April, when the UN Secretary General, Kofi Annan, the American Secretary of State, Colin Powell, the Russian Foreign Minister, Ivanov, and the Spanish Foreign Minister, Piqué, issued a declaration in Madrid. This was the beginning of what was soon named the *Quartet* effort.

The initial declaration stipulated as follows:
1. IDF operations inside the occupied territories must be stopped immediately;
2. the IDF must withdraw from the occupied cities and from around the Arafat headquarters;
3. Israel must show respect for international humanitarian principles and give access to humanitarian organisations;
4. Israel must desist from the exaggerated use of force;
5. the IDF must respect civilian lives;
6. Arafat must do his utmost to stop attacks against innocent Israelis;
7. the PNA must do its utmost to dismantle terrorist infrastructures;
8. Arafat must convince his people to stop terrorism and the PLO leader must authorise his representatives to reopen talks with Israel on security.

While the start was a fairly positive one in Spain, Denmark had hoped that during her Presidency in the second half of 2002, more progress could be expected, perhaps finalised at the EU Summit in Copenhagen in December 2002. The basic idea was that the plan should comprise a concrete *road map* towards the independence of

Palestine, which all nations seemed to accept, including even such difficult features as the question of Jerusalem, which had been avoided in the Oslo agreements and other accords so far, without any positive result. It was thought that with the aim of independence fixed for June 2005, all elements could be discussed and negotiated before this date.

However, because of the sad developments in Israel and the occupied territories with Palestinian terror and brutal Israeli retaliation attacks, which we have described amply above, there was no prospect of the Summit in Copenhagen furthering the peace process. It was therefore postponed —with regret — until after the elections in Israel on 28 January 2003.

Nevertheless, in his capacity as Chairman of the EU Foreign Ministers' Council, the Danish Foreign Minister, Per Stig Møller, visited most of the involved countries in order to promote a long-term solution on the basis of the *road map*.

Since there was not much hope to be derived from these elections in Israel, which was soon confirmed, as we have seen above, we may conclude that the goodwill shown by the powerful nations and the UN has been, if not in vain, at least limited to useful preparatory work. At the time of writing there is no prospect that a final settlement can be agreed upon.

In a so-called *non paper* presented by the Danish Presidency in October 2002,[305] it is said, "Lessons learned from the Madrid and Oslo process suggest that a clear, detailed and unequivocal **road map** has to be worked out to ensure that permanent status negotiations will be concluded before June 2005. The EU should pursue an active role within the Quartet to hold its partners to the commitment to work for a Palestinian statehood within that time frame".

The June 2005 limit had been mentioned in President Bush's speech regarding the Middle East on 24 June 2002, and soon after endorsed by *the Quartet* at its meetings of 16 July and 17 September, during the Danish EU Presidency, thus giving the transition period a validity of three years from the first documented date.

The plan was to divide the preparatory work into three phases:

A pre-election phase, with a view to carry through reforms in the territories, including the creation of a post of Prime Minister[306] and the calling of a peace conference.

---

305 A *non-paper* is used by diplomats to indicate a proposal or outline of a plan that is not yet an official paper, but only a draft, giving an idea of the concept. It may have a somewhat official character, though, if its author is indicated, but may also be seen more as an anonymous paper, having neither an author or even a date sometimes. A sort of *guinea pig* paper.

306 Probably in order to change the domineering leadership of Arafat and prepare for his succession. The PLO leader accepted the decision, and Abu Mazen was appointed Prime Minister.

The IDF should begin a withdrawal, and no new settlements or expansions of the existing ones in the territories would be allowed. International observers should control the Palestinian elections.

A post-election phase, until the establishment of the Palestinian state with provisional borders refers to the elections planned (then) for January 2003 and the formation of a new Palestinian Authority with a new legitimacy.

The final phase, after the formation of the Palestinian State with preliminary borders until the creation of the (real) Palestinian state. It is stipulated that the pre-1967 borders must be accepted with the possibility of only negotiated modifications (proportional exchange of territory); Jerusalem is mentioned as the capital city of both states, and the question of the refugees must be solved in a just, viable and gradual way.

Whereas the USA was more inclined to respect Sharon's wish to ensure security before any other movement that was to take place according to the plan, the EU and the other participants wanted parallel actions with regard to the various subjects and reciprocal steps by the opponents. But the war between Palestinians and Israeli forces that was going on throughout the years 2002 – 2004, as we have seen, gave (and still gives) absolutely no impetus to work seriously for the peace plan, however clear the *Road Map* may look. Without a minimum of goodwill between the parties no progress can take place.

In April 2003, around the US-led victory in Baghdad, it seemed as if President Bush had accepted the suggestion put forward by his ally in the war, British Prime Minister Tony Blair, who wanted an assurance that the West would work for a solution to the Palestinian problem. This condition was also endorsed by another ally of the USA in the war against Iraq, the Spanish Prime Minister Aznar as mentioned above. This combined effort therefore gave a new impetus to the revival of the Road Map. Despite his original negative attitude, Sharon came under pressure during his visit — yet another — to Washington in early May 2003, when he gave President Bush his (qualified) acceptance of the *Road Map* plan to a peaceful settlement of the Conflict.

As mentioned above, H. Pundik concluded (15 May) in *Politiken* that the Road Map process had ended in a ditch because of a collision with the Israeli Prime Minister.

In October 2003, the result of a private initiative, to which I will refer in more detail below, showed that a group of Israelis had agreed on a peace proposal with some Palestinians – a very interesting initiative that, not unexpectedly, was almost immediately rejected by the Sharon government. Thomas Friedman's cynical comment was: "A glimpse of sanity that infuriates Sharon".[307]

In the same month the Sharon government — once again — defied a UN Gen-

---

307 *Herald Tribune*, 17 November 2003.

eral Assembly resolution (of 21 October) asking Israel to stop the building of the already mentioned huge wall separating Israel from the occupied territories. This wall is being constructed in such a way that it leaves many Palestinians cut off from their own fields and also expands the Israeli territory at the cost of the already small Palestinian area.

In November 2003, four former *Shin Bet* (Secret Service) leaders issued a serious warning against the bellicose policies of Sharon. The *Herald Tribune* (on 19 November) calls them "Four Wise Men in Israel", and their message was essentially to point out that "the Israeli government was dealing solely with the question of how to prevent the next terrorist attack, ignoring the question of how we get out of the mess we find ourselves in today". They also asserted: "We are on the way to a catastrophe". The former chiefs recommended the acceptance of one of the proposed peace plans (either the Road Map or the recent, private Geneva accord). Other officials and military persons have also recently warned the government on and off against the retaliation attacks on Palestinian targets, often killing innocent people and frustrating and angering the local population.

The former Security adviser to President Carter, Zbigniew Brzezinski, wrote an article of warning in the *Herald Tribune* on 15 November 2003, stating that "if this continues, Israel will become increasingly like Apartheid South Africa — the minority dominating the majority, locked in conflict from which there is no extraction [...T]he US must identify itself with peace and help those who are the majority in Israel who want peace".

At the end of 2003, Sharon toyed with the idea of a complete separation between Israel and the occupied territories, if the *Road Map* failed, but this desperate idea was rejected by almost all sides. His former Foreign Minister, Simon Peres publicly told Sharon that the Prime Minister was constructing a wall of declarations instead of taking the necessary decisions (in the direction of peace).[308]

---

308 Quoted from el *País*, 20 December, 2003.

XX. Latest Developments

2004 – 05

The year 2004 began with an initiative by the Israeli President, Moshe Katsav, who invited the Syrian President to come to Jerusalem and discuss peace. First of all, we have to recall that the Head of State in Jerusalem is supposed to be apolitical, and Katsav did not seem to have coordinated his proposal with the Prime Minister, who was quick in denouncing the Syrian reply, which was — as could be expected — negative. As I have pointed out above, the Syrian President had no wish to imitate the late Egyptian President, Sadat, whose spectacular initiative we have examined above. The young President in Damascus had no desire, either, to change his father's ways and would therefore not give in to such melodramatic moves. At any rate, the Syrian Foreign Minister recalled that Damascus needed a guarantee from Jerusalem that negotiations could resume from where they had stopped in the aftermath of the Madrid conference when they had almost come to a fairly positive end, entailing that Israel would withdraw entirely from the Golan. It is also a fact that these negotiations were stopped — not by Damascus, but by Peres soon after he took over from Rabin in November 1995.

Also in January, Israel agreed to an exchange with *Hisbollah* of some dead bodies in Arab hands for the release of several Palestinian prisoners in Israel. This macabre business was not the first that was organised — through German mediation — and it had probably only very limited political repercussions.

In February, Sharon again threatened to totally separate the Palestinians from Israel if it were not possible to reach an agreement with the new Prime Minister, whom Sharon had declared he was willing to meet. His above-mentioned negative declaration was probably due to pressure from right-wing circles in the difficult internal political climate in Jerusalem, and carried little value and did not impress the Americans, either.

The violence continued almost unabated, and in late March, the IDF managed to kill the *Hamas* leader, Sheikh Yassin, in his wheelchair; he was the old so-called spiritual leader who had been set free after the intervention by King Hussein some years earlier and mentioned above. The reaction to this assassination was one of strong disapproval from many countries and by the UN Secretary General, whereas the USA only reminded the public that the Sheikh had been a leading figure in a terrorist organisation. At the same time, the US innocently declared that it had received no warning from Israel beforehand that this event was being prepared.

In early April, Sharon was even more defiant, telling the world that he would delay the establishment of a Palestinian state for many years. This followed an earlier declaration to the effect that Israel was willing to withdraw all the Jewish settlements and the IDF from Gaza, and these two elements must be seen together. By withdrawing [only] from the difficult Gaza area, the occupation of which had been very costly over recent years, Israel hoped to be able to keep the other and more valuable occupied territories, i.e. the West Bank in particular. At the same time, Sharon once again accused and warned Arafat, but the PLO leader reciprocated that a [limited] withdrawal from the Gaza could in no way be acceptable to the Palestinian cause. What else could one have expected?

In early May, in an interview with the Egyptian newspaper *Al Ahram*, President Bush assured that the US was still aiming at the creation of a Palestinian State, but that the dates fixed by the *Road Map* (before the end of 2005) were no longer realistic because of the continuous violent crisis. He also declared that he would soon be sending Prime Minister Qurei a personal letter. So if there was no longer any contact with Arafat, the new Prime Minister was seen as an acceptable partner. Not surprisingly, Arafat — once again from his still isolated headquarters — criticised the American demonstration of understanding for the manoeuvrings of Sharon to postpone any concession to the Palestinians. In the same month, 13 Israeli soldiers were killed by *Hamas*, and one of the sad results was that in retaliation, the IDF destroyed so many houses in Gaza that more than 1,000 Palestinians became homeless. The *International Herald Tribune* wrote that "the world had seen horrifying scenes of death as an Israeli tank and helicopter opened fire on a group of Palestinian demonstrators, including children".[309] The newspaper also wrote of "Sharon's obsession with appearing characteristically tough, lest his desire to withdraw be taken for a sign of weakness".

Almost at the same time, 100,000 persons demonstrated in Tel Aviv in favour of a complete Israeli withdrawal from Gaza and for a renewed dialogue with the Palestinians. Those in favour of peace had apparently not died out entirely, which was also demonstrated by various opinion polls. Many ordinary people felt it necessary to support Sharon's idea, made after heavy US pressure, to get out of Gaza, especially because it was opposed by many right-wing forces behind the government. The plan had therefore just been rejected by the Likud Party.

The American Secretary of State, Colin Powell, met the Palestinian Prime Minister in Jordan in May and assured him that President Bush was still committed to the establishment of an independent Palestinian state.

---

309 *International Herald Tribune* 21 May 2004.

In June, Sharon survived a vote in Parliament to save his plan for a withdrawal from Gaza, and an agreement was made with Egypt on a better control of the borders. But many observers claimed that the compromise, which was reached after many difficulties in the Knesset and saved the Sharon Government for the time being, was very vague because it delayed any withdrawal well into the following year. Israel, therefore, could not carry through the promised immediate withdrawal. Almost at the same time, the IAF launched an attack on *Hisbollah* positions inside Lebanon, not far from Beirut, thereby renewing those military engagements and retaliation attacks that were more frequent before the withdrawal of the IDF, in 2000, from the southern parts of Lebanon.

In the same month, Sharon could breathe more easily because the case against him on corruption charges, which had threatened his political position, was abandoned by the relevant legal authorities, mostly for lack of evidence.

In July 2004, after having deliberated the case over several months, the International Court in the Hague decided that Israel had no right to carry through its plan for finishing the building of the wall or fence dividing the occupied territories from Israel, especially those sections that were built inside what was never accepted as being Israeli territory. In those occupied territories Israel was asked to dismantle the newly built installations, whether they were in the form of a huge wall in concrete or a barbed-wire fence.

All in all, this *Iron wall*, to use an old Zionist expression, which had been built over the last two years and remained controversial in Israel itself, reminded one of the dividing wall through Germany which was built in 1961 and demolished only in 1989. The verdict of the International Court was of course a moral victory for the Palestinians but could not be enforced legally since it had no binding effect. It was the UN General Assembly that in 2003 passed a resolution condemning the wall and at the same time asked the International Court to decide whether the establishment of the wall was in accordance with international law. The Supreme Court of Israel had just before this international verdict called upon the Israeli authorities to respect as much as possible the rights of the Palestinians whose land had been invaded or divided by the wall. The government in Jerusalem, which had not wanted to defend its case before the International Court (because it did not accept its authority in the matter) defied the verdict — not unexpectedly — and declared that it would only accept the findings of the Israeli Supreme Court. 200 out of the planned 700 kilometres had already been erected at the time of the verdict, and it is altogether a very costly affair, not only for those Palestinians affected, but for Israel, for which the wall costs almost $1,000 million. The EU threatened Israel to cancel the agreement between Israel and the Union, if the government in Jerusalem continued the building despite the negative verdict. As a result, Israel became more aggressively negative towards the EU, which had supported the verdict of the International Court. The Israeli government has always maintained that the

Wall is necessary in order to protect itself against terrorist attacks and thereby to save lives.

Because of these new difficulties, internally and internationally, Sharon found it necessary to begin talks about a new coalition government, one that would involve Labour ministers.

If the Sharon Government had internal political difficulties, Arafat, too, was facing new challenges from younger politicians who found that the isolated leader, or *Rais* as he was called, did not understand the necessity of reform for the Palestinian society. Many had been upset because the *Rais* had nominated his own cousin, Musa Arafat, as responsible for the security in Gaza. Nepotism and corruption were surely old elements of the PLO set up and many accused Arafat of being the leader in this field, as well. It came to a new crisis when the Prime Minister threatened the President with his resignation, and eventually Arafat had to accept handing over some of his powers on security to Prime Minister Qurei or Abu Ala, as he is also called.

Many Palestinians were brutally cut off from home when the IDF blocked the frontier to Gaza and left 2,500 out in the wilderness of the desert in the scorching heat of July. Several Arabs were wounded and three died in a retaliation attack in the same area, confirming that the violence continued from both sides. It is not my intention, however, to give a full list of all those bloody episodes that harmed people on both sides of the conflict in its last phase until recently.

The month of August ended with a particularly cruel *Hamas* suicide attack on two buses in Israel, killing 16 and wounding around a hundred; one result was that in addition to the usual retaliation attacks, Sharon used the opportunity to declare that he would *not respect* the Road Map and also *not vacate* those settlements, as he had otherwise promised. While he had earlier been forced by Washington to abide by the above plan, which he had initially rejected or met with so many conditions that it amounted to a rejection, he now more diplomatically emphasised that it was not realistic for the time being to enforce it.

In September, the IDF killed at least 20 militant Palestinians, most of them members of *Hamas*, and the organisation must have lived in fear of new attacks, often facilitated by superior Israeli technical means. Not only was the Arafat camp weakened because of internal splits, but also the radical fractions, such as *Hamas* and *Jihad*, had increasing difficulties. The government in Jerusalem got away with its harsh methods because the world focused on the increasing violence in Iraq, where the population did not seem to appreciate their so-called liberation. But despite these suppressive methods by the IDF, *Hamas* seemed to increase its potential.[310]

In early October 2004, fighting in the Gaza reached unheard of proportions,

---

310 See *Berlingske Tidende* 24 September 2004.

involving many IDF tanks (200) in their onslaught against terrorists in northern parts of the strip, who had sent missiles into Israel. The government in Jerusalem did not refrain from accusing the Head of UNRWA, (the important UN agency supporting the Palestinian refugees) Peter Hansen, a Dane, of aiding Palestinian terrorists; to prove it, the IDF showed photos of unspecified "weapons" being carried into ambulances of the organisation. Hansen denied this, of course, but he may have provoked the Israelis by saying — in an honest way — that he could not guarantee that there were no *Hamas* members in his 24,000-people large agency. Later, however, the Israeli authorities had to admit that they could not prove their accusation against the UNWRA. Probably the photos showed only stretchers, the normal inventory of an ambulance. The Israeli reaction confirms the sensitivity of the Jerusalem government with regard to the UN and its various bodies in the area. Hansen, on his side, could often tell stories emphasising all the impediments which he and his UNWRA personnel were met with by the IDF.[311]

The UN Secretary General asked for an apology for the wrong accusation — a request the Israelis would hardly ever consider — and he also demanded that the IDF stop their incursions into the Gaza, while at the same time requesting the Palestinians to stop sending missiles into Israel, the reason behind the onslaught. A resolution to that effect was vetoed by the USA in the UN Security Council, and an adviser to the Prime Minister in Jerusalem was blunt enough to admit in the Israeli paper, the *Haaretz*, that the Sharon Government purposely aimed at destroying any real peace plan granting Palestine full independence.[312]

On 7 October, another dramatic event took place, this time in the Egyptian part of the Sinai, near the border with Israel. More than 30 innocent victims were killed and over 100 wounded, many of them Israeli tourists. The Danish newspaper, *Politiken* (11 October) found that the attack was characteristic for *al-Qaeda*, perhaps in collaboration with Egyptian terrorist cells. The aim was not only to kill Israelis, but also to weaken the pro-Western image of Egypt in general, through an attack on the important tourist industry in the country, which had been hit severely before in the early 1990s. At any rate, many observers find that President Mubarak had already seen his influence diminished in the Arab world and on the international scene, and this onslaught was the latest blow to the ageing President (born in 1928, the same year as Sharon).

A recent (October 2004) count of casualties during the second *intifada* showed the sad figure of 4,340 dead Palestinians (the majority) and Israelis, over the last four years, more than in many formally declared wars.

When opening the winter session of Parliament on 11 October, Sharon declared in his defiant way that there could be no question of proceeding with the *Road Map*

---

311 I have heard this confirmed by him, who is no longer head of the UNWRA.
312 Quoted from the newspaper *Urban*, 7 October 2004.

as long as the Palestinians did not live up to their obligations to stop terrorism. In a leading article a few days later, on 14 October, the above-mentioned *Politiken* stressed that against the background of the dramatic military events killing so many in the Gaza, it was necessary for the USA and the EU to remind Sharon of his promise to leave Gaza, and the sooner the better. The newspaper added that this must be regarded only as a first step, since Israel should vacate all the occupied areas and only in this way ensure that the conflict would be eased and eventually lead to real peace.

In another realistic comment on the military interventions in the occupied territories, the Israeli newspaper *Haaretz* wrote on 14 October that it was easy enough (for the IDF) to occupy Palestinian towns, but it was never easy to vacate them again and at the same time insure Israel against any new terrorist attacks.[313]

In Lebanon, a political crisis arose in September – October concerning the prolongation of the term of President Emil Lahoud, a man trusted by Damascus. It was surely the dominant Syrian neighbour who asked for this prolongation, normally not allowed by the Constitution. With around 20.000 Syrian soldiers still in the country, Damascus had maintained her political influence there. Many protested inside and outside the Lebanese Parliament, but a majority vote assured Lahoud's prolongation as President for a second term of three years. (The normal term is six years not to be prolonged. Yet the first president after the Civil War, Elias Hrawi, who began his initial term in 1989, had already been prolonged under Syrian pressure, until Lahoud took over in 1998.) Several ministers resigned, though, and eventually also the Prime Minister, Hariri, a sort of Lebanese Berlusconi, a very rich magnate. He had served 10 years combined in the twelve-year period 1992 to 2004, but was never at ease with President Lahoud. The latter now asked the old politician from the north, Omar Karame, to take over until the coming elections, soon to be held. The only other Prime Minister than Hariri in the post- civil war period was Selim Hoss, in the two-year period from 1998 to 2000.

None of the politicians mentioned have been able to change the difficult economic situation for the better, but the fragile balance between the political parties and different ethnic groups seems to have been upheld. The change of government in Lebanon may not have much importance as such in the region, except that of focusing on the role of the autocratic government in Damascus as the dominant one in both countries. With the increasing pressure from Washington — the victor over Iraq — on Damascus, it may be a question of time before Syria will understand the necessity of relinquishing some, or rather all of its domination over little Lebanon. It is high time. (see below)

On 24 October, Sharon obtained his government's approval on compensations to the Jewish settlers withdrawing from the Gaza. This was an important element

---

313 *Politiken* 16 October 2004.

Saad Hariri, son of the slain former Prime Minister of Lebanon, Rafic Hariri (see picture left), during press conference in Beirut the day after the end of the Lebanese Parliament elections.

in the withdrawal plan that was soon approved by the Knesset, with 67 voting in favour and 45 against.

In an interesting comment in the *International Herald Tribune* on 25 October, Thomas Friedman, in a critical mood, stresses that when Rabin wanted to get out of the occupied territories, it was in order to make *peace with the Palestinians*. "When Sharon offers to withdraw from the Gaza it is in order to make *peace with the Jews* [my emphasis]. At the same time his aids have made it clear that in getting out [...] it is in order to entrench Israel even more deeply in the West Bank and the Jewish settlements there. In the face of this plan, the Bush team is silent".

The month of October 2004 ended with the dramatic news of the serious illness of the PLO leader, Arafat, who was travelling to Paris to receive full medical treatment in a French military hospital.

The Death of Arafat

Yassir Arafat died on 11 November 2004 at the age of 75, less than two weeks after he had been hospitalised in Paris. His death is an event of momentous importance in our conflict perspective, because with him, the first and foremost of the Palestinian leaders was gone. We shall not enter into any discussion here on what was the main cause of his death, which was surrounded by some mystery in the days following his demise. "Had he been poisoned?" it was asked. At any rate, the PLO leader had long had health problems and after all had had a fairly long life, full of struggle and difficult challenges. Let us leave the speculation on the cause of death to medical historians, some of whom still discuss the cause of death of Napoleon in 1821.

Even during his stay in the French hospital, a severe suicide attack took place in Tel Aviv, killing three Israelis and wounding 30 more. It was vindicated by the PFLP, which claimed it as revenge for the 150 Palestinians who were killed in the sole month of October, mostly in Gaza. The suicide attack enraged the Sharon government, of course, and gave rise to new fear in the Israeli population.

During his long fight over the last 30 years for the creation of an independent state of Palestine, Arafat had hoped eventually to die in its capital, Jerusalem. Had Yitzhak Rabin not died nine years earlier at the hands of an Israeli assassin, Arafat might have reached his goal, which was at least within sight in the last years, especially after the UN, the EU and even the US President had openly supported the idea of an independent nation of Palestine, living in peace along Israel, within the original borders of British Palestine.

A funeral with military honours took place in Cairo on 12 November 2004, in the city in which Arafat had lived for several years. Many heads of state and government were present at the ceremony, but no public at large was allowed (due to the state of emergency in Egypt) before his body was taken by plane to his final burial place in Ramallah, the city in which he had lived his last three years encircled by the occupying power, and more and more isolated from the outer world.

As I have written above, Arafat was a Byzantine figure, much more a fighter than a politician, and an old-fashioned autocrat, usually ignoring the necessities of dialogue, openness and freedom of speech. That he was probably also personally corrupt[314] and allowed corruption to a large extent does not necessarily mean much in our political setting, since he was no exception in the Arab world in this respect and never lost his popular appeal with the people. We have to accept that with him at the head, there was hardly ever any chance of establishing a real democracy in his coming state, still to be born. But for the stubborn fight against Israel or the *intruding Zionist nation* as he saw it, Arafat was certainly a necessary element, without which no new (Palestinian) state might ever have been envisaged. It was a pity that neither of the two leaders, Arafat and Barak, who met with President Clinton in 2000 – 2001 to find a viable solution, were at the height of the situation.

---

314 See, for instance, Jakob Andersen's recent book *Blodig Jord* [Bloody Soil], Copenhagen, 2004, pp. 119 - 120.

Probably Arafat was the more inflexible of the two, and also the one who lacked the vision of the necessity of compromise in a situation when a real solution had come into sight.

But had he been able to see the multitudes, the many, many thousands around his coffin when he was laid to rest in Ramallah, he would have smiled, even if he had also known that several persons were wounded in the chaotic ceremony. The multitudes confirmed that this was a leader in his own right, hailed in the same way as the late Egyptian leader, Nasser, when the masses followed him to his ultimate resting place.

The death of Arafat is certainly a new element that may launch the prospect of peace after so many vain efforts. Just as the assassination of Rabin in November 1995 closed any real hope for years, we may assume that the same turn-around may occur, but this time in a positive way, with the death of Arafat.

An election was immediately called to choose Arafat's successor, and it was obvious from the start that Abu Mazen, the first Prime Minister, had the best chances. In him even the Sharon Government saw a possible collaboration partner. In order to allow for a thaw in the frozen relationship, the Israeli Prime Minister decided that Palestinians in East Jerusalem might participate in the vote. That the new Palestinian leadership wanted to create a better relationship not only with Israel, which Abu Mazen initially stressed, but also with Syria, can be seen from the fact that Abu Mazen and Abu Ala went to Damascus and reached an agreement on a better understanding, soon after Arafat's death. The relationship had long been very difficult, especially before the death of President Hafez Assad in 2000.

The outgoing US Secretary of State, Colin Powell, went to Jericho in December to have talks with the transitional leaders, promising to support the coming elections. During the transition period before the election of the coming president in Palestine, there was a certain stand-still in the violence, but it was broken by *Hamas*, which on 12 December launched a spectacular attack against an Israeli border station, utilising a specially dug secret tunnel and killing fours soldiers and wounding many more. Because it was made in such a sophisticated — militarily speaking — and cruel way, it came as a complete surprise to the border control post. At least no civilian casualties seem to have been involved this time.

At the end of the year, the two main parties in Israel, the Likud and the Labour Party, agreed on a new try for a coalition government with the ever emerging Simon Peres to be deputy Prime Minister — at the age of 82, quite a venture. Sharon was forced to accept the inclusion of the Labour Party because some of the right-wing members of the Knesset had vetoed further concessions to *the other side*, even opposing the withdrawal from the Gaza.

January 2005 began with a new wave of violence, just before the elections for a new Palestinian president, to take place on 9 January. A *Hamas* attack on an IDF barracks on 5 January, carried out despite the appeal by the coming president to avoid such meaningless violence, wounded 12 soldiers.

The election was carried through peacefully and with the participation of more than 50%, — some sources mentioned 66% — of the electorate (higher than in most US elections). Mahmoud Abbas, alias Abu Mazen, 69 years old, won more than 62% of the votes as opposed to the other main candidate, Barghouti, who secured less than 20%. The latter was in Israeli custody, and realistic voters would therefore not vote for him.

The new leader had thus had an election that was almost faultless, witnessed also by former US President Jimmy Carter, who said it was "a remarkably wonderful election".[315]

But despite this very positive result, President Abu Mazen has several challenges in front of him. First of all he has to create a better administration, including monitoring organs that can combat corruption, especially in the security forces, where the Byzantine ways of Arafat had led to the creation of almost 30 different organisations, often fighting among themselves. The fact that the new leader has to dominate the radical organisations like *Hamas* and *Islamic Jihad*, in order to be able to enter into real negotiations on peace, will probably be the most difficult challenge for him. Many terrorist attacks in the first weeks of his government have already demonstrated the negative way of thinking of these hard-line Palestinian fighting brigades, as mentioned above.

The second and last Prime Minister under Arafat, Qurei or Abu Ala, was immediately re-appointed by Abu Mazen, and there are positive new signals in many circles, especially from abroad. Sharon has thus expressed his willingness to meet the new Palestinian leader, and he has also set some Palestinian prisoners free. President Bush has likewise declared that Abu Mazen will be welcome in Washington, unlike Arafat, who was never received by Bush. The new Secretary of State, Condoleezza Rice, has recently been to the Middle East area and, according to the press, she asked Sharon to be prepared to take difficult decisions. Washington was also instrumental in organising a meeting between Sharon and the new Palestinian President, in Sharm el Sheikh, in Egypt, which took place on 8 February. This meeting had been well prepared by officials and seems to have brought about an agreement on a standstill in the violence from either side, thus promising a negotiated cease-fire. If only the radical fractions on the Palestinian side will abide, there is hope that a new *modus vivendi* can be found.

We have come a long way from the beginning of the conflict, and the last four years — since Sharon became Prime Minister — have seen the worst cases of violence and a complete freeze in the peace process. But at the time of finalising this last chapter, there is more hope than there has been for a long time. If real peace

---

315 See the *International Herald Tribune*, 11 January 2005.

is probably not round the corner, at least there is some faint light at the end of the tunnel, especially after the Israeli withdrawal from The Gaza in mid 2005.

Peace-loving people in Israel who had lost hope for a long while may now revive and issue strong signals, in order to persuade the political majority to use this new opportune moment to enter into a final *land for peace* settlement with the new Palestinian leadership. The USA and the EU will hopefully also know to profit from the new political climate after Arafat's death and the advent of a more flexible leader.

Israelis in general should recall that, at the Arab League summit meeting in Beirut in March 2002, all the member states passed a resolution implying the acceptance of Israel in the Middle East, on the conditions set by the UN SC resolution 242; they should also remember the late Egyptian President's words to the Jewish state, in Jerusalem, when Sadat declared: "We welcome you in this area".

We know that polls in Israel have shown that there is a majority who would rather vacate the occupied territories in order to secure peace than prolong an illegal occupation which is very costly to all involved and creates hatred and more violence, of the worst kind. All experience shows that violence cannot be eliminated by military means. Over the last four years it has been proven once again. We may also hope that the Sharon government will finally accept the good advice from President Bush to treat the Palestinian people with the dignity they merit and need, just as the Jewish people were, when their independence was found — at last — in 1947, and approved by a majority in the UN. The other side, and especially the radical organisations like *Hamas* and *Jihad* must also show respect for a cease-fire agreement, because if they do not, terrorism of the worst kind will only turn the clock back again.

XXI. Independent Peace Efforts

1. The Geneva Accord of 2003

The most important independent initiative in recent years has been the one supported by the Swiss government, resulting in the Geneva Accord that was made public, first in October and later in more detail in December 2003. It is in keeping with the 10-years' older Oslo Accord that was also based on an independent initiative but was soon endorsed by the Israeli government and by the PLO, as we remember. In the case of the Geneva Accord, the Sharon government immediately shot down the valuable initiative, but it may still get the chance to become an important basis for further talks, when the peace process may be resumed between Israel and Palestine.

The Accord was signed on 12 October 2003, in a hotel near the *Dead Sea* in Jordan, after three years of difficult negotiations. Its main negotiator on the Israeli side was Yossi Beilin (also behind the Oslo Process), former Minister of Justice under Barak; and many of the twenty Palestinian signatories, led by Yasir Abed Rabbo, were among the closest of Arafat's collaborators and of the two first Prime Ministers of Palestine, Abu Mazen and Abu Ala respectively. There is therefore no doubt that it has been signed by delegates representing a wide portion of the Palestinian leaders. Thus Sharon's angry accusation against the Accord seems even more to be lacking in sense, when he continues to deny having any serious peace-loving Palestinian opponents.

The main elements in the 44-page Accord are as follows:

Israel must withdraw from the occupied territories and limit its own territory to within the borders before the 1967 war. Jerusalem will be the capital of both states; the Jewish parts (including the sacred *Wailing Wall*) will come under Israeli authority, the Arab parts (including the *Haram al Sharif* or *Tempel Mount* with the holy Mosques) under Palestinian authority. The refugee problem must be solved, granting compensation to those refugees who want resettlement and cannot be repatriated. The parties agree that they will try their best to organise repatriation and resettlement in those countries that are willing to receive the refugees, including Israel. At the time of the writing of this book, no further details are available, and, at any rate, given the negative attitude of the Sharon government, there is no chance of success in a near future for this accord. However, it constitutes an important positive step in the bilateral conflict.

2. The Copenhagen Declaration of 1997

Another interesting effort was the Louisiana Initiative that was prepared in Denmark in 1996,[316] and which still tries hard to follow up on the *Copenhagen Declaration* that was approved in January 1997. This initiative, creating the International Alliance for Arab-Israeli Peace, was supported by the Danish government and later also by the EU. It aimed at creating an atmosphere of better understanding between intellectual circles in the former enemy countries. The initiative first comprised Egypt and the PLO, in addition to Israel of course, but eventually also included Jordan, whereas Syria and Lebanon not only declined invitations to attend, but also opposed or punished those intellectuals who very cautiously tried to recommend to their respective governments that they permit participation.[317] In Egypt a violent debate on the subject divided some of the initial participants, but in Jordan King Hussein's acceptance of the initiative made it less controversial than in Egypt.[318] Under the right-wing governments in Israel, especially the one led by Sharon, participation in such extra peace efforts has become rather controversial.

In July 1999, a peace conference was organised in Cairo under the title "Arab-Israeli Peace — Time to Act, in order to demonstrate that the people on both sides [...] are a constituency for peace and can work together to support it". It was attended by several statesmen, such as President Mubarak, UN Secretary General Kofi Annan, Moustafa Khalil, Simon Peres and the special EU Envoy to the Middle East, Miguel Moratinos, in addition to the ambassadors in Cairo of Russia, the USA and Denmark among others. This conference took place at an opportune moment

---

316 The already-mentioned Herbert Pundik was among those taking the initiative, together with the leader of the *Louisiana Museum* near Copenhagen who helped a great deal with the infrastructure. In the year 2000, the European Peace Prize, *Pro Humanitate*, was awarded to this initiative.

317 I personally know of one Syrian journalist who was also a civil servant and who, in very careful wording, and in a non-Syrian Arab newspaper, recommended that it was time perhaps not to look only negatively on the Copenhagen Initiative. He was dismissed from his job in the Ministry of Culture and got an inferior one in the National Library. He would have had a worse fate if he had written such an article previously when Israel was still regarded a non-entity in Syria.

318 I was instrumental in presenting the project to the authorities in Amman.

after the takeover of Prime Minister Barak in Israel, allowing for initial optimism with regard to the resumption of the peace progress.

Since then the Arab-Israeli climate has again taken a turn for the worse, and substantially so; the Copenhagen initiative has therefore recently run into more difficulties than anticipated, because of the lack of progress in the efforts for real peace. In almost a good-humoured way, the Copenhagen Declaration spoke of "peace as such a serious matter that it is not advisable to leave it to governments alone". This is a slogan that it is hard to accept in a country like Syria, where any foreign policy guidance must come from the government above and not be inspired from citizens below. The well-known Syrian professor Sadik al-Azm, recently retired and always trying to promote understanding with other countries without provoking his own government, wrote an article not long ago in the New York Review of Books.[319] He states among other things that the Arab reaction to the Copenhagen initiative was "overwhelming, diversified, loaded with deep rooted feelings and often biased in a nasty manner". When he speaks of Arabs in general, he means only the intellectuals, most of them outside Syria and Lebanon, because in the heavily controlled Syrian system, knowledge of such non-authorised undertakings was difficult to obtain. Azm's main philosophy in this regard can be expressed with the title of his recent article, "Modern Arabs and Hamlet", in the ISIM Newsletter, 5/00. He describes the modern Arabs as living in the past, dreaming of their old proud history and forgetting how to modernise and improve their governments and the like.

In May 2003 a new meeting was organised in Copenhagen by the Louisiana Initiative, and delegates from the four participating countries, Israel, Egypt, Jordan, and Palestine issued a joint declaration urging the international community, including *the Quartet* and especially the USA, to do its utmost to solve the Arab-Israeli problem. They advocated respect for the following elements:

Security for both parties; human rights; the withdrawal from all territories occupied in 1967, including Jewish settlements there (with a few agreed exceptions); commonly agreed borders, again with a reference to those prior to 4 June 1967; Jerusalem as the joint capital for the two nations (Israel and Palestine); a just solution to the refugee question; and the involvement of a third party to monitor the respect for the agreement.

Whatever the merits of this *Louisiana Initiative*, and I naturally find them praiseworthy, we have to admit that in the climate of open confrontation or war in the region today, there is not much chance that understanding between the warring factions will grow out of this project. In an account of a recent Arab Journey, organised in the second half of 2003 by *Det Udenrigspolitiske Selskab* of Copenhagen to the countries around Israel, it is stated that in Egypt, many liberal Egyptians who had earlier supported the process told a deceived Danish audience, especially H.

---

319 On 15 June 2000.

Pundik, that there was no prospect for the furthering of the Copenhagen process just now or in any foreseeable future.

As it will be seen, all of these independent initiatives base themselves on UN resolution 242, which grants *land for peace*, and also try to solve the other important outstanding problems such as refugees and Jerusalem, which were not solved by the Oslo Accord.

3. International Folk High School

The International Folks High School in Denmark has also supported an open dialogue on how to create a better understanding between the former enemies. In this connection seminars have been organised in Cyprus, Denmark, Egypt and Jordan between groups of teachers and others who have gathered to debate the possibilities of improving links between themselves despite the increasingly cool atmosphere, especially during the Netanyahu and now Sharon governments. These meetings have also been organised with financial contributions from DANIDA (The Danish International Development Agency). A regular publication called *Crossing Borders* is issued, and in a recent issue, the Israeli student Kobi Elzera Kiryar Yam, terms the general attitude of Israelis towards the original Arabs in the nation as nothing less than "racist".[320] Ben-Ami, the above-mentioned Foreign Minister under Barak, admits that this is often the case, but he does not use the word "racism",[321] which I also prefer to avoid, since negative comments from outsiders can hardly help in the finding of a solution.

This Danish-supported process of meeting with people from *the other side* has parallels in other countries, of course, and they are all praiseworthy, but unfortunately will not change the political pattern in any measurable way, at least not in the near future.

4. Neve Shalom

In Israel itself a remarkable initiative was taken as early as in 1970 by the Catholic monk, Bruno Hussar. It is called *Neve Shalom*, and is placed near the famous cloister

---

[320] No.10 from September - October 2000. He writes: "Most of the Jewish citizens of Israel treat the Arabs in a racist way [...]. I argue that the Jewish majority should and must behave to the Arab minority in an honest and fair way. There is a duty to give the Israeli-Arabs the chance to participate more fully in the life of the country".

[321] "Arab citizens of Israel have no real equality with Jews and cannot exercise their formal rights. We have to change that", op.cit., p. 35.

of Latrun — only 15 kilometres from Jerusalem. It was meant to be a school for everybody, for Arabs and Israelis alike, and a school for peace, it was said by its founder. Jakob Andersen writes a positive paragraph on this interesting venture in his already quoted book, but unfortunately must add that it has been fully ignored by the various Israeli governments. He stresses, therefore, that it has hardly had any impact on the political process. Nevertheless, the Danish journalist also finds that the school gives the visitor a fine impression of *common sense* in an otherwise sad world of conflict. He adds that Hilary Clinton came to the place as the President's wife and gave a speech there.[322]

---

322 Op.cit., p. 10.

Postscript

After the main portion of this manuscript was handed in to the publishers, a serious development occurred in Lebanon, not least in regard to its relationship with its mighty neighbour, Syria.

A violent bomb attack on 14 February 2005 killed the former Prime Minister, Rafic Hariri, and several others, and this brutal onslaught naturally caused an outcry in Lebanon. This episode soon developed into a new crisis, not only internally in Lebanon, where the government had to resign because of violent attacks, but also in its relationship with Syria. Many people, led by the opposition parties in the Lebanese Parliament, accused Syria of being behind the attacks — an accusation that was of course immediately denied by Damascus, but endorsed by the USA and many other outsiders. They called for an independent body to examine who was behind the attack, and later, an international commission of inquiry was indeed set up. At the time of writing this postscript, no final result has yet emerged. But no doubt the UN and other observers kept the situation under tight scrutiny. The Damascus government had long been under strong pressure from Washington because of US suspicion against Syria that it was helping the terrorists in Iraq. This pressure was soon increased from many sides and has already given a positive result. In the first half of 2005, the Syrian troops, already reduced in numbers over the last years, have been fully withdrawn from Lebanon that could thus finally celebrate her full independence. Thereby the UN resolution 1559 from September 2004, sponsored by France and the USA (for once in agreement) was fulfilled.

Internally in Lebanon the cabinet crisis that was the result of the resignation of Prime Minister Omar Karame could not be solved for a long time, but has quite recently (in the second half of April 2005) been settled with the nomination of Nigib Mikati as the new Prime Minister. In the wake of the massacre that killed Hariri, several other bomb attacks occurred in Lebanon — mostly against Christian establishments — but lately internal troubles fortunately seem to diminish; most observers deny that there is a risk of a new civil war.

The withdrawal of the Syrian troops that should be finished before the end of April is a momentous new development and a fortunate indication of a new pattern in the Middle East. Now a higher respect for the independence of smaller states seems to emerge and may be combined with an enhanced focus on democracy, which the USA has demanded in the wake of the Iraq war, and which seems to be followed by slow signs of improvement in the governmental pattern in many countries, such as Egypt, Saudi Arabia and probably also in Syria following the pressure from abroad. Hand in hand with the recently reached cease-fire between the Palestinian "terrorist" groups and Israel, there is at the close of my writing signs of an improvement, if not of a final settlement in sight yet. But there is more hope now than there has been for a long time.

SELECTED BIBLIOGRAPHY

Abu-Odeh, Adnan JORDANIANS, PALESTINIANS and THE HASHEMITE KINGDOM, United States Institute of Peace, Washington, 1999
Ajami, Fouad THE ARAB PREDICAMENT, Cambridge, 1981
Albright, Madeleine, MADAM SECRETARY, A MEMOIR, Miramax Books, New York, 2003
Ammoun, Denise HISTOIRE DU LIBAN CONTEMPORAIN, Fayard, 1997
Andersen, Jakob BLODIG JORD, Høst og Søn, Copenhagen, 2004
Andersen, Lars Erslev og Peter Seberg ET NYT MELLEMØSTEN, Syddansk Universitetsforlag, Odense, 2003

Ball, George W. ERROR AND BETRAYAL IN LEBANON, Washington, 1984
Bamford, James BODY OF SECRETS; ANATOMY OF THE ULTRA SECRET NATIONAL AGENCY FROM THE COLD WAR, New York, 2001
Bitterlein, Lucien GUERRES ET PAIX AU MOYEN ORIENT, Jean Picollet, Paris, 1996
Bjøl, Erling FRA MAGTENS KORRIDORER, Politikens Forlag, Copenhagen, 1994
Borchsenius, Poul BEN-GURION, Copenhagen, 1956
Brooks, Geraldine, SLØR OG BEGÆR (translated from NINE PARTS OF DESIRE) Gyldendal, 1995
Brown, L. Carl DIPLOMACY IN THE MIDDLE EAST, Tauris, London-New York, 2001
Butt, Gerald THE ARABS, Tauris, London, 1994, 1997

Chamieh, Jebran TRADITIONALIST, MILITANTS and LIBERALS in PRESENT ISLAM, The Research and Publishing House, Beirut, Montreal, 1977
Churchill, Randolph, THE SIX DAY WAR, Heinemann Ltd, London 1967
Corm, Georges, LE PROCHE-ORIENT ÉCLATÉ, Gallimard, Paris, 1999

Eban, Abba AN AUTOBIOGRAPHY, Random House, New York, 1977

FREDSPROCESSEN I MELLEMØSTEN, Udenrigsministeriets temahefte, Copenhagen, 2000

Friedmann, Thomas FROM BEIRUT TO JERUSALEM, Anchor Books, New York, 1989 (1995)
Fromkin, David A PEACE TO END ALL PEACE, First Owl Edition, New York, 2001

Hansen, Carlo KAKTUSSENS LAND, Klim, 2001
Hiro, Dilip, DICTIONARY OF THE MIDDLE EAST, Macmillan Press Ltd, 1996
Hirst, David and Beeson, Irene SADAT, A BIOGRAPHY, London, 1981
Hourani, Albert DE ARABISKE FOLKS HISTORIE (Translated from the History of the Arab Peoples), Gyldendal, 1991
Hussein, King of Jordan UNEASY LIES THE HEAD, New York, 1962

Jensen, Michael Irving og Laursen, Andreas ARAFATS PALESTINA, Odense Universitetsforlag, 2000

Kassir, Samir LA GUERRE DU LIBAN, Karthala-Cermoc, Beirut, 2000
Khazen, Farid el THE BREAKDOWN OF THE STATE IN LEBANON, 1967-76, Tauris, London, 2000
Klein, Claude ISRAEL, Editions du Felin, Paris, 1990

Lewis, Bernard THE MIDDLE EAST, 2000 YEARS OF HISTORY, Phoenix Press, 1995, 2001
Lewis, Bernard WHAT WENT WRONG, Weidenfeld and Nicolson, London, 2002

Malik, Habib C. BETWEEN DAMASCUS AND JERUSALEM, Washington Institute for Near East Policy, 2000
Meir, Golda MY LIFE, Futura, London, 1975, 1979
Morris, Benny RIGHTEOUS VICTIMS, Vintage Books, New York 2001

Ostrovsky, Victor and Hoy, Claire BY WAY OF DECEPTION. A DEVASTATING INSIDER´S PORTRAIT OF THE MOSSAD, Canada, 1990

Peres, Simon BATTLING FOR PEACE , Random House, New York, 1995
Pundik, Herbert, DET ER IKKE NOK AT OVERLEVE, ERINDRINGER. Gyldendal Copenhagen, 2005

Quandt, William B. PEACE PROCESS, The Brookings Institution, Washington, 2001

Rabin, Yitzhak THE RABIN MEMOIRS, University of California Press, 1979, 1996
Rahbek, Birgitte EN STAT FOR ENHVER PRIS, Fremad, Copenhagen, 2000

Sadat, Anwar, IN SEARCH OF IDENTITY, AN AUTOBIOGRAPHY, Harper and Row, New York,1978
Satloff, Robert B. FROM ABDULLAH TO HUSSEIN, Oxford University Press, 1994
Seale, Patrick HAFEZ ASSAD, THE STRUGGLE FOR THE MIDDLE EAST, Tauris, London, 1988
Seidenfaden, Erik DEN HELLIGE KRIG OM DET HELLIGE LAND, Based on articles in *Information*, 1956
Shlaim, Avi THE IRON WALL, Penguin, London, 2000
Shlomo, Ben Ami, CUAL ES EL FUTURO DE ISRAEL, Madrid, 2002
Simonsen, Jørgen Bæk DET RETFÆRDIGE SAMFUND, Samleren, Copenhagen, 2001
Simonsen, Jørgen Bæk POLITIKENS ISLAM LEKSIKON, Copenhagen, 2001
Stone, Robert DAMASCUS GATE, New York, 1998

Tabor, Hans DIPLOMAT BLANDT POLITIKERE, Copenhagen, 1995

Wedeen, Lisa AMBIGUITIES OF DOMINATION, The University of Chicago Press, 1999

Zisser, Eyal ASAD'S LEGACY, New York University Press, 2001

The above Bibliography only refers to the most important books which I have studied or read; not all are quoted in my manuscript.

For those interested in more informative material, I may refer my readers to the very complete lists of books to be found in the two most recent and erudite books I have read and often quoted above, *Righteous Victims* by Benny Morris and *Iron Wall* by Avi Shlaim. The authors are both history professors (in Israel and Oxford respectively) and have been able to use archives in Israel up to then under secrecy restrictions. As sources of information they are therefore second to none and most valuable - many former ones have thus become rather obsolete.

- **Abdullah, Crown Prince/King of Saudi Arabia**: 224.
- **Abdullah, Emir/King of Jordan**: 44, 45f, 56, 60 and 209.
- **Abdullah II, King of Jordan**: 187 and 240.
- **Abed, Dr. Samith el-**: 209.
- **Abu-Odeh, Adnan**: 112, 114 and 187.
- **Adenauer, Konrad**: 86.
- **Ajami, Fouad**: 167.
- **Ala, Abu**: 180, 224, 238, 250, 255f and 259.
- **Albright, Madeleine**: 198 and 210.
- **Allenby, General**: 45.
- **Allon, Yigal**: 106.
- **Armey, D.**: 229.
- **Amit, Meir**: 97.
- **Andersen, Jakob**: 263.
- **Annan, Kofi**: 228, 241, 243 and 260.
- **Aoun, Michel**: 152.
- **Arafat, Musa**: 250.
- **Arafat, Yassir**: 14, 92, 111, 116, 126, 159, 163-166, 173, 176, 179-182, 185, 189, 192, 194f, 201, 203f, 207-211, 213-216, 218-226, 228ff, 232-240, 243f, 248, 250, 253-257 and 259.
- **Assad, Bashar**: 113, 207 and 240.
- **Assad, Hafez**: 16, 109, 113, 123-127, 132-135, 143, 148, 169, 177, 197, 203-207 and 255.
- **Azm, Sadik al-**: 261.
- **Aznar**: 226 and 237.
- **Azouri, Najib**: 43.
- **Baker, James**: 171, 176 and 178.
- **Balfour, Arthur James**: 27.
- **Ball, George W.**: 146.
- **Barak, Ehud**: 16, 39, 184, 188, 193, 199, 201ff, 205-213, 224, 232, 254, 259 and 261f.
- **Barghouti**: 256.
- **Beeson, Irene**: 161.
- **Begin, Menachem**: 36, 52, 55, 92, 97, 105, 117, 143ff, 149, 155f, 158f, 161-164, 166, 169, 171, 179, 181, 186, 191, 213 and 220.
- **Beilin, Yossi**: 179 and 259.
- **Ben-Ami, Shlomo**: 39, 174, 201, 205, 208, 209, 211 and 262.
- **Ben-Gurion, David**: 30ff, 34ff, 50-53, 56f, 60, 63, 65, 67-78, 81-89, 91, 97, 99, 105, 107, 196 and 220.
- **Bernadotte, Count**: 61, 178 and 220.
- **Bevan, Aneurin**: 52.
- **Bin Laden**: 219.
- **Blair, Tony**: 237 and 245.
- **Blinkenberg, Jane**: 11.
- **Bourgès-Maunoury**: 78.
- **Boutros-Ghali**: 159.
- **Brezhnev, Leonid**: 123.
- **Brzezinski, Zbigniew**: 164, 204, 246 and 264.
- **Bunche, Ralph**: 61.
- **Bush, George W.**: I: 14, 16ff, 171, 175ff, 181, 186.
- **Bush, George W.**: II: 208, 215ff, 219f, 222, 224, 226-229, 231f, 235, 236, 244f, 248, 253 and 256f.
- **Bustani, Butrus al**: 42
- **Carter, Jimmy**: 18, 156, 162ff, 166, 246 and 256.
- **Chamberlain, Neville**: 156 and 193.
- **Chamoun (President)**: 137f.
- **Chenab (Christian General)**: 138.
- **Cheney**: 222.
- **Christopher, Warren**: 180.
- **Churchill, Winston**: 33 and 51f.
- **Clinton, Bill**: 16, 180ff, 186, 192, 194, 199, 207f, 210, 216f and 254.
- **Clinton, Hillary**: 263.
- **Cook, Robin**: 17.
- **Corm, Georges**: 140f, 148-152 and 167.
- **Dahlan, M**: 234.

- **Darwin, Charles**: 88.
- **Dayan, Moshe**: 68f, 71f, 75-78, 80f, 85, 97f, 101, 102, 105, 128ff and 135.
- **Doran, Michael**: 74.
- **Dreyfus**: 23.
- **Dulles, Allen**: 85.
- **Dulles, Foster**: 75 and 85.
- **Eban, Abba**: 68, 71, 83, 96f, 99f, 106, 117 and 131.
- **Eden, Anthony**: 78.
- **Eichmann, Adolf**: 86.
- **Eisenhower, Dwight D.**: 83, 85, 87, 99, 114 and 138.
- **Elazar, David**: 130.
- **Eliezer, Ben**: 234.
- **Ellemann-Jensen, Uffe**: 179.
- **Erekat, S.**: 235f.
- **Eshkol, Levi**: 89, 93, 96f, 99 and 105ff.
- **Fadlallah, Sheikh Muhammed Hussein**: 147.
- **Fahd**, King: 170.
- **Fahmi, Ismail**: 161.
- **Feisal, King of Saudi Arabia**: 132.
- **Feisal, Prince/King of Iraq**: 32, 44 and 45.
- **Fink, Lillian and Dan**: 10.
- **Foighel, H.**: 210.
- **Freedland, Jonathan**: 18.
- **Friedman, Thomas**: 36, 38f, 151, 206, 227, 235, 245 and 253.
- **Gads Fond**: 10.
- **Gaulle, Charles de-**: 85, 99, 138 and 177.
- **Gemayel, Amin**: 146f and 152.
- **Gemayel, Bashir**: 143ff and 146.
- **George, Lloyd**: 25f and 31.
- **Ghadafi, Muammar Abu Minyar**: 49 and 123.
- **Gibly**: 72.
- **Goldstein, Baruch**: 39.
- **Gorbachev, Mikhail**: 177.
- **Grosman, David**: 236.
- **Guevara, Ernesto Che**: 141.
- **Habash, George**: 92.
- **Habib, Ambassador**: 146f.
- **Haig, Alexander**: 144 and 167.
- **Hammarskjöld, Dag**: 76.
- **Hansen, Peter**: 251.
- **Hariri, Rafic**: 196, 252f and 265.
- **Hariri, Saad**: 253.
- **Hassan, Prince**: 102 and 127.
- **Heikal, Muhammed H.**: 157.
- **Herzl, Theodor**: 22-25 and 29.
- **Hiro, Dilip**: 157.
- **Hirst, David**: 160.
- **Hitler, Adolf**: 51, 88, 156 and 193.
- **Hirschfeld, Yair**: 179.
- **Hobeika, Elie**: 146 and 224.
- **Holst, Johan J.**: 180.
- **Hoss, Selim**: 152, 177, 226 and 252.
- **Hrawi, Elias**: 196 and 252.
- **Hussar, Bruno**: 262.
- **Hussein, King of Jordan**: 16, 46, 93, 96, 101f, 106, 108f, 112ff, 127, 129, 170, 172f, 183, 185, 188, 192f, 197ff, 247 and 260.
- **Hussein, Saddam**: 9, 14, 146, 175f, 185 and 236f.
- **Hussein, Sharif**: 29, 44 and 46.
- **Husseini, Haajii Muhammed Amin al-**: 51, 55 and 92.
- **Indyk, Martin**: 210 and 235.
- **Ismail, Hefez**: 122.
- **Ivanov**: 243.
- **Jabotinsky, Zeev**: 33ff, 47, 52, 67 and 231.
- **Jarring, Gunnar**: 118.
- **Johnson, Lyndon B.**: 99, 115 and 117.
- **Jumblatt, Kamal**: 137 and 143.
- **Kadil, Ibrahim**: 163.
- **Kaplan, Eliezer**: 52.
- **Karame, Omar**: 252 and 265.

- **Kassir, Samir**: 141f.
- **Katsav, Moshe**: 225 and 247.
- **Kawakibi, Abd al-Rahman al-**: 42.
- **Kennedy, John F.**: 87ff.
- **Khaddam, Abdul Halim**: 142.
- **Khalidi, Yusuf Zia-el**: 24.
- **Khalil, Moustafa**: 260.
- **Kissinger, Henry**: 39, 118f, 121f, 126, 131-134 and 155f.
- **Lahoud, E.**: 239 and 252.
- **Larsen, Roed**: 180.
- **Lavon, Pinchas**: 71ff and 76.
- **Lawrence of Arabia**: 44 and 45.
- **Lenin, Vladimir**: 141.
- **Levy, David**: 199 and 201.
- **Lykketoft, M.**: 212 and 217.
- **Majali, Abdel Salaam al-**: 186.
- **Malley**: 210.
- **Marx, Karl**: 141.
- **Mazen, Abu**: 237f, 255f and 259.
- **Medzini, Meron**: 120.
- **Meir, Golda**: 32, 46, 56, 76ff, 82f, 86, 89, 96f, 107, 109, 115, 117-122, 127-132, 135 and 196.
- **Melchior, M.**: 204 and 218.
- **Milosovic, Slobodan**: 146.
- **Mittchell**: 217, 224, 226, and 229.
- **Mollet, Guy**: 78.
- **Moratinos, Miguel**: 241 and 260.
- **Morris, Benny**: 30, 47, 53, 55, 59ff, 63, 70, 75f, 82, 93, 95ff, 100, 127-130, 139, 147, 172 and 180.
- **Mubarak, Hosni**: 161f, 192, 199, 218, 251 and 260.
- **Muhammed, the Prophet**: 40f and 49.
- **Møller, Per Stig**: 244.
- **Narkiss, Uzi**: 98.
- **Nasser, Gamal Abdul**: 47ff, 70, 73f, 76ff, 81, 84, 91f, 95ff, 101f, 108f, 111f, 115-121, 124, 137, 140f, 157, 161, 167 and 255.
- **Nasser, Sheif**: 102.
- **Neguib**: 49
- **Nehru, Jawaharlal**: 48.
- **Netanyahu, Benjamin**: 10, 113, 188-199, 201-204, 206, 208f, 211f, 224, 234f and 262.
- **Nixon, Richard M.**: 115, 117ff, 123, 130 and 133f.
- **Oldenburg, Christian**: 10.
- **Ostovsky, Victor**: 212.
- **Peel, Lord**: 31f, 35, 47 and 50f.
- **Peres, Simon**: 38, 75, 78, 171-174, 179f, 189-193, 196, 201f, 204, 212f, 219f, 224f, 230f, 233f, 246f, 255 and 260.
- **Pfaff, William**: 209 and 227.
- **Picot, F. G.**: 28, 31 and 44f.
- **Pinochet, Augusto**: 146.
- **Piqué**: 223, 228 and 243.
- **Powell, Colin**: 224, 225, 229, 243, 248 and 255.
- **Pundak, Ron**: 179 and 210.
- **Pundik, Herbert**: 11, 107, 179, 219, 237, 245 and 262.
- **Qurei**: 248, 250 and 255.
- **Rabbo, Yasir Abed**: 259.
- **Rabin, Yitzhak**: 39, 81, 89, 93, 96-99, 101, 103, 105, 117ff, 121ff, 129, 135, 143, 157, 171ff, 174, 177, 179-182, 186, 189-193, 196, 198, 201f, 205, 208, 247 and 253ff.
- **Rahbek, Birgitte**: 143 and 208.
- **Reagan, Ronald**: 144, 166f, 170f, 186 and 217.
- **Rice, Condoleezza**: 256.
- **Rida, Rashid**: 43.
- **Rogers, William**: 112, 115 and 117f.
- **Rothschild, Lord**: 26f.
- **Sadat, Anwar**: 121-127, 132-135, 144, 155-170, 181f, 185ff, 204f, 218, 247 and 257.
- **Sadiq, Muhammed**: 125.

- **Samuel, Sir Herbert**: 27.
- **Saud, Ibn**: 46f.
- **Schultz, George**: 170.
- **Scott, C. P.**: 25.
- **Seale, Patrick**: 124ff, 135 and 203.
- **Shaara, Farouk**: 178.
- **Shamir, Yitzhak**: 38, 61, 92, 146, 169, 171-174, 176-179, 186, 191 and 220.
- **Sharett, Moshe**: 52, 65, 67-77 and 107.
- **Sharon, Ariel**: 9, 14-18, 34, 71, 74f, 102, 143-147, 149, 172, 191, 199, 207ff, 212f, 215-238, 240, 245-257, 259f and 262.
- **Shishakli, Adib al-**: 69.
- **Shlaim, Avi**: 32, 34, 36, 53, 55, 57f, 60f, 63, 65, 68ff, 72-75, 78, 82, 84, 86ff, 96, 103, 105-108, 115, 117, 146, 158, 172, 178, 183, 190ff, 195ff and 216.
- **Shuquiri, Ahmad**: 91.
- **Simonsen, Jørgen Bæk**: 11.
- **Stone, R.**: 107.
- **Sukarno**: 48.
- **Sykes, Sir Mark**: 28, 31f and 44f.
- **Tabor, Hans**: 103.
- **Talal, Prince/King of Jordan**: 58.
- **Tito, Josip Broz**: 48.
- **Toukan, A.**: 219.
- **Truman, Harry S.**: 68.
- **Vance, Cyrus**: 165.
- **Velux fonden**: 10.
- **Weizmann, Chaim**: 25f, 28, 32-36, 46 and 52.
- **Wilson, Harold**: 100.
- **Wilson, Woodrow**: 25.
- **Yaalon, Moshe**: 220.
- **Yam, Kobi Elzera Kiryar**: 262.
- **Yassin, Sheikh**: 198 and 247.
- **Yassin, Deir**: 55f.
- **Yaziji, Nasif**: 42.
- **Zahri, A.**: 218.
- **Zaim, Husni**: 65 and 69.
- **Zapatero**: 241.
- **Zinni, A.**: 221 and 227f.